Geoffrey of Monmouth

Twayne's English Authors Series

George D. Economou, Editor

University of Oklahoma

TEAS 509

CAMDEN'S DRAWING OF THE GLASTONBURY LEAD CROSS, WHICH
CLAIMS TO MARK THE BURIAL PLACE OF ARTHUR, FROM *BRITANNIA*
(1607).

Geoffrey of Monmouth

Michael J. Curley

University of Puget Sound

Twayne Publishers • New York
Maxwell Macmillan Canada • Toronto
Maxwell Macmillan International • New York Oxford Singapore Sydney

Twayne's English Authors Series No. 509

Geoffrey of Monmouth
Michael J. Curley

Twayne Publishers
Macmillan Publishing Company
866 Third Avenue
New York, New York 10022

Maxwell Macmillan Canada, Inc.
1200 Eglinton Avenue East
Suite 200
Don Mills, Ontario M3C 3N1

Library of Congress Cataloging-in-Publication Data

Curley, Michael J., 1942–
    Geoffrey of Monmouth / by Michael J. Curley.
      p.   cm. — (Twayne's English authors series)
    Includes bibliographical references and index.
    ISBN 0-8057-7055-0
    1. Geoffrey, of Monmouth, Bishop of St. Asaph, 1100?–1154.
Historia regum Britanniae.   2. Great Britain—History—To 1066–
–Historiography.   3. Merlin (Legendary character)   4. Arthurian
romances—Sources.   7. Arthur, King.   I. Title.   II. Series.
DA140.G49C87   1994
936.2'007202—dc20   94–14513
                                                 CIP

The paper used in this publication meets the minimum requirements of American National Standard for Information Sciences—Permanence of Paper for Printed Library Materials. ANSI Z3948–1984.∞

10 9 8 7 6 5 4 3 2 1 (hc)

Printed in the United States of America

For Sandy, Austin, and Brendan

Contents

Preface

Geoffrey of Monmouth is difficult to overlook. To the nonspecialized reader, he is best-known today as the twelfth-century author who first gave literary shape to the legend of King Arthur with his portraits of the great warrior-king, the boy-prophet Merlin, the beautiful queen Guinevere, the traitorous Mordred, and the host of knights who gathered around the fated court at Caerleon. Geoffrey was the channel through which the Arthurian matter passed to Wace, the originator of the concept of the Round Table, and to the French poets who so brilliantly elaborated the *matiére de Bretagne*. Without the *History of the Kings of Britain*, Shakespeare could not have composed *King Lear* or created Owen Glendower in *Henry IV, Part I* as the Welsh *miles gloriosus* spouting Merlin's prophetic skimble-skamble stuff. The seed that Geoffrey sowed was harvested by Malory and Tennyson, by T. H. White and Mary Stewart.

In fact, Geoffrey has become so integral to our understanding of Arthurian literature, that we forget how controversial his history originally was. From its appearance in the midtwelfth century to the present day, the *History of the Kings of Britain* has aroused strong emotions. Many of Geoffrey's fellow historians were clearly stung by the way that his work eclipsed their own. Upon being shown a copy of Geoffrey's *History of the Kings of Britain* at the monastery of Bec in 1139, Henry of Huntingdon stated that he was stupefied to see this great book because his own inquiries about the history of Britain from the time of its settlement by Brutus down to the invasion by Julius Caesar had turned up no information whatsoever, either written or oral. Gerald of Wales, himself a man of vivid imagination, rarely passed up an opportunity to indict Geoffrey for his lack of veracity. In his *Journey through Wales*, Gerald tells the story of the prophet Meilyr, who lived in the vicinity of Geoffrey's beloved Caerleon and who was frequently tormented by demons. If a copy of Saint John's Gospel were put in Meilyr's lap on such occasions, Gerald recounts, the demons would flee immediately. On the other hand, if a copy of Geoffrey's *History of the Kings of Britain* were put in the place of John's Gospel, the unclean spirits would eagerly alight upon the book and remain there an unusually long time. The existence of the anonymous Variant Version of the *History of the Kings of Britain* shows that the effort to rewrite Geoffrey's history to bring it into closer conformity to Bede's *History of the English Church and People* was under way in Geoffrey's own lifetime.

No wonder Henry of Huntingdon was astonished when he was shown Geoffrey's book. In an age when the authority of established histories was still powerful, an account of an obscure people, which seemed to spring fully grown from the imagination of its author, was bound to evoke astonishment. Henry found in the *History of the Kings of Britain* a continuous history of the Britons, where before there had been only scraps. A closer examination would disclose that the *History of the Kings of Britain* indeed, did not ignore the standard authorities on British history, but rather sought to subvert, contradict, and displace them.

The *History of the Kings of Britain* provided a cure for amnesia. In the smithy of his fervid imagination, Geoffrey set about to forge the missing links in the chain of memory concerned with the British past. Attentive readers of the *History of the Kings of Britain* would discover that one of Geoffrey's chief tools in the recovery of Britain's early history was simply an aggressive revision of earlier authors: Caesar, Gildas, Bede, and Nennius, among others. Combined with Geoffrey's keen sense of narrative technique and dramatic structure, his revisionist strategies imparted a certain plausibility to his history. So many vivid stories, such circumstantiality and completeness, such a novel viewpoint. Could this be all wrong?

Moreover, Geoffrey appealed to his contemporaries' waxing confidence in the efficacy of human will and desire as the true shaping forces in history. His characters are driven by passion, greed, rivalry, a thirst for glory and adventure, a restless spirit, and a consciousness of their origins. Above all, they are imbued with a sense of their own autonomy and the possibility of self-realization.

Although not written primarily for an oppressed and beleaguered people, the *History of the Kings of Britain* is certainly about their past, their rise to prominence, and their fall from greatness. The glittering pages of Geoffrey's history paint a picture of early Britain as a rival to Rome in the greatness of its temples, baths, roads, and laws, in the military valor of its leaders and in the grandeur of its conquests. For his immediate audience, the Anglo-Norman aristocracy, linked to the British through a common legendary Trojan ancestry, the *History of the Kings of Britain* was a reminder of the fragility of human institutions and culture. For the Welsh and the Bretons, Geoffrey held out the faint promise of restoration.

This book is intended for the nonspecialist reader who wishes to know something of Geoffrey's career, the strategies that guided him in composing the *History of the Kings of Britain* and the *Life of Merlin,* and something of the lasting appeal of Geoffrey's view of the human condition. Geoffrey's works have been many things to many people: history, fiction, folklore, mythology, satire, epic, tragedy, comedy. I have tried to give the reader a feel for the richness and the variety of approaches to Geoffrey, as well as a sense of his place in the intellectual and political world of the twelfth century.

I would like to acknowledge the many friends, colleagues, and students whose conversations over the years have enriched my understanding of Geoffrey's works. In particular, the hospitality of the Centre for the Advanced Study of Celtic at the University of Wales, Aberystwyth, offered me the full range of its scholarly resources during the 1982–83 academic year. My residence in Wales was supported by the Arnold L. and Lois Graves Award. I have received invaluable guidance from J. Caerwyn Williams, Marged Haycock, Bobi Jones, and A. O. H. Jarman. My undergraduate students at the University of Puget Sound and the teachers who have journeyed to Tacoma in the summers to read Arthurian literature with me under the auspices of the National Endowment for the Humanities have convinced me of the need for this book. Finally, this book could not have been written without the expert services of Christine Fisher of the Collins Library at the University of Puget Sound and Jean Brooks, who patiently typed countless revisions of the original manuscript.

Michael J. Curley
University of Puget Sound

Chronology

1154–1189   Reign of Henry II.
   1155   Geoffrey of Monmouth dies. Wace's *Roman de Brut* appears.
1157–1158   Henry II leads successful Welsh campaign.
1198–1201   William of Newburgh's *Historia rerum Anglicarum* appears.

Chapter One

The Life and Career of
Geoffrey of Monmouth

Details of the life of Geoffrey of Monmouth come to us from several sources of variable reliability. Geoffrey was witness to seven charters concerned with properties in the vicinity of Oxford between 1129 and 1151. The manner in which he identified himself, along with what is known of the careers of his cosignatories, reveals much about Geoffrey's life. The dedications and epilogues to Geoffrey's three known works: *The Prophecies of Merlin (PM)*, *The History of the Kings of Britain (HRB)*, and *The Life of Merlin (VM)* provide further particulars. We have reliable information too, on Geoffrey's ordination and appointment as bishop of Saint Asaph's (Flintshire, North Wales), as well as the date of his death. Beyond these sources, one can draw inferences about Geoffrey's background from his name and from the early history of Monmouth, almost certainly the place of his birth. The Welsh chronicles transmit muddled, but perhaps not entirely unreliable, information concerning Geoffrey's life. Finally, modern scholars still debate over Geoffrey's authorship of parts of the *Book of Llandaff.*

Geoffrey appears to have identified strongly with his place of origin because he styles himself "of Monmouth" once in the *PM,* twice in the *HRB,* and once in the *VM.*[1] He also shows a partiality in the *HRB* for places in the vicinity of Monmouth. To cite but one instance, in rewriting Nennius's account of the death of the tyrant Vortigern, Geoffrey transferred the scene from Demetia (South Wales) to the ancient hilltop fortress of Little Doward (Cloartius), on the banks of the Wye River quite close to Monmouth.[2] In Geoffrey's day, Monmouth was under the jurisdiction of Robert, Earl of Gloucester (made earl in 1122; died in 1147), the natural son of Henry I, and one of the dedicatees of the *HRB.*[3] The town fell under Norman domination shortly after the Conquest and was ruled by William FitzOsbern, Earl of Hereford (1067) and Lord of Breteuil, who lost no time building castles in Monmouth and four nearby locations in order to protect the Norman settlers of this district of the marches. William's son Roger succeeded him in 1071, but was deprived of his lands in an unsuccessful rebellion against the Conqueror, and Monmouth passed thereafter into the hands of the Breton Wihenoc of Dol. On the basis of the favorable portrait of the Breton people in the *HRB,* some scholars have speculated that Geoffrey's family was Breton and may have originally settled in Monmouth under Wihenoc (Tatlock, 1974, 396–402, 443; Chambers, 24; Lloyd, 1942, 466–68). Wihenoc retired to the religious life and was succeeded by his nephew William FitzBaderon. The Monmouth church was dedicated in 1101 and was given to the Benedictine abbey of Saint Florent de Saumur, 35 miles west of Tours. Geoffrey was probably born around 1090–1100 and educated in the Monmouth priory, and may possibly be "Geoffrey the scribe" (*Gaufridus scriba*) to whom a Monmouth charter makes mention around 1120.[4]

In the seven surviving Oxford charters and deeds to which Geoffrey was witness, he signs himself "Geoffrey Arthur" consistently in the first five, which date from 1129 until about 1150.[5] We may assume that he left Monmouth to take up residence at or near Oxford during the 1120s. Geoffrey's signatures during this period prove William of Newburgh incorrect when he jibed that Geoffrey acquired the nickname (*agnomen*) Arthur as a consequence of having passed off the fables of King Arthur as genuine history in the *HRB*.[6] Lloyd is probably correct to suggest that Arthur was Geoffrey's father's name, which he used as a young man until his own professional identity became secure (Chambers, 23).[7] Arthur was an uncommon, though not unknown, name in Wales, but was apparently more widespread in Brittany (Lloyd, 1942, 466–67).[8] This may be further evidence along with the settlement of Bretons under Wihenoc in Monmouth, that Geoffrey's family was of Breton origin.

In a deed of Walter the archdeacon to Godstow Abbey (January 1139), Geoffrey Arthur's name appears with the title *magister (mag. Galf. Arturus)*, indicating his position as teacher (Salter, 383). While Oxford at this time did not yet possess a university, lectures by this date are known to have been given there by Theobald of Étampes, who also used the title *magister,* as early as 1101–17, and in 1133 Robert Pullen moved to Oxford from Paris to lecture on theology (Tatlock, 1974, 442, Salter, 385). Consequently, the title *magister* probably indicated that Geoffrey taught in one of the Oxford clerical schools of the day, possibly as a secular canon at Saint George's College, the Augustinian school within the church of Saint George inside Oxford Castle where his friends Walter the archdeacon and Robert of Chesney were both associates. The College of Saint George was dissolved and given to Oseney, the nearby Augustinian house, around 1149 (Tatlock, 1974, 441; Salter, 385).[9]

The evidence of the Oxford charters suggests also that Geoffrey belonged to a close-knit group of scholars, prelates, and noblemen connected to Lincoln and Oxford, and that among these were men such as Bishop Alexander of Lincoln and Archdeacon Walter of Oxford, who cultivated a taste for history and had access to books. While we must be skeptical about Geoffrey's claim that Walter gave him "a very ancient book in the British language" from which he translated the *HRB,* Oxford and Lincoln were undoubtedly important urban networks through which books and information were constantly passing and where enterprising authors could find patrons and colleagues. We must also bear in mind that vast private and monastic libraries were rare in Geoffrey's day. Access to books was a chancy affair at best and often depended on one's personal contacts and the proximity of the courts, schools, and monasteries among which manuscripts regularly circulated for consultation and copying.

In addition to being a growing center of intellectual activity during the early twelfth century, Oxford was also the scene of some important political events. King Stephen held a council at Oxford during the summer of 1139 and there arrested Alexander, bishop of Lincoln, and Roger, bishop of Salisbury, among others.[10] In December 1142 Stephen forced the empress Matilda to flee from Oxford Castle by night and to seek refuge in nearby Wallingford. All things considered, Oxford was a good place to write a history of the kings of Britain, and Geoffrey probably composed the *PM* (ca. 1135) and the *HRB* (ca. 1136–38) here.

Among the patrons, friends, and colleagues Geoffrey came to know in his Oxford days were some of the most influential and learned men of twelfth-century England. He dedicated the *PM* to Alexander, bishop of Lincoln (1123–48), stating that Alexander was chief among those who urged him to publish Merlin's prophecies (*HRB,* 171). Later, in the prologue to the *VM,* however, Geoffrey expressed his disappointment in not receiving a reward from Alexander for his labors (*VM,* lines 7–9).[11] The *HRB* itself was dedicated to two patrons: Robert, Earl of Gloucester (d. 1147), natural son of Henry I, and Waleran, Count of Mallent (1104–66), both of whom Geoffrey praised in fulsome terms for their learning and martial valor (*HRB,* 51–52). Walter, archdeacon of Oxford (d. 1151), from whom Geoffrey claims to have received the "very ancient book in the British language," which he translated as the *HRB,* was Provost of Saint George's College, where Geoffrey himself may have taught (Lloyd, 1942, 464–65; Chambers, 23). Geoffrey's affiliation with Walter dates back at least to 1129, when both men served as witnesses to the foundation charter of Oseney Abbey (Salter, 383); their names appear together spread over the next 22 years on five other documents concerning properties in the vicinity of Oxford (Salter, 383–84). Robert of Chesney, the dedicatee of the

VM, was a canon of Saint George's and later, in 1148, became successor to Alexander as bishop of Lincoln, where he served until his death in 1167.[12] Robert was also a cosignatory in 1151 with Geoffrey and Walter to a grant of land in Knolle (Salter, 385). The signature of another Monmouth native, Ralph of Monmouth, appears as witness with Geoffrey on four charters connected with the Oxford area, the first dated January 1139, the remaining four dating from the years 1150–51 (Salter, 383–84). As a canon of Lincoln Cathedral, Ralph confirms Geoffrey's close association with that city along with Alexander and Robert of Chesney. Roger of Almary, precentor of Lincoln, also appears on charters with Geoffrey in 1129 and 1142 (Salter, 383). In January 1139 Geoffrey and Robert, bishop of Exeter (1138–55), were witnesses to a deed made by Walter the archdeacon to Godstow Abbey at the dedication of that house (Salter, 383). Robert was traveling at the time in the retinue of King Stephen, who was present at the dedication ceremony. This is probably the same Robert, bishop of Exeter, who in his own turn commissioned the scholar John of Cornwall to translate the prophecies of Merlin from the British language into Latin sometime during the early 1150s.[13]

Did Robert and Geoffrey discuss Merlin or the *HRB* at the time of their meeting at Godstow, or the place of Cornwall, over which Robert had jurisdiction, in the early history of Britain? Possibly. The *PM* was probably finished before 1135 and may have circulated as a separate book sometime shortly thereafter (Chambers, 27–28; see ch. 3). The *HRB* itself, which incorporates the *PM* as the seventh book, was seen by Henry of Huntingdon at the monastery of Bec in Normandy in January 1139 and could have been known to Robert of Exeter by this same date (Tatlock, 1974, 433–34).[14] Among historians, Geoffrey also may have known personally Caradoc of Llancarfan, the author of a life of Gildas, and thought by some to have been one of the authors of the *Book of Llandaff*.[15] In the explicit to some of the manuscripts of the *HRB,* Geoffrey assigns to Caradoc the task of continuing the history of the Welsh kings from Cadwallader to his own day. In the same place he assigns the history of the Saxon kings to William of Malmesbury and Henry of Huntingdon, although he commands them not to meddle in British history because they lack the book in the British language, which Walter the archdeacon gave to Geoffrey (*HRB,* 284). Whether Geoffrey knew these men personally is unclear.

In the last two Oxford charters, dating from 1151, Geoffrey replaced the name Arthur with his new title "bishop" or "bishop elect" of Saint Asaph (Salter, 384; *Gaufridus episcopus sancti Asaphi, Gaufridus electus sancti Asaphi*). The bishopric of Saint Asaph was a relatively new one in

Geoffrey's day. In fact, the first bishop appointed to the church (1143), was Geoffrey's predecessor, Gilbert. In Gilbert's day, the church was apparently called the church of Llanelwy after the Elwy River. Geoffrey was the first to be called bishop of Saint Asaph, but it is unlikely that he ever traveled to North Wales to take up residence.[16]

The uprisings of Owain Gwynedd against the forces of Henry II made that part of Wales a scene of violent conflict during the 1150s. The humble church of Saint Asaph, in any case, was scarcely suited to a man of Geoffrey's urbane and scholarly character.[17] The *VM*, however, was probably completed early in the 1150s and contains material associated with the life of Saint Kentigern, the supposed founder of Saint Asaph's. This suggests a close connection in the later period of Geoffrey's life between his literary and his ecclesiastical career.

Geoffrey was ordained at Westminster on 16 February 1152 and consecrated bishop of Saint Asaph eight days later at Lambeth by archbishop Theobald.[18] In November or December 1153 he was among the bishops who witnessed the Treaty of Westminster (signing his name *Galfrido de S. Asaph episcopo*)[19] between Henry and Stephen, which ended the civil war and guaranteed Henry's right as successor to the crown.

Later Welsh tradition as represented by the so-called *Gwentian-Brut* adds a number of details to the final period of Geoffrey's biography.[20] It correctly states, for example, that Geoffrey became bishop in 1152 and goes on to claim that he died in his house in Llandaff and was buried in that town before ever assuming his episcopal functions. It also asserts that Geoffrey was the foster son of Uchtryd, "Archbishop" of Llandaff, his father's brother, and that Geoffrey served as archdeacon of the church of Saint Teilo in Llandaff, where he was the teacher of "many scholars and chieftains." Lloyd demonstrated that none of the *Gwentian-Brut* can be dated before the sixteenth century and that it owed its presence in the *Myvyrian Archaiology of Wales* (1801–7), an often-reprinted anthology of Welsh literature and history, to the notorious forger Iolo Morganwg, which is the nom de plume of Edward Williams (Lloyd, 1942, 462–64). As its title implies, the chronicle was to glorify the history (or pseudohistory) of Gwent, in part by connecting illustrious personages such as Geoffrey with local religious institutions, particularly with Llandaff.

In spite of its suspect character, however, the *Gwentian-Brut*'s biography of Geoffrey may preserve some genuine traditions. Residence in or around Wales, rather than at Oxford, during the period of composition of the *VM* (ca. 1150) might explain how Geoffrey came into contact with genuine Welsh traditions that unquestionably stand behind the

portrait of Merlin in the *VM*.[21] Uchtryd, who was bishop, not archbishop, of Llandaff (1140–48), did have a nephew called Geoffrey, but this
man was already a priest at Saint Peter's in Gloucester in 1146, some six
years before Geoffrey of Monmouth was ordained (Chambers, 22;
Tatlock, 1974, 447, note 50). The author of the *Gwentian-Brut* perhaps
unknowingly equated these two Geoffreys. Tatlock is right to insist that
Geoffrey was no Llandaff booster, but this does not exclude his living or
being buried there. Similarly, the idea that Geoffrey taught "many scholars and chieftains" at Saint Teilo, may possibly be a distortion (deliberate?) by a Gwent partisan of Geoffrey's teaching career at Oxford.

Gwenogvryn Evans's claim that Geoffrey was the author of parts of
the *Book of Llandaff* also rests on rather uncertain ground.[22] While most
of the compiling of the charters, deeds and saints' lives of the great *Book
of Llandaff* was carried out during the episcopacy of Urban of Llandaff
(1107–33), and under Urban's direct supervision some of the material,
such as the *Life of Dubricius* (Dyfrig), the founder of Llandaff, was completed after Urban's death, perhaps during the 1150s,[23] when Geoffrey
may have been living in or near Wales (E. D. Jones, 154–55).

Unfortunately, the dating of the relevant portions of the *Book of Llandaff*
is still far from settled,[24] and a date after 1155 would of necessity exclude
Geoffrey as author if his obit in the *Brut y Tywysogyon* is correct. Then there
are the obvious discrepancies between the *HRB* and the *Book of Llandaff*.
The latter claims Dubricius to have been the founder and first bishop of the
church of Llandaff and states that upon his death he was succeeded by Teilo
(Evans, 1979, 69, 107). In the *HRB*, however, Dubricius is appointed to the
vacant metropolitan see of Caerleon by King Aurelius; he later crowns
Arthur at Silchester, appears at Arthur's plenary court at Caerleon as Primate
of Britain and Papal Legate, resigns his archbishopric to become a hermit,
and is succeeded by Arthur's nephew David (*HRB*, 198, 212, 227, 230). At
the same time, according to the *HRB*, Teilo, a "celebrated priest of Llandaff,"
succeeded Samson as archbishop of Dol in Brittany (*HRB*, 230). While
writing the *HRB*, Geoffrey could not have been unaware of Urban's efforts
to exploit the traditions of the early saints of Wales for the aggrandizement
of the church of Llandaff. His association of Dubricius with the bogus archi-
episcopal see of Caerleon, rather than with Llandaff, and his decision to
make Teilo succeed Samson at Dol, rather than Dubricius at Llandaff, seem a
rebuff to Urban's pretensions. Perhaps Geoffrey changed his view of things during the 1150s and became a champion of Llandaff, but this seems very unlikely.

The Welsh chronicle, *Brut y Tywysogyon*, states that Geoffrey died in
1154 (rightly, 1155).[25]

Chapter Two

The History of the Kings of Britain: Introduction and Non-Arthurian Material

This chapter begins with a discussion of date, dedications, and prologue of the *HRB*, and goes on to discuss the contents of books 1–6, from the story of Brutus's coming to the Island of Britain to the confrontation between Vortigern and Merlin. The following two chapters will discuss the prophecies of Merlin and the Arthurian matter of the *HRB*.

Historia Regum Britanniae: Date and Dedications

Geoffrey must have begun the *HRB* sometime before 1135. He informs us that he interrupted work on the history before he had reached the point where Merlin confronts Vortigern and his magi, in order to provide Alexander, bishop of Lincoln, with a translation of the prophecies of Merlin, which he then inserted into the history in its present place (book 7). He then returned to the narrative, picking up once again the confrontation between Vortigern and the boy-prophet.

The original version of the *PM* alludes to events down into the reign of Henry I. In certain manuscripts of the prophecies, however, a sentence (beginning *Vae tibi neustria,* "Woe to you Normandy") is added, which clearly alludes to the disposal of the king's body following his death on 1 December 1135. Whether this sentence was added by Geoffrey or someone else, we cannot know, but it entered the manuscript tradition at an early date, apparently as an effort to "update" the prophecies. Its presence indicates that the book of prophecies was completed before the king's death (see chapter 3 for further discussion). How much before, we cannot tell. Assuming that Geoffrey had been at work on the *HRB* for a while before 1135, we might conjecture that he began the *HRB* in 1133 or 1134, perhaps even somewhat earlier.[1]

The *HRB* was in circulation by January 1139. On his way to Rome in the retinue of Archbishop Theobald, Henry of Huntingdon stopped at the abbey of Bec in Normandy. While there, Robert of Torigni, a monk of Bec and a great lover of books, showed Henry a copy of the "great book of Geoffrey Arthur." In a letter of the same year to his friend Warin Brito, Henry described the contents of the book, which he says he was astonished to find (*stupens inveni*).[2] In fact, we know that the Leyden MS BPL 20 copy of the *HRB* was at Bec sometime before 1154, and some have suggested that this may possibly be the very version of the history that Henry saw (Chambers, 30, 47; Faral, 2:20–23; Tatlock, 1974, 311–13 and 433, n. 3; for a contrary view, see Wright, 1991, 89–90).

Efforts to be more precise about the date before which the *HRB* was completed have rested on the evidence of the three dedications that accompany the work.[3] The majority of the manuscripts of the *HRB* have a single dedication to Robert, Earl of Gloucester, whom Geoffrey praises in fulsome terms for his learning, martial virtue, and high ancestry and whom he asks to correct his work.

A smaller number of manuscripts have dual dedications: one group is dedicated to Robert and Waleran, Count of Mallent, while one other manuscript (Bern, Burgerbibliothek, MS 568; Wright, 1984, xii, n. 18) is dedicated jointly to King Stephen and Robert. Much debate has ensued over the chronological order of the dedications. Griscom thought that the dual dedications preceded the dedication to Robert alone, but this view has been called into question by Chambers, Tatlock, and Wright. Initially, Robert and Waleran were both supporters of Stephen in his conflict with Matilda, but Robert broke with Stephen in 1138 and went over to the side of Matilda, while Waleran continued to support Stephen until 1141 (Griscom, 42–95). A joint dedication to Robert and Waleran would make little political sense, one could argue, after 1138, when their allegiances were divided. This dedication would push the date of completion of the *HRB* back to 1138, which would be consistent with Henry of Huntingdon's being shown a copy of the work at Bec in 1139. The dedication to Stephen and Robert would also point to a date between April 1136, when Robert allied himself with Stephen, and June 1138, when he broke with him. Consequently, we can safely conclude that the *HRB* was probably begun a year or so before Henry I's death in 1135 and was certainly in circulation by 1139.

As for the vexed question of the order of the dedications, the current view seems to be that Geoffrey first addressed the work to Robert alone, then went on to add to this a dedication to Waleran. He then rewrote for the king the original dedication to Robert and revised the dedication to Waleran, with necessary changes, for Robert.[4] Additional evidence supporting the view that the *HRB* was originally dedicated to Robert alone comes from within the *HRB,* where Geoffrey addresses himself to a single "noble duke" (Thorpe, 257; *consul auguste*).

Also in support of Robert as the original dedicatee is the prominent place Geoffrey assigned to Gloucester in his history, such as his claim that Gloucester was one of the chief cities of Arthurian Britain and that it was an episcopal see in those days (it actually acquired its first bishop under Henry VIII). Of all the dedicatees, in any event, Robert is the most likely to have actually read Geoffrey's book. Sometime before 1147 Robert lent a copy of Geoffrey's history to Walter Espec of Helmesley (d. 1153), who in turn, passed it on to Raul Fitz-Gilbert and his wife Custance, who gave it to the poet Gaimar to put into verse for his *History of the English* (*L'Estoire des Engleis*) (Tatlock, 1974, 208, 453).[5]

If Robert were the original dedicatee, the *HRB* could have been dedicated to him as early as 1135 (Chambers's view) or as late as 1138 (Wright's opinion). The fact that Henry of Huntingdon was astonished to be shown the *HRB* in 1139 would weigh in favor of the later date because as Tatlock pointed out, Geoffrey would have had difficulty keeping his work secret from Henry for very long. Both authors were working in the same field, and both were under (or in Geoffrey's case, aspiring to be under) the patronage of the same man, Alexander, bishop of Lincoln.

The dual dedication in the Bern manuscript to Robert of Gloucester and Stephan of Blois may have been written for a presentation copy, that is, for a single occasion, and only entered the manuscript tradition by chance (Griscom, 90–94; but see Wright, 1984, xiv–xv).

Whatever their value as a guide to the dating or as an indication of Geoffrey's attempt to keep pace with the political allegiances of his day, the surviving dedications to the *HRB* were attempts by Geoffrey to curry favor with powerful and wealthy men in an effort to gain patronage and preferment. Geoffrey's bitter remarks in the preface to the *VM* on Alexander of Lincoln's lack of response to his translation of the *Book of Prophecies* (*PM*), amply demonstrate that the prefaces were practical appeals and not mere literary adornments.

The dedications also indicate the kind of audience for whom Geoffrey wrote the *HRB* and reveal Geoffrey's doggedness in seeking patronage where he could find it. The dedicatees were some of the principal players among the Anglo-Norman aristocracy in the civil dispute over succession to the throne of England following the death of Henry I. Whether the multiplicity of dedications arose as Geoffrey attempted to keep pace with the quickly shifting sands of political allegiance is hard to say. If any of the patrons whose favor Geoffrey sought ever bothered to read the *HRB* (and there is no evidence that they did), they would have found in it a message tracing the periods of decline in British history precisely to the kind of internecine strife which characterized political affairs following the death of Henry I and in which they were among the chief antagonists.

The Very Ancient Book

Geoffrey begins his preface by claiming that, outside the works of Gildas and Bede, he was unable to discover any account of the kings of Britain, either of the kings who came before the Incarnation, or those such as Arthur, who came after it. Yet the deeds of these men were worthy of eternal praise and were joyfully proclaimed by many people as though they were written down.

He then goes on to claim that Walter, the archdeacon of Oxford, gave him a "certain very ancient book in the British language" (*quendam Britannici sermonis librum uetustissimum*), which set forth the deeds of the kings of the British from Brutus, the first king of the Britons, to Cadwallader, the son of Cadwallo. He also states that this book was written in a beautiful style and contained a continuous and orderly narrative of events. At Walter's request, he translated the book into Latin in his own rustic style, not wishing to collect "ornamented words among other men's gardens" or to draw his reader's attention to style in place of substance. Ironically, nothing could better describe Geoffrey's actual method of composing the *HRB,* as we shall see, than the metaphor of harvesting words among other men's gardens.[6]

The *HRB* has two other references to the ancient book. The first of these comes in book 11, when Geoffrey is about to describe the battle between Arthur and Mordred (Thorpe, 258). The details of this conflict, Geoffrey states, came to him from the book in the British language, as well as from Walter himself, "a man most learned in all branches of history." The final reference to the ancient book comes in the epilogue included in some of the manuscripts of the *HRB*. There, Geoffrey warns his contemporaries, William of Malmesbury and Henry of Huntingdon, to say nothing about the kings of the Britons because they do not possess the book in the British language that Walter brought *ex Britannia,* an expression of uncertain meaning, but probably meaning "out of Brittany," rather than "from Wales" (Thorpe, 284, n. 1).

These claims about the very ancient book have been greeted with understandable skepticism by generations of readers (Chambers, 55 ff.).[7]

To begin with, spurious claims of access to books containing secret or hidden knowledge were commonplace in the Middle Ages (Tatlock, 1974, 424–25). Moreover, no such continuous historic narrative in the British language has come down to us from Geoffrey's day or before. The Welsh *Bruts* are all later than Geoffrey and many of them are clearly influenced by him. A careful study of Geoffrey's sources indicates, however, that he made free use of Gildas, Bede, Nennius, the Welsh genealogies, the Bible, various saints' lives, and Virgil, among others. Apart from the genealogical tracts, none of these are in Welsh or Breton (the two languages most readily designated by the term *Britannica sermo*) and none of them constitutes the continuous type of history of the Britons that Geoffrey claims to have merely translated. Geoffrey Ashe, however, has recently reopened the case for Geoffrey's ancient book by hypothesizing the existence of a now lost account of the continental campaigns of the fifth-century British king Riothamus, whom Ashe identifies with Arthur. He thinks that this hypothetical book influenced both Geoffrey and the Latin *Legend of Saint Goesnovius* (eleventh century?), preserved in the fourteenth-century *Chronicle of Saint Brieuc,* and that it would be a prime candidate for Geoffrey's "very ancient book."[8]

There is the problem of Geoffrey's knowledge of the language in which such a book would have been written. Geoffrey took pains to scatter evidence of his knowledge of the Welsh language throughout the *HRB,* but most of these passages have to do with the meaning of place and personal names and do not imply more than a superficial knowledge of the language on his part. He knows that the prefix *kaer* means "fortress" or "city," the term *mais* (Modern Welsh *maes*) means "field," *map* means "son of," the epithet *pendragon* translates literally as a "dragon's head," and so on (Tatlock, 1974, 28).[9]

A deeper knowledge might be inferred from his clever (and possibly tongue in cheek) etymology of the Welsh word for their own language, *Cymraeg.* Geoffrey claims that the Trojan language was called "Crooked Greek" (*curuum Grecum*) until the time of Brutus, when it was changed to British (*Britannica*) to commemorate the island's Trojan founder, just as the land itself was called Britain and the people Britons for the same reason (Thorpe, 72). If this *jeu d'esprit* is Geoffrey's own invention, rather than common "academic folk etymology," as Brynley Roberts believes, it displays Geoffrey's awareness of two Welsh words, *cam,* "crooked," and *Groeg,* "Greek," and demonstrates, perhaps more importantly, knowledge of Welsh initial consonantal mutation (lenition) that would cause the consonant *G* to be dropped from *Groeg* when the prefix *cam* was attached to form the word *camroeg, close enough for Geoffrey, I suppose, to *Cymraeg*.[10] One wonders for whose benefit Geoffrey told this story. It would make no sense at all to an audience without command of both Latin and Welsh and hence would make little sense to any but a mere handful of members of Geoffrey's Anglo-Norman audience. It was either, therefore, an insider's joke to be shared by a few cognoscenti, or it was already an established etymology whose linguistic basis was well known.

As for Walter of Oxford's role in the genesis of the *HRB*, Walter and Geoffrey were friends and cosignatories on a number of documents, as shown in chapter 1. The office of archdeacon was a very public one, exposing its holder to contact with many people, including the learned. It is unthinkable that Geoffrey was playing a hoax without Walter's knowledge. Did they cook up the story of the ancient book together? This seems unlikely. Both men were too much in the public eye and too dependent on the will of others to risk being unmasked and exposed to ridicule (Crawford, 1982, 158).[11] A more likely explanation seems to be that Walter, being a person, as Geoffrey says, "well informed about the history of foreign countries," passed on to Geoffrey a compilation of documents, some of which, such as the Welsh genealogies, were in Welsh, but did not require a profound knowledge of the language to be read and that Geoffrey used these sources, among others, when composing the *HRB*. His claim to have been given a very ancient book in the British language, would then not be entirely untrue. Characterizing lists of kings and rulers as "continuous" might not be far from the mark either, although these scarcely could be taken as continuous narratives or be characterized as having a lovely style. There is nothing improbable about Geoffrey's claim that Walter brought this book from Brittany (*ex Britannia*), although this statement occurs only in some of the manuscripts of the *HRB*.

A close examination of Geoffrey's methods of composition shows that he drew on at least one source in the "British" language, namely, the Welsh genealogies. The sequence of kings who follow Leir is revealing. They are Cunedagius, Rivallo, Gurgustius, Sisillius, Iago (the nephew of Sisillius according to Geoffrey), then Kinmarcus, son of Sisillius, Gorboduc, and finally Gorboduc's sons Ferrex and Porrex. Geoffrey was not making up these names. Apart from Ferrex and Porrex, each of them can be found among the names in the genealogies printed in Bartrum,[12] although this precise sequence is not found outside of Geoffrey. Ferrex and Porrex are unknown outside Geoffrey, but they look to be duplicated forms of the same name, Ferrex being possibly an aspirated form of Porrex.

On the framework of this genealogical material, Geoffrey interspersed as much historic/legendary matter as he could find or invent in order to flesh out his narrative and to provide a continuous account of the succession of leaders of early Britain. Stuart Piggott has shown that Geoffrey sometimes simply took over genealogical lists in undigested form, as though sensing an obligation to include them, although not completely understanding their meaning.[13] Geoffrey filled out the guest list of Arthur's Pentecost ceremony at Caerleon for example with names that derived from a genuine native source in the British language and had the look and sound of authenticity for the period. That he left this list in such a raw form indicates that he did not expect his audience to protest or know any more than he did about the fragmentary nature of the genealogy.[14]

It seems unlikely that a single source will ever be identified as Geoffrey's "very ancient book in the British language." As demonstrated by the survey that follows, Geoffrey's manipulation of his known sources shows a certain uniformity of purpose. If he also possessed a now lost Welsh or Breton king list or account of Riothamus's campaigns in Gaul, we can be sure that he would have turned those sources to his own unique ends.

Description of Britain

The *HRB* begins with a description of the island of Britain, which is derived largely from Gildas's *De excidio Britonum* (*On the Destruction of Britain*), a tract written during the sixth century probably in South Wales; the description also shows occasional borrowings from Bede and Nennius. Geoffrey was seldom content to follow his sources slavishly. He breaks Gildas's description, which is in one long and dense sentence, into a more fluid sequence of six shorter and more manageable sentences,[15] and rearranges the contents of the passage in a more logical order. He places Gildas's comments on the decayed condition of Britain's 28 cities, for example, at the end of the description of the geography and the fertility of the land. Unwilling to accept Gildas's view that Britain's cities were wholly obliterated by the ravages of the Saxon invasions, he interjects that while many cities have fallen into decay, others still contain the shrines of saints and the companies of holy men and women.

To Gildas's description he adds a list derived from Bede and Nennius concerning the peoples who inhabit the island, but Geoffrey adds the Normans to the head of the list as the fifth people (followed by the

Britons, Saxons, Picts, and Scots), stressing one of his principal concerns in the *HRB,* the passage of dominion over the Island of Britain. Here, too, Geoffrey adds his observation that the Britons fell victim to the Picts and Saxons as a punishment from God for their arrogance. To Gildas's list of the two principal rivers of Britain, the Thames and the Severn, Geoffrey adds a third, the Humber. Both Geoffrey and Gildas stress the richness of Britain's land and its suitability for pasturage, but Geoffrey adds information (probably from Bede's *History of the English Church and People*) on the abundant mineral deposits of the land and the flowers which provide home for bees and honey. He mentions its woodlands, so beloved to the Normans and the abundance of fish in its streams. Both Gildas and Geoffrey portray Britain as the conventional *locus amoenus,* the garden of delight, and evoke the topos of the paradisial quality of the place. While Geoffrey passes over Gildas's comparison of Britain to a bride bedecked with jewels in the *HRB,* he later exploits the potentialities of the image of Britain as a garden. Set apart from, but close to, the continent, Britain will project throughout her history a fatal allure to her neighbors, Trojans, Romans, Saxons, Africans, Normans, who will be inexorably drawn to her lovely, fecund, and all too vulnerable land.[16]

Legend of Brutus

The story of the settlement of Britain by the legendary Brutus and his followers was designed by Geoffrey to provide the British with a glorious heroic past, on a par with that of the classical people. Thus, Geoffrey's foundation legend claims that Britain was settled by Aeneas's grandson Brutus, who was exiled from his homeland in Italy after killing his father in a hunting accident. During his wanderings, Brutus lands on the island of Leogetia, where in a deserted city, along with the augur Gero and 12 elders, he sacrifices to Diana in one of her temples. The goddess delivers a prophecy instructing them to go to an island in the sea beyond Gaul, uninhabited now except for a race of giants. This place will be a new Troy, and from Brutus will descend a race of kings to whom the whole world will be subject.

Later in their voyages near the Pillars of Hercules, Brutus and his company are joined by other Trojans, the descendants of Antenor, and their leader, Corineus, a man fond of battling giants. During their travels, Corineus provokes Goffar, the Pictish ruler of Aquitaine, by hunting in the king's forest without the king's permission. In a series of fierce battles, Brutus and Corineus defeat Goffar and his allies in a fierce slaughter at a city later called Tours after one of Brutus's men, Turnus, who was buried there. Fearing reprisals after their victories in Gaul, and mindful of Diana's prophecy, Brutus sails next to the "promised island," landing at Totnes. Delighted by the beauty of the place, the Trojans decide to settle there. They drive the giants into mountain caves, divide the land among themselves, begin to cultivate the fields; they change the name of the place from Albion to Britain and their language from Crooked Greek to British. Meanwhile Corineus busies himself with his favorite pastime, giant wrestling, and rids his portion of the island of giants, particularly the nastiest of the lot, named Gomagog. Corineus defeats him in a wrestling match, hoists him onto his shoulders, and running swiftly to the coast, hurls him into the sea. The place thereafter down to the present day was called Gomagog's Leap.[17] Brutus builds his capital on the banks of the river Thames, calls it *Troia Nova* (New Troy), later known as Trinovantum, and gives his folk a law code. These events occurred when Eli ruled in Judea; the sons of Hector in Troy; and Aeneas Silvius, son of Aeneas, in Italy.

The foundation legend thus assimilates the British people into the dignified civilization of the ancient Mediterranean, and at the same time, draws them into the legendary past of the French and the Normans.[18] Trojan origins were first claimed for the French in the seventh-century *Chronicle of Fredegar,* through the eponymous Francion, who supposedly attempted to construct a New Troy not far from the banks of the Rhine. Other versions, such as that found in the *Liber historiae Francorum,* trace the ancestry of the Franks back to Priam and Antenor, the founders of the city of Sicambria in Pannonia.[19] Henry of Huntingdon mentions that the legend of French descent from the Sicambrian Trojans was fully explained to Henry I, who had inquired about the origins of the French people, while on campaign in France in 1128 (Arnold, 1879, 248–49). Geoffrey's Norman audience itself had its own Troy foundation legend, modeled on that of the Franks, and first provided them by Dudo of Saint Quentin around 1015–20, and in a somewhat different form about 50 years later by William of Jumièges in his *History of the Normans* (Faral, 1:288–93). Thus, Geoffrey was linking the Normans and the British through a common racial ancestry and set of pseudohistoric traditions. The arrival of the Normans on the shores of Britain in 1066, then, could be interpreted as a rejoining of peoples connected by race and history but separated by the Saxon incursions.

Geoffrey follows the broad outlines of the legend of Brutus as he found it in Nennius (829–30), where the story occupies but a scant and muddled couple of pages. Geoffrey inflated Brutus's brief *curriculum vitae* as found in the *Historia Brittonum* to mini-epic proportions in the *HRB,* where it occupies some 20 pages in Thorpe's translation. But he refashioned Nennius's account in order to fit it into the larger structure of the *HRB*. Geoffrey introduced the intimation that Brutus was conceived before the marriage of his father and mother, perhaps wanting to link Brutus by anticipation to the later heroes of the history, Merlin and Arthur, both of whom were conceived in compromising circumstances. In the *HRB*, Brutus kills his father while the two of them are hunting together in the forest, a detail that could scarcely fail to call to mind for Geoffrey's audience the death of King William Rufus, struck down accidentally by an arrow while hunting in the New Forest in 1100. Geoffrey works into the legend another parallel to contemporary affairs, the hated Norman forest laws, by having Corineus slay Goffar's messenger Himbert with a crushing blow to the head with his bow when Himbert confronts Corineus over his illegal hunting in the king's forest.[20] Geoffrey gives to Assaracus[21] mixed Trojan-Greek blood and claims that his Greek half-brother was attempting to take his castles away from him on the grounds of Assaracus's being born to his father's concubine. The theme of family rivalry, particularly between brothers, here broached for the first time, will play an important role in the *HRB*'s concern over political instability and could not fail to strike Geoffrey's contemporary readers with its relevance to their own political condition. The same could be said for the problem of mixed populations, of which Assaracus's case is a synecdoche and a foreshadowing of Vortigern's fatal infatuation with the Saxon woman Renwein, daughter of Hengist.

Once having accepted Nennius's legend of Brutus as the eponymous founder of Britain, however, Geoffrey had to establish a plausible career for him. And what better model to follow in constructing the details of Brutus's wanderings than his celebrated great-grandfather Aeneas? The *Aeneid* provided Geoffrey with authentic information about what the life of an exile in the Mediterranean around the time of Aeneas Silvius might have been like. Of course, Geoffrey pretends that his information comes from Gildas and Homer, but this literary shell game is merely part of his pretense to possess information of impeccable authority unavailable to other historians. The *Historia Brittonum*, in any case, often circulated under the name of Gildas rather than Nennius in Geoffrey's day, hence his attribution of the Brutus story to Gildas may not be as much of a false lead it initially appears to be.

Geoffrey's "invention" of Brutus's saga should be seen as precisely that, an invention, or a discovery of the past as Geoffrey's audience conceived the past to have been in Brutus's day. To fill in the gaps of Nennius's account, Geoffrey turned to a variety of ancient and medieval sources to recreate an authentic scenario of yet another Trojan comeback. The migrations of Francion and the Sicambrian Trojans were already part of the pseudohistoric past of the Franks and the Normans. The *Aeneid* informed Geoffrey that the Trojan *diaspora* had established many communities around the Mediterranean following the destruction of their city. Helenus's descendants, whom Brutus rallies to his side with the help of Assaracus, were Geoffrey's projection onto one of these communities found in book 3 of the *Aeneid,* in which Aeneas and his men are welcomed to the shores of Chaonia by Andromache and Helenus. Helenus built a "little Troy" (*parvam Trojam*) here after the assassination of Pyrrus. In attempting to recreate the details of Brutus's exile, Geoffrey logically assumed that his hero would encounter the later generation of Helenus's Trojan offspring. As an exile destined to found another Troy on the banks of a far off city,[22] Brutus might well have received, as did his great-grandfather before him, a prophecy announcing his glorious future. Where Aeneas learned from Apollo on the island of Delos that his house was destined to "rule all coasts," so too, does Brutus discover from Diana on an uninhabited Grecian island that "the whole earth would be subject to the kings" who would be born to his offspring (Thorpe, 65).

The Latin classics also provided Geoffrey with precise information on the incubation rituals that Brutus could be assumed to have followed when seeking Diana's will. Geoffrey's description of this ceremony carefully recreates authentic procedures and proper Latin ceremonial vocabulary: the donning of fillets, the pouring of libations to the goddess, the ninefold reiteration of the invocation (which Geoffrey composed for Brutus in proper Latin distichs), the procession around the altar four times, the sleeping on the skin of a hind before the altar, and so forth. The details come probably from *Aeneid* 7:110 ff. or Statius's *Thebaid* 4:443 ff., or other such descriptions in classical sources. Here in the career of Brutus, as so often is the case in the *HRB,* when Geoffrey was faced with the absence of concrete evidence of what had occurred, he attempted to supply what might have occurred.

The same can be said of Brutus's berserker companion Corineus after whom Cornwall comes to receive its name. Given Geoffrey's naive (or ironic) fondness for eponymy as a form of historic research, the presence in the *Aeneid* of the ancient name Corynaeus as one of Aeneas's companions proved irresistible. Corineus's heroic fury owes something to his counterpart in *Aeneid* 12, who smashes a charred torch into the face of his Latin adversary Ebysus before plunging a sword into his flank. He also has something in common with Hercules of Lucan's *Pharsalia,* who defeats the cave-dwelling Libyian giant Antaeus in a wrestling match by holding him away from the earth, the source of his strength. Like the Cornish giant Gomagog (or Goegmagog), Antaeus lived in a cave and gave his name to a place, though not as a result of being slain by Hercules.[23]

The first part of the *HRB* attempts, therefore, to create a plausible account of Brutus's exile and wanderings, by "harvesting ornamented words" from various classical and medieval gardens. The epic machinery of this first part of the *HRB* establishes the work as a kind of British prose chanson de geste. Brutus's career sets the standard of British heroism that will be followed by his successors, Belinus, Brennius, Caratacus, Aurelius Ambrosius, Utherpendragon, and, of course, Arthur, who will retrace Brutus's path by carrying the triumphant golden dragon standard back across the channel to defeat the Roman legions in Gaul and to envision capturing the city of Rome itself, from which his ancestor was driven as an exile centuries before. Imbued with the same martial fury of Brutus and Corineus, Arthur's career will be distinguished also by the setting of new standards of civilized behavior, and by waging two gigantomachies on Mont-Saint-Michel and on Mount Aravia (= Mount Snowdon?).

Trojan dominion over the new land, which was sanctioned by Diana's prophecy, now comes to be ratified by purifying the land of the miasma of giants. Nennius makes no mention of giants in his account of Brutus's arrival in Britain. The giants symbolize for Geoffrey, as the Cyclopes do for Homer, an impediment to civilized life as represented by the cultivation of the land, the rule of law, and the construction of cities.[24] The giants dwell in caves, leave the land uncultivated, and attack the newly arrived Trojans when Brutus is celebrating a religious festival.[25] When the land has been cleared of giants, the Trojans erect their New Troy on the banks of the Thames and establish themselves as the island's first humans, or at least, as the first inhabitants of the island to possess human culture.[26] The legitimacy of their sovereignty over the island is thus deeply rooted and is best symbolized by their building cities, instituting laws, and cultivating the land. No subsequent invader will ever find the land totally vacant and have such unqualified claim to rule it.

Early Britain

Once having established the Trojans as the first to introduce civilized life into Britain, Geoffrey had to show next how that civilization grew and evolved and made its mark on the history of the land. Chronologically, he had to account for the period from the Trojan foundation, the "first coming," as it were, to the "second coming," the arrival of the Romans under Julius Caesar, in the year 55 B.C., a particularly formidable task because this period of British history was virtually a blank page in Geoffrey's usual sources. But it was also a splendid opportunity for Geoffrey to provide a detailed view of pre-Roman Britain where other historians were largely silent.

Geoffrey seems to have taken inspiration initially from Bede's method in the *De temporum ratione* of providing a strict annalistic and synchronistic framework for history. Thus, he tells us that Locrinus reigned for 10 years and his wife Gwendolen for 15 years; their reign was contemporary with the prophet Samuel in Judea, Aeneas Silvius in Rome, and Homer in Greece. Locrinus's son Maddan came to the throne next and reigned for 40 years, after which his son, Mempricius, a sodomite and tyrant, held sway for 20 years before being eaten alive by wolves. This period corresponded to the reigns of Saul in Judea and Eurysthenes in Sparta. And so on. But the attempt to associate the history of Britain with the great events of world history soon proved onerous to Geoffrey. After the rule of Cordeilla's nephew Cunedagius, simultaneous with the founding of Rome by Romulus and Remus, Geoffrey rarely gives either regnal years or synchronisms.

Again, faced with the extreme paucity of information on this long period of British history, Geoffrey assigned a prominence to the careers of certain kings out of all proportion to the length of their reigns. In fact, the history of King Leir and the exploits of the brothers Belinus and Brennius occupy about half of the narrative space in the *HRB* between the paired "arrivals" of the Trojan Brutus and the Roman Julius Caesar on the shores of Britain. A single page suffices, on the other hand, to list the reigns of the 34 kings between Elidurus and Lud (Thorpe, 105–6).

Another strategy was simply to trace to British origins many of the most prominent features of the cultural map of Britain. The roads, cities, monuments, baths, ports, as well as the country's legal and religious traditions were all well in place, according to the argument of the *HRB*, during the period of British sovereignty and long before the advent of Roman civilization in Britain. What the blank page of history could not yield, Geoffrey's rich imagination and resourcefulness supplied.

The topography of Britain provided Geoffrey at least with plausible names on which to build his narrative. From the three regions of Britain came the names of Brutus's sons: Locrinus (Welsh *Loegr,* "England"), Kamber (Welsh *Cymry,* Latin *Cambria,* "Wales"), and Albanactus (Latin

Alban/Albania, "North Britain"). Similarly, the Humber River yielded up its supposed eponym, Humber, king of the Huns, who drowned in its waters while fleeing Locrinus. Humber's female counterpart is Habren (Welsh *Hafren,* the Severn River), illegitimate daughter of Locrinus and Estrildis, who was thrown into the river that came to be named after her.[27] The city of York (Latin *Eboracum*) was founded by Ebrauc, Bath by Bladud, Carlisle by the British King Leil, not by the Romans as William of Malmesbury thought,[28] and so on. Geoffrey conjured various adventures for these persons out of literary sources and folklore. King Bladud, the eponymous founder of Kaerbadum (Bath), was the British techno-hero who built the famous baths in that city[29] and even attempted to fly. Supposedly a contemporary of Elijah (who was swept up into the heavens in a chariot of fire), Bladud enjoyed a similar, if less transcendent and successful, aerial adventure. Like Icarus and Simon Magus, Bladud's momentary career as an aviator ends in disaster.[30] He crash-lands on the pinnacle of the Temple of Concord and is dashed to pieces.[31]

Welsh traditions may have contributed some information about the significant achievements of the folk of pre-Roman Britain. A case in point is Geoffrey's culture hero Dunvallo Molmutius, son of Cloten, King of Cornwall, who becomes king of all of Britain and who establishes the Molmutine Laws. Dunvallo, however, may have already been an established figure in Welsh traditions, whose career received a particular spin in the *HRB.* Geoffrey credits Dunvallo with instituting the law of sanctuary in Britain, and including the roads leading to the sanctuaries in the same law. During Dunvallo's reign the kingdom was rendered so peaceful that banditry and robbery ceased, and "no one dared to do violence to his fellow" (Thorpe, 89). Following his burial in Trinovantum (London) beside the Temple of Concord, which he erected as a tribute to his own code of law. According to Geoffrey, Dunvallo's law code was rendered into Latin by Gildas and later translated by King Alfred into English, along with another British law, the *Lex Martiana,* invented by Marcia, the learned wife of the British king Guithelinus.

No doubt Geoffrey intended all of this to come as a great surprise to his readers. His revisionist strategy was to attribute to British sources the monuments of culture in the island of Britain assumed to have derived from the later arrivals in the land. Geoffrey's contemporaries in the field of history, such as William of Malmesbury and Henry of Huntingdon, knew nothing of Dunvallo Molmutius or Marcia. Henry of Huntingdon described the four principal roads of Britain, but did not know that there was one from Saint David's to Southampton (Arnold, 1879, 12).[32]

Onto the character of the British Cordeilla, Geoffrey also projected a certain measure of contemporary political anxiety. During the time he was writing the *HRB,* and immediately after its appearance, the question of a woman's exercising political power had particular importance. On 1 January 1127, Henry I, being without legitimate male issue, proclaimed his daughter Matilda his heir and compelled his magnates to swear allegiance to her on this and on several subsequent occasions. On the death of Henry I on 1 December 1135, however, Matilda's cousin, Stephen of Blois, returned to England, where he was enthusiastically received by the citizens of London and crowned king by William of Corbeil, archbishop of Canterbury. Matilda's claim to the throne was championed particularly by her half-brother, Robert of Gloucester,[37] Geoffrey's patron and one of the dedicatees of the *HRB.*

The parallels between Matilda and Cordeilla are close, but not exact. Like Cordeilla, Matilda was married by her father to a Frenchman, Geoffrey of Anjou; her rival to the throne was a close male relative, her cousin, rather than a nephew or nephews in Cordeilla's case. Like Cordeilla, too, Matilda mounted a stiff resistance against her adversary. While maintaining that Cordeilla stands for Matilda would be reductive, it is unlikely that these parallels were entirely unpremeditated on Geoffrey's part, or that they could fail to impress his contemporaries.

The succession of a woman to the crown by hereditary right was, needless to say, completely without precedence in Norman or French politics but was cause for considerable worry in twelfth-century England.[38] The *HRB* suggests, however, that the custom was established early in the history of Britain. Both Cordeilla and Helen, daughter of Coel, succeed to the throne when their fathers die without legitimate male offspring. In fact, Helen is educated by her father in such a manner as to prepare her for the role of monarch.[39] Gwendolen rules Britain for 15 years after overthrowing her husband Locrinus. She then passes the scepter on to her son Maddan. Marcia, following her husband Guithelinus's death, reigns as queen-regent until her son Sisillius reaches his majority.

Cordeilla then numbers as one of four queens in the *HRB,* along with Gwendolen, Marcia, and Helen, who govern Britain and who are famed for their wisdom, righteousness, and fidelity. Ultimately, however, when left without the support of husband or father, Cordeilla cannot resist the combined might of her nephews, and she commits suicide. As an anticipation of Britain's future, the story of Leir and Cordeilla suggests that Britain's internal divisions during a time of weakened authority or lack of restraint will prove fatal. As a view of things likely to occur after the death of Henry I, the story is not reassuring. It suggests that baronial ambitions might be held in check by Matilda with a combination of wise political alliances and decisive military action. But Matilda was no Cordeilla. In the anarchy that followed the death of Henry I, the story of Leir and his three daughters proved tragically prophetic.

The Brothers Belinus and Brennius

The most protracted episode in the pre-Roman section of the *HRB* concerns the careers of Belinus and Brennius, the two sons of Dunvallo Molmutius. Unlike the story of Leir and Cordeilla, the core of this story was well-established in the writings of the ancient historians themselves and in the digests of Roman history composed by Orosius and Landolfus Sagax. The sacking of Rome by the Senonian Gauls under the leadership of Brennus naturally drew Geoffrey's attention as one of the most glorious exploits of the Gallic peoples. As might be expected, however, Geoffrey molded the historic Brennus to his own purposes. In the *HRB* Brennus appears as the British prince Brennius,[40] brother to Belinus,[41] and accomplishes a wide range of dramatic exploits (as does Belinus) unattested by ancient authorities but that lead up to and follow the celebrated sack of Rome.

The story of Belinus and Brennius concerns the rivalry that arises between the two brothers following the death of their father Dunvallo. The magnates of the country judge that Belinus should be crowned king according to the "Trojan custom" of the privilege of the firstborn (*primogenitus*). Belinus rules Loegria, Cambria, and Cornwall, while Brennius is left with the territory north of the Humber as far as Caithness. When discord between the two brothers breaks out again, Brennius goes into exile, achieving remarkable success in Scandinavia and France, where he marries the daughter of Segnius, king of the Allobroges, and inherits the kingdom upon Segnius's death. Returning to Britain, Brennius prepares to attack Belinus. Tonuuenna, mother of Belinus and Brennius, however, steps between the two armies and, baring her breasts, makes a moving appeal to the two brothers, thereby bringing about a reconciliation. The two brothers return to Trinovantum and resolve to join their forces together to invade Gaul and subject all of its provinces to their power.

The rivalry of the two brothers dramatizes growing tensions in the *HRB* at this point. Their father had left behind the Temple of Concord, in which he himself was buried, as a monument to the peace made possible in his day by the rule of law. The terms *concordia* and *discordia* run like a leitmotif through the first part of the story of Brennius and Belinus, which concludes with the reconciliation of the two brothers and an agreement to inaugurate a mighty imperial venture. Great are the fruits of Concordia. The role of their mother Tonuuenna is crucial.

Faral and Tatlock are probably right to state that Geoffrey derived the scene in which she steps between the rivals with breasts exposed from a similar scene featuring Jocasta in book 7 of Statius's *Thebaid* (Faral, 2:134; Tatlock, 1974, 305, n. 1; *Thebaid*, 7:470 ff.). The differences are important, too. Jocasta fails to bring her warring sons together, while Tonuuenna not only reconciles them, but enunciates a private theory of social mobility unknown to Jocasta, but which must have struck Geoffrey's audience as particularly relevant to contemporary life. Geoffrey traces the brother's rivalry to the practice of primogeniture, which he makes out to be yet another ancient Trojan custom. In point of fact, primogeniture was a fairly recent practice in twelfth-century England and was only becoming customary among the nobility in Geoffrey's own day. William Rufus, the second of William the Conqueror's three sons, not Robert Curthose, the eldest, ruled England following his father's death; and Rufus himself was succeeded by the Conqueror's third son, Henry Beauclerc (Henry I). A scene much like the reconciliation of Belinus and Brennius, minus the mediation of the mother, did occur in 1101 at Alton, between the armies of Henry and Robert Curthose, the eldest of William the Conqueror's sons. Their informal verbal agreement was ratified at Winchester and confirmed by oaths (Tatlock, 1974, 355–56).[42] But it did not last. Henry later seized Robert and kept him securely in prison for 28 years (1106–34) until his death. The reconciliation of Belinus and Brennius, on the other hand, conforms to the ideal of Concord as established by their father and championed by their mother. The united brothers inaugurate one of the golden ages of early British history, which serves as a model for Arthur's reign at a later period (Thorpe, 233). Significantly, Belinus, the British king, defeats the Norwegians in battle and brings the Danes under his domination as tribute-paying subjects. He thus conquers the peoples who would later harass and dominate England and overcome the English.

Tonuuenna's speech of reconciliation justifies primogeniture on the basis of its encouragement of salutary competition and the spirit of adventure; her words probably offered cold comfort to the many disgruntled younger sons in Geoffrey's audience.[43] Brennius is the very model of the modern self-made entrepreneur pulling himself up by his bootstraps, seeking supplemental income in martial as well as marital enterprises. The energy of such actual vagabond dispossessed younger sons, the *milites peregrini,* often expressed itself in violent activities such as crusades and warfare, but also in a particularly intense form of legacy-hunting among widows and daughters of the wealthy nobility.[44] Brennius marries his way into economic opportunity and waits anxiously for Segnius to die without a male heir, which he obligingly does.

The first part of the story of Belinus and Brennius, therefore, is a fantasy in which an inherently unstable set of family property arrangements in twelfth-century England is optimistically resolved in accord with the increasingly widespread practice of primogeniture. The combination of power bases in the inherited wealth of the eldest son (Belinus) and in the newly acquired possessions of the entrepreneurial cadet (Brennius) makes possible the brothers' grand imperial undertakings.

Geoffrey took his account of the Gauls defeat of the Romans and subsequent sack of Rome largely from Orosius (fifth century)[45] and perhaps from Landolf Sagax (eleventh century).[46] Most important, however, is the British perspective from which Geoffrey tells the familiar story. In both sources, of course, there is no mention of Belinus, who is Geoffrey's own creation, and in both Orosius and Landolf, Brennus is the Gaulish leader of the Senonians, not a British exile in command of the Allobroges.[47] Orosius used the sack of Rome by the Gauls to emphasize how far more furious and destructive it had been than the recent Gothic sack of the city in A.D. 410, the occasion that prompted Saint Augustine to write his *City of God.* Picking up on this Orosian theme, Geoffrey stresses the unbridled fury of the attack by Brennius and Belinus. He tells how they erected a gibbit in front of the city's gate and hanged 23 Roman hostages in an effort to get the city to capitulate. He understandably passed over the passage in Orosius in which the Gauls are said to have been bought off for 1,000 pounds of gold; and he chose not to follow Livy (5, 49) or Landolf (Crivellucci, 1, 23) in describing how the Gauls were later overtaken by Camillus, who cut them down and recovered the ransom price and stolen military insignia. All traces of Roman perseverance and heroism connected with the attack of the Gauls, such as the famous stories about Manlius and the Capitolian geese, or the flamen Gaius Fabius Dorsuo's defiantly completing the prescribed religious rites on the occupied Quirinal Hill, both of which are told by Livy (5, 46) and Landolf (Crivellucci, 22–23), find no place in Geoffrey's account. The British-Gallic adventure in Italy ends when Belinus returns home, and Brennius dies after subjecting the people of Italy to unheard of cruelty. Geoffrey passes quickly over Brennius's later deeds and his death, claiming that they had been treated adequately already in Roman history.

The conquests of Brennius and Belinus in the *HRB* demonstrate the capacity of the early Britons to subject the greatest civilization of the ancient world to their power. Later, Arthur will look back to these exploits when he contemptuously dismisses Lucius's demand that Britain pay tribute to Rome (Thorpe, 233). Yet, no lasting empire results from the brothers' conquests. Instead, having established British military dominance, Belinus returns home to rule Britain during a golden age of peace and prosperity that will never again be equaled (Thorpe, 100). He restores cities, ratifies Dunvallo's laws, even builds new cities, such as Kaerusk, which later the Romans rename *Urbs Legionum,* the City of the Legions (Caerleon). When he dies, Belinus's ashes are placed in a golden urn and set atop a great tower over Billingsgate (*Belinesgata*), the gateway of Trinovantum named in his honor. The *HRB,* in other words, contradicts the notion that the Romans were the first to bring significant material culture to Britain. On the contrary, Geoffrey asserts, they inherited from the British much of what has been erroneously taken to be marks of their industry and ingenuity. Even the celebrated obelisk in the Circus of Nero in Rome containing the ashes of Julius Caesar, or the Column of Trajan in which the bones of the emperor were enclosed in a golden urn (both of which were well-known to twelfth-century pilgrims), had their precursor in Belinus's burial tower (Faral, 2:137; Tatlock, 1974, 371–72; Arnold, 1879, 24).

Geoffrey follows the same revisionist strategy in listing the achievements of the more than 40 successors of Belinus down to Cassivelaunus and the period of Roman occupation. The great walls, baths, and amphitheater of Caerleon, still impressive though in ruins in Geoffrey's day,[48] were originally built, according to the *HRB,* not by the Romans, but by Belinus and were augmented by his son and successor, Gurguit Barbtruc. Lud, the son of Heli, similarly oversaw the construction of houses, palaces, and public buildings in Trinovantum, of such splendor that the city was unrivaled for its beauty in his day, and ultimately came to be named Kaerlud (hence Kaerlundein, London) after him. The Anglo-Saxon Mercian Laws were mere translations by King Alfred, of British originals authored by Marcia, the wise wife of Gurguit's successor Guithelinus, who governs Britain during the minority of her son Sisillius.

The rulers who follow Belinus all have plausibly British sounding names, which Geoffrey did not invent but selected principally from Nennius (Guithelinus, Eldol), or from the Welsh genealogies (Arthgallo,

Ingenius, Enniaunus, Isuallo), although not in the order found there. Occasionally a fragment of Welsh tradition can even be discerned behind the stark list of rulers. Digueillus, for example, who "cared above all for the fair administration of justice among his people" may actually be a garbled form of Higuel Bonus, the British king mentioned in the *Annales Cambriae* under the year 950 (Thorpe, 106; Hutson, 1978, 43; Nennius, ed. J. Morris, 49, 91). Higuel Bonus is Hywel Dda ("Hywel the Good"), the historic tenth-century Welsh ruler, known to scribes of the law code that circulated under his name as "prince" or "king of all of Wales" (Jenkins, 1). The names of two of the kings in this section of the *HRB*, Peredurus and Rederchus, will appear once again in Geoffrey's *VM*.

Taken as a whole, the list of rulers following Belinus is intended to prove the existence of a long and continuous line of British sovereigns, among whom are a rich assortment of law-givers, builders, generous, wise, forgiving men, as well as traitors, sadists, and tyrants. The names and deeds of the vast majority of these rulers and most of their predecessors, too, were in all likelihood utterly unknown to Geoffrey's contemporaries. Their stories opened an entirely new page in the history of Britain and of Europe itself. The *HRB* revealed for the first time the existence in pre-Roman Britain of a dignified culture with ancient roots and a rich material, military, and cultural history on a par with the better-known civilizations of Northern Europe and the Mediterranean.

With Cassivelaunus and the invasion of Caesar, the reader would be entering somewhat more familiar ground.

Roman Britain

Unlike the careers of Leir and the successors of Belinus, the Roman period in Britain was relatively well-known to Geoffrey's audience. It had been described in part by Caesar himself, of course, in his *Commentaries* on the Gallic War, manuscripts of which were in the library at Bec in Geoffrey's day,[49] but also by Orosius, Gildas, Bede, and Nennius. Geoffrey's contemporary Henry of Huntingdon had only a few years earlier described this period as part of his survey of Roman emperors in his *History of the English,* the first version of which appeared in 1129 (Arnold, 1879, 16–37).[50] Henry had mainly followed Bede's account of the Roman conquest of Britain as he was instructed to do by his patron, Alexander, bishop of Lincoln. Out of these sources (one might even say in the face of these sources), Geoffrey spun his own characteristically unique version of the Roman presence in Britain.

By the time Geoffrey came to recount Caesar's first invasion, he had firmly established his vision of Britain as a highly civilized nation enjoying the protection of an ancient code of native laws, an elaborate system of roads, beautiful cities, impressive monuments, baths, a complete urban culture, in other words, a worthy rival of Rome itself. The *HRB* would have us believe that upon arriving on the shores of Britain, the Romans discovered an advanced civilization very much like their own. This was not Caesar's view. Although admiring the British for their valor on the field of battle and for their uncanny skill at chariot warfare, Caesar regarded the people of Britain essentially as barbarians. They painted themselves blue with woad, kept wives in common, and were given to the practice of human sacrifice under the auspices of the druids. Gildas, though himself a member of the British race, bitterly denounced both the ancient Britons and their contemporary progeny. Gildas claimed that British cowardice in war and infidelity in peace had become proverbial and stated that the ancient Britons turned their backs and ran at the approach of the Roman armies (Winterbottom, 18). The inherent instability of this people in Gildas's view made them especially vulnerable during the early Christian period to the poison of Arianism. Bede inherited Gildas's attitude toward the British, but added the stain of Pelagianism to the list of their inveterate vices (Bede, trans. Sherley-Price, 49–50).[51]

Geoffrey, in other words, had his work cut out for him. In order to invert the traditions of Caesar, Gildas, and Bede, he invented from whole cloth, characters and events found nowhere in earlier authorities on Roman Britain and entirely reversed the received view on established events. He was particularly clever at filling in the many gaps in the scrappy historic record of Roman and early Christian Britain with evidence of the country's distinguished past. Who was there to gainsay him? Most continental annalists only deigned to speak about Britain when it played its occasional part in continental affairs. Bede wrote about the Romans in Britain merely as a preface to his main interest in the English church and people. Gildas's fulminations against the British yielded little concrete history. Nennius provided a framework, not a history. Moreover, Geoffrey seems also to have relished the opportunity to contradict accepted authorities, even eyewitnesses such as Caesar.

Where Caesar in the *Commentaries* remarks on how little anyone in Gaul seemed to know about the British beyond that they regarded themselves as the indigenous inhabitants of the island,[52] Geoffrey conjures up a scene for the *HRB* on the eve of the Roman invasion in which Caesar muses on the common Trojan ancestry that links the Romans and the British (Thorpe, 107). He resolves to send a message demanding tribute rather than make war on the British, observing that "we must not shed the blood of our kinsmen, nor offend the ancient dignity of our common ancestor Priam" (Thorpe, 107). Geoffrey has Cassivelaunus respond to Caesar's message in high rhetorical style, scolding the Roman leader for insulting their "common inheritance of noble blood [that] comes down from Aeneas to Briton and Roman alike" (Thorpe, 108). His people, Cassivelaunus remarks, are completely unaware of what it means to live under the yoke of slavery.[53]

Geoffrey turned to Nennius for the view that Caesar required three rather than only two attempts to subdue the British. Caesar tells how his two expeditions to Britain were imperiled by his loss of ships to storms in the Channel. Geoffrey makes no mention of this. Conversely, in the *HRB* British military genius is solely responsible for the defeat that the Romans suffer in their first two landings. In the first encounter (55 B. C.), the Briton Nennius (Geoffrey's invention) takes Caesar's sword, Yellow Death, away from him in face-to-face combat and nearly kills Caesar before he himself is slain. During the second campaign (54 B. C.), according to Caesar and later authorities, the British implant sharp stakes along the banks of the Thames and in the river bed beneath the water in order to prevent the Romans fording the river. At Caesar's command, however, the troops simply enter the water, cross over unmolested, avoiding the stakes, and drive the barbarians into the forest (Caesar, 5, 18; Orosius, 6, 9, 282–83; Bede, trans. Sherley-Price, 41; Nennius, 23). Geoffrey has quite a different perspective on this. In the *HRB* the Romans sail up the Thames unaware of the stakes the British have fixed on the river bottom, and run the hulls of their ships upon them, causing thousands of their soldiers to be drowned (Thorpe, 111–12). Rather than retreating, as the earlier authorities would have it, the British troops in the *HRB* account follow Cassivelaunus in an assault on the Roman survivors, outnumbering them three to one, ultimately causing Caesar to flee in his ships back to Gaul with his remaining men.

The Romans' third invasion is successful only because the British are betrayed by one of their own leaders by the name of Androgeus, who writes a craven letter to Caesar complaining of Cassivelaunus's unfair treatment of him.[54] Androgeus's surprise rear attack on Cassivelaunus's army while it is engaged with Caesar's legions is the turning point of the war. Cassivelaunus is forced to retreat to his hill fortress and ultimately surrenders to Caesar, but the two men become friends thereafter, and Caesar spends the winter in Britain.

Geoffrey had also to concoct a line of distinguished British kings to fill the vacuum in the historic record between the Caesarian (55/54 B.C.) and the Claudian (A. D. 43) conquests (Thorpe, 118–19). Tenvantius succeeds Cassivelaunus and is followed by Cymbelline, who is reared in the household of Caesar Augustus, and pays tribute to Rome of his own free will, even though he need not do so. Almost as an afterthought, Geoffrey mentions that the birth of Jesus took place at this time. The Claudian conquest in the *HRB* is occasioned by the refusal of Cymbelline's son Guiderius to pay tribute. When Guiderius is slain through the treachery of the Roman Lelius Hamo (eponym of Southampton), his brother Arvirargus takes over.

Arvirargus is another Gaulfridian creation whose grandiose deeds were invented by Geoffrey almost out of thin air. Actually, Geoffrey culled Arvirargus's name out of Juvenal's Fourth Satire and invented a glorious career for him, as champion of the British against the Romans in the time of Claudius, and for his daughter Genvissa.[55]

Geoffrey used all of his inventiveness, in other words, to overturn the conventional view of the Roman conquest of Britain as his audience was likely to find it in previous sources. The British emerge in his account as the equals of the Romans in all things. The land was brought under Roman domination only with the greatest of difficulty and never completely accepted its role as a tribute-paying province. The Britons marry into noble Roman families, are educated in the courts of the Roman nobility, fight as lieutenants to Roman generals elsewhere in the Empire, and distinguish themselves as builders of cities.[56] With the advent of Christianity under Lucius, great-grandson of Arvirargus, and the persecutions of the Christians under Diocletian, the animosity between the Britons and the Romans intensifies. Asclepiodotus, Duke of Cornwall,[57] revolts against the cruelty of Allectus, the Roman governor of Britain, and massacres Romans in London.[58] Britain is distinguished for its Christian martyrs, especially Saints Alban and Amphibalus[59] at Saint Albans and Julius and Aaron in Geoffrey's favorite City of the Legions.

Geoffrey also attacked Bede's picture of early Christian Britain as having only two cities with metropolitan status, Canterbury and York. Geoffrey knew from reading Bede that Canterbury achieved its eminence as a result of the missionary activities of Augustine, sent to convert England by Pope Gregory. Geoffrey insists that Canterbury was a late arrival and that the earliest Christian administrative arrangement had London, York and the City of the Legions as the original sees of the archbishops of Britain. Moreover, the *HRB* shows the continuity of

British and Roman administrative centers by making the 28 cities of
Britain mentioned by Nennius into residences of Roman flamens, which
thereafter become the sees of the earliest bishops. The significance of
these dispositions for the politics of Geoffrey's own day, will be discussed
in chapter 3, but here we need only remark that Geoffrey was supplying
information on the administrative structure of early Christian Britain
that directly contradicted Bede.

With the reign of Constantine, the son of Helen, Rome's debt to
Britain becomes even more clear. The Constantine (Constantine the Great)
whose career is described in the *HRB* is quite different from the one mentioned in Bede, whose mother is concubine to Constantius, the Roman
governor of Gaul and Spain, not the wise daughter of Coel, the British
king, and wife of Constantius. Always alert for opportunities to supply evidence of Britain's glorious role as a cradle of civilization, Geoffrey added
the story of the migration to Constantine's court of the many Roman
exiles who flee the cruelty of the dictator Maxentius. His comments on
Constantine's Britain, in fact, sound very much like what William of
Malmesbury had to say about England as a tranquil refuge for foreign
exiles under Henry I, and Geoffrey may have intended this detail in his
account of Roman Britain as flattery to the king.[60] In any case, Geoffrey's
Constantine responds to the cries for justice and becomes the second
Briton (half-Briton actually), counting Belinus and Brennius as one, to
conquer Rome. He overthrows the dictator Maxentius and goes on to
become "overlord of the whole world." In his train, three Britons ascend to
the rank of senators. In keeping with the *HRB*'s focus on secular matters,
Geoffrey makes no mention of the legend of Helen's discovery of the true
cross or of her son's favoritism toward Christians in the Western Empire.

The final crisis for Roman Britain begins with the ascent of the half-
British Roman senator Maximianus[61] to the throne of Britain. Geoffrey's
sources for Maximianus's career, Gildas, Bede, and Nennius, agreed in
blaming the decline of Britain on Maximianus's depleting the island of
its soldiers in his bid for the purple. Left without military protection, the
island falls prey to the Picts, Irish, Norwegians, and Danes, all precursor
invaders to the Saxons. To his sources, however, Geoffrey adds the character Conanus Meriadocus. After first battling against Maximianus,
Conanus is finally reconciled to him and departs with him to Gaul where
he is rewarded by Maximianus with the kingship of Armorica. The land
he rules over becomes a "second Britain," itself preserving the flower of
the British race, while the island of Britain is being ravaged by a series of
ruthless invaders.

Among Maximianus's many acts of inhumanity, according to Geoffrey, was the extermination of all the males of Armorica in order to restock the land with trustworthy Britons. He initiates an out-migration of 30,000 British soldiers and 100,000 ordinary men and women. In addition to this group, an additional component of 11,000 British women is brought over by Conan as wives for his troops because he does not wish to mix the blood of his race with that of the Gauls. Unhappily a storm scatters their ships at sea, drowning some and driving others into the hands of enemies along the coast of the continent; the most abominable of these are Wanius and Melga, leaders of the Picts and Huns, who seize the British women and, when their sexual advances are spurned, slaughter them all.

The story of the lamentable fate of the British maidens was taken by Geoffrey from the well-known legend of Saint Ursula and the 11,010 virgins, versions of which date back to the tenth century and earlier.[62] The story is closely associated with the city of Cologne, where Ursula was martyred, along with the girls dedicated to virginity who accompanied her on pilgrimage, after she rejects Attila's proposal of marriage. Given the great popularity of the Ursula legend in Geoffrey's own day as a result of the supposed discovery of the relics of the martyrs in 1106, this is one of his most audacious appropriations of preexisting material. Displacing the story from its traditional location in Germany, Geoffrey recasts it as part of the Breton settlement legend. Moreover, he desacralizes the legend by making the women the intended (and some even eager) brides of their own countrymen, the British soldiers in Armorica. Martyrdom in the cause of Christian virginity is replaced by martyrdom in the cause of racial purity. And as if inviting the reader to relish this little prank of his, Geoffrey preserves a vestige of the story's original purpose by allowing that some of the women leaving Britain preferred to remain virgins rather than marry.

For the scenes of the final collapse of Britain, Geoffrey used the account in Gildas (Winterbottom, 21–25). All of his sources stressed the responsibility of Maximianus, the "madness of Maximianus" (*vesania Maximiani*) in Geoffrey's phrase, for draining the island of its youth and vitality (Thorpe, 147). Left behind are the pitiful remnants of a once great culture, now exposed to the full fury of the surrounding barbarians. The Romans come to their aid, leaving behind a protective wall in the north, and instructions on how to construct weapons and organize an army, but ultimately they inform the British that they must defend themselves or lose their lives and liberty. Geoffrey adds to this a speech by Guithelin, archbishop of London, urging the remaining citizens to learn the ways of war. He enunciates a bracing theory of social mobility, observing that men can change their stations in life, that a soldier (*miles*) can be born to a peasant (*rusticus*) or a peasant to a soldier, and so on. But Geoffrey seems to have set up this theory in order to knock it down. Subsequent events show that Guithelin's hope is misplaced. "It is easier for a kite," Geoffrey comments later, "to be made to act like a sparrow-hawk than for a wise man [*eruditus*] to be fashioned at short notice from a peasant [*rusticus*]" (Thorpe, 146). The piteous scene of the miserable commoners being dragged to their death from their defensive positions atop the Roman walls is borrowed from Gildas, as is the final appeal for help to the Roman general Agicius that goes unanswered (Winterbottom, 23–24).

The Romans in Geoffrey's *HRB* take much from Britain, but bring very little of lasting value to it. Their legacy was to introduce a slow poison into the political fabric of the island by drawing the British into a web of imperial rivalries and by siphoning off the island's vitality. Their most devastating stroke was to deprive Britain of its military elite in time of great peril in order to support the personal ambitions of a ruthless tyrant. The idea that the Romans precipitated Britain's loss of sovereignty was not original with Geoffrey. His contribution was to construct an elaborate and convincing image of the dignified civilization of Britain that the Romans left in ruins. His depiction of this second Trojan advent to the shores of Britain begins with Cassivelaunus's proud declaration of the British people's love of liberty and ends with the devastation of the country following the mass exodus of their warriors, the only genuine guarantee of liberty.

In calling up his own version of Britain under Roman dominion, Geoffrey offered the island's most recent conquerors a sober lesson in the consequences of vanity, greed, ambition, and rivalry. His humanism expresses itself here in the belief that mankind lives in a world of human agency and has the power to damn or redeem itself at least in part by understanding history, the mirror of its folly and wisdom. Recovery of Britain's lost liberty would be slow and painful.

The Saga of Vortigern

In order to bridge the gap in his sources between the Britons' appeal to Agicius and the career of Vortigern, Geoffrey borrowed the story of two brothers, Constantine II and Constans, from Bede (Bede, trans. Sherley-Price, 1, 11, 50). Bede's Constantine is a British usurper, "a common trooper of no merit" whose incompetence causes "great harm to the commonwealth." He is killed at Arles by command of the Emperor Honorius; his brother, Constans, whom Constantine has made a Caesar, is later dispatched at Vienne. Geoffrey's Constantine, on the other hand, is brother to King Aldroenus of Brittany and is said to have been a man "skilled in military affairs." He is sent to Britain by Aldroenus in response to Archbishop Guithelin's appeal for help in defending Britain against the barbarians. Constantine returns to Britain, is crowned at Silchester by Guithelin, marries, and later begets three sons, Constans, Aurelius Ambrosius, and Utherpendragon. After ruling Britain for 10 years, Constantine is killed by a Pict. Constans is then lured out of the monastic life by the clever Vortigern, leader of the Gewissei, and quickly becomes Vortigern's tool. This elicits Geoffrey's sardonic comment that "what he [Constans] had learned in the cloister had nothing to do with how to rule a kingdom" (Thorpe, 152). Vortigern convinces Constans to confederate with the Picts, who soon learn that Vortigern is the real power among the Britons. Vortigern gains their loyalty with lavish gifts, and soon induces them to murder Constans.[63] The tutors of the youthful Aurelius Ambrosius and Utherpendragon, sensing danger, flee with their charges to Brittany. Vortigern immediately crowns himself king. Fearing attack from Aurelius and Utherpendragon, Vortigern allies himself with the brothers Hengist and Horsa, who have been exiled from their Saxon homeland.

The principal source of Geoffrey's saga of Vortigern is Nennius's *Historia Brittonum,* chapters 35–50. By the time Nennius wrote, Vortigern (Nennius calls him *Guorthigirn*) had come to shoulder nearly all the blame for the devastations wrought by the Saxon invasions. Gildas and Bede had their own versions of the British tyrant, and in Geoffrey's own day, Henry of Huntingdon (1129) had retold the story, largely out of Bede, but also with some borrowings from Nennius (Arnold, 1879, 37–40). This was the perfect opportunity for Geoffrey to shed new light on this familiar story from the perspective of the "British book," especially because the pieces of the saga of this supposedly traitorous British ruler had been very imperfectly welded together by Nennius.[64] It would be fair to say, in fact, that the story of Vortigern in the *Historia Brittonum* remains more in the nature of fragments, the miscellaneous character of which was recognized not only by Geoffrey, but also by the medieval redactors of the text.[65] Geoffrey did not need to scruple, therefore, over taking liberties with Vortigern's legend as he found it in Nennius.

As has long been recognized, the names of the exiled brothers Hengist and Horsa mean *mare* and *stallion,* respectively. The two brothers are euhemerized horse divinities, a duplicated version of the same god who brought fertility and plenty to the Germanic people.[66] Both Nennius and the *Anglo-Saxon Chronicle* trace the brothers' lineage back to Woden, while in southeastern English dynastic tradition Hengist and Horsa were honored as the twin founders of the royal house of Kent. Like Brennius and Conan Meriadocus, they are noble young men who have been forced by circumstances to "seek a living for themselves" (Thorpe, 156).

As Vortigern soon discovers, however, they were also pagan worshipers of Mercury/Woden. Understanding the Saxon arrival in Britain as a kind of miasma helps to appreciate why Vortigern as host to the exiles, and later as brother-in-law to Hengist through his marriage to Renwein, is in a sense contaminated by their presence. Aldhelm (ca. 640–709) lamented in his letter to Geraint, the British king of Domnonia (Devon and Cornwall), that the bishops of Dyfed (South Wales) went so far as to refuse even to eat with the Saxon clergy; they ordered that the plates and cups shared in the refectory be "purified with grains of sandy gravel, or with the dusky cinders of ash."[67]

In Nennius, Saint Germanus's three visitations to Britain alternate with the various Saxon *adventus* and are intended to illustrate the holy man's power over two corrupt kings, Benlli (or Belinus) and Vortigern. Germanus's presence in the *Historia Brittonum* may be the product of propaganda arising from the tensions between Mercia and Powys (Vortigern's base of power) during the seventh and eighth centuries (Kirby, 51–52, 59). Nothing could be more in keeping with Welsh hagiographical conventions than to conscript a saint into service in dynastic disputes, and this appears to be the case with Germanus. Vortigern's fiery death in his tower is brought about in the *Historia Brittonum* by Germanus's fasting against the tyrant (Tatlock, 1974, 3:34–35).[68] For Nennius, the saint is the principal catalyst in the king's demise.

Not surprisingly, Geoffrey relegates the role of Germanus to the periphery. He reduces Germanus's three visitations to one and even that has as its sole purpose in the *HRB* the suppression of Pelagianism. The entire account of the opposition of Germanus and Vortigern, so integral to the *Historia Brittonum* version, is thus brushed aside by Geoffrey. Gone, too, is Vortigern's incestuous union with his daughter, the event that provided motivation for Germanus's second visit to Britain in

Nennius. In its place, Geoffrey invents the story of Vortigern's infatuation with Hengist's sister Renwein, including the celebrated excursus into the origin of Saxon toasts (*drincheil* and *wasseil*), their marriage, and Renwein's poisoning of her stepson Vortimer.[69]

Having demoted Germanus from the rank of chief agent in Vortigern's status degradation, Geoffrey replaced the saint with the "boy without a father" (Merlin) by transferring Vortigern's meeting with Merlin to its present crucial place in the story. His purpose was clearly to deflate the hagiographical character and perspective of the *Historia Brittonum* and to redeploy the remaining material into two essentially secular narratives.

First, instead of opposing the tyrant for his marriage to a pagan princess and his incestuous union with his own daughter, Merlin foretells Vortigern's death as the inevitable result of his lack of political wisdom: "You made a fatal mistake when you betrayed their [Constantine II's sons] father and invited the Saxons to your island" (Thorpe, 186). (This is not strictly faithful to Geoffrey's own version in which a Pict murders Constantine; Vortigern betrays Constans not Constantine.)

Second, Aurelius and Eldol, both of whom have strictly political and personal grudges to settle with Vortigern, lay siege to his fortress on Mount Cloartius, and when all else fails, burn it and the king to ashes. Their motivation for attacking Vortigern and the means they use to bring him down are strictly human. By replacing Germanus with Merlin and by substituting the human agency of Aurelius and Eldol for divine intervention in response to Germanus's fast, Geoffrey betrays here as elsewhere in the *HRB* his underlying philosophical assumption that human will is the principal force that governs history.

Geoffrey also introduced some minor changes to make Vortigern's saga more meaningful to his audience. Vortigern's messengers find Merlin at Carmarthen (Modern Welsh, *Caerfyrddin*; Medieval Welsh, *Kaermirtin*) rather than at "campus Elleti" in the district of Glywysing as in Nennius. Glywysing is the ancient district between the Tawe and the Usk, a region quite close to Monmouth. Carmarthen is the old Roman town (Moridunum) on the Towey River in South West Wales. The usual explanation for Geoffrey's displacement of the setting is simply that he was struck by the similarity of the name Myrddin/Mirtin and the name of the town Kaermirtin. Some scholars believe that Geoffrey was the first to make this association, while others believe that he was merely following an earlier Welsh eponymic tradition connecting the prophet Mirtin with the town Kaermirtin. Mirtin/Myrddin was known as a prophet of stature in South Wales as early as the *Armes Prydein* (ca. 930), but we know little about the places where his legend was cultivated during this period. Perhaps Geoffrey was also motivated to shift this scene to Carmarthen, feeling that its dignity as a Roman town was especially suitable for the new prominence he had decided to bestow on Nennius's legend of the boy without a father. He seems to have held Caerleon in similar respect for its status as a Roman legionary city.

Geoffrey also invents Vortigern's magus Maugantius, who knowingly explains that Apuleius's *De Deo Socratis* tells us all about the *incubi demones,* and their sexual escapades with humans (it doesn't).[70] Geoffrey makes Merlin's mother out to be the daughter of the king of Demetia,[71] and also gives the name Dinabutius to the anonymous playmate of the boy without a father in Nennius, no doubt wishing in part to concretize what Nennius had left vague.

Similarly, Geoffrey levels the awkwardness of Nennius's account of the uncovering of the two fighting *vermes* (worms, serpents). Nennius appears to be fusing together two different versions of the fighting animals, one in which they were encased in two jars and another in which they were folded together in a single cloth. Geoffrey was too good a storyteller to let such awkwardness pass. He discards the cloth and has the beasts discovered within the two separate jars.

The Sacrifice of the Boy without a Father

One of Geoffrey's boldest revisions to Nennius was to give the name *Merlin* to the fatherless boy-prophet. The boy goes unnamed in the *Historia Brittonum* until the end of chapter 42 following his explanation of the meaning of the battle between the red and white dragons. When Vortigern asks him his name he replies, "I am called Ambrosius." The text then adds, "that is to say, he was shown to be [or "in British" according to the Vatican recension (Dumville, 95)] Emrys the Overlord" (*Embreis Guletic*), a statement that looks very much like an interpolation intended to provide the Welsh name for the lad (Embreis/Emrys = Ambrose; *Guletic* = Welsh *gwledic* = overlord, leader). To the king's next inquiry about his family background, Ambrosius answers, "My father is one of the consuls of the Roman people." This statement, of course, boldly contradicts what we have previously learned about the boy, namely, that he is "without a father." Nennius was probably cobbling together bits of information about Ambrosius's youth from disparate sources without attempting to resolve their contradictions. Nennius has

Vortigern give over the fortress on Mount Eryri and all the kingdoms of western Britain to Ambrosius before he goes north with his wise men to the region called Gwynessi, where he builds a city called Caer Gwrtheyrn.

Geoffrey changed all of this. For the *HRB* he devised two people named *Ambrosius*. One, Merlin Ambrosius, was the boy-prophet who had no father; the other, Aurelius Ambrosius, was one of the three sons of Constantine II, and hence, a man of noble Roman blood. Distinguishing the boy Merlin Ambrosius from Aurelius Ambrosius solved the internal contradiction of the Nennian version. Aurelius Ambrosius in Geoffrey returns from his refuge in Brittany and helps Eldol to burn Vortigern in his tower on Mount Cloartius. Merlin Ambrosius remains the mysterious boy without a father.

Vortigern's councilors insist that the only way to ensure the stability of his tower is to sprinkle it with the blood of a boy without a father. Such foundation-sacrifices have been documented as far back as the Yin Dynasty of the second millennium B. C.,[72] and reflexes of them can apparently be found in Insular Celtic foundation legends during the medieval period related to Emain Macha in Ireland[73] and Saint Columba's monastery on Iona.[74] Savory's excavations at Dinas Emrys did not turn up any evidence of human sacrifice at that site,[75] but Alcock thinks that the skeleton of a young man discovered beneath an Iron-Age rampart at Cadbury was "a dedicatory sacrifice intended to bless the later rampart."[76] Given the opposition of Rome and the Church of Rome to human sacrifice, the association of Vortigern with the practice is an index to the fierce scorn with which British traditions commemorated (or execrated) his career.[77]

Geoffrey's placing the episode of the sinking foundation at the nadir of Vortigern's kingship underscores the rupture in the vital link between king and land.[78] Whether Geoffrey or Nennius actually believed that the land itself revolted against the stewardship of a corrupt king or whether they simply used this ancient belief as metaphor for the alienation of Vortigern from the moral basis of sovereignty is uncertain. Surely they both conceived of Vortigern's crumbling fortress as a fitting metaphor for the dissolution and decay of British society during the insecurities of the fifth century.

The crime of Constans's murder is on Vortigern's hands, and his marriage to Renwein places him among the unclean Saxon exiles. To Nennius, the withdrawal of Germanus's ecclesiastical approval from the king signals his loss of power. To Geoffrey, however, Merlin's exposure of

the ignorance of the king's wise men exposes Vortigern's empty authority. The unmasking of the king as victim falls to Merlin, too. After aston-
ishing the assembly with the ambiguity of his lengthy prophecies (see
chapter 3), Merlin accedes to Vortigern's desire to know his own end,
first by predicting that the sons of Constantine will burn him in his
tower and then foretelling that death threatens him also from the Saxons
themselves. An audience accustomed to perceive historic events as reit-
erations of biblical types would naturally associate Merlin's confrontation
with Vortigern's magi with the story of Moses' and Aaron's conflict with
the magicians of Pharaoh (Exodus 7:8–13), the contest between Elijah
and Ahab's prophets of Baal (1 Kings 18:17–40), or the conflict of
Daniel with the enchanters of Nebuchadnezzar and Belshazzar (Daniel
2). Vortigern meets his end in Geoffrey's *HRB* at the hands of Aurelius
Ambrosius and Eldol, Duke of Gloucester, who burn him in his tower on
Mount Cloartius (Doartius) in the Wye valley, a location very near to
Monmouth (Tatlock, 1974, 72). Before the king's death, Aurelius makes
a stirring speech indicting Vortigern as the guilty one uniquely responsible for all the misfortunes that have befallen the British folk.

Vortigern's consumption by fire and dispersal into the air is the final
cathartic gesture, which enables the land to be restored to peace and
unity. The encounter with Merlin on the flanks of Snowdon serves also to
identify Merlin as the new prophetic authority. Merlin, who deflects violence from himself onto the king, is to Vortigern what Teresias is to
Oedipus: an intended victim whose clarity of understanding reveals the
king himself as the source of chaos.

The Stonehenge Episode

The raising of Stonehenge in the *HRB* is linked to the sinking of
Vortigern's tower by the simple thematic device of associating Merlin
with the foundation of the two edifices. Vortigern is unable to construct
his tower because of an underlying structural weakness, the presence of
a pool in which two dragons sleep in their stone enclosures. This architectural instability is surely in part a metaphor for the political deca-
dence of the tyrant's reign: Vortigern's crimes, simply put, undermine
the edifice of British sovereignty. The fortress on Mount Snowdon is a
monument to his corruption and impiety, just as the raising of
Stonehenge to those massacred at Mount Ambrius is an act of piety on
the part of Aurelius. Merlin stands as the common link between these
two diametrically opposed foundation efforts. Vortigern's sinking foun-

dation is a synecdoche also for the devastations he has brought on the churches and cities of Britain. By contrast, Aurelius's first proclamation following the defeat of his enemies is that the churches and cities of the country be rebuilt. Thus, having made Merlin the "boy without a father," Geoffrey also implicitly began his career as the master-builder who frustrates Vortigern's *aedificium vanitatis* and magically erects Aurelius's *aedificium pietatis,* beneath which the victims of the massacre of Mount Ambrius will forever sleep. As a deliberate parody of Vortigern's failure to build his tower on Snowdon, the Stonehenge episode is intended to mark a turning of the wheel of history from the rule of a *tyrannus* to that of the *rex pius.*

The sequence of events in the Stonehenge episode is easily recognizable as a reprise of the scene on Snowdon. Aurelius's workmen fail to come up with a fitting monument to commemorate their fallen comrades. Tremorinus, archbishop of the city of the Legions, steps in to propose that Aurelius consult Merlin about the enterprise because "there is no one else in your kingdom who has greater skill, either in the foretelling of the future or in mechanical contrivances" (Thorpe, 195). Aurelius sends messengers forth to seek out Merlin. Having traveled through the country, they find him at last in the region of the Gewissei at the Galabes Spring (shown by Tatlock, 1974, 74–75, to be a place not far from Monmouth itself). He is warmly greeted by Aurelius who requests that Merlin foretell the future. Merlin refuses to debase his prophetic talents in trivial displays for fear that the spirit of prophecy will withdraw from him in time of need, but he agrees to help Aurelius construct a sepulcher for the dead. Given the repetitive plot structure of the Stonehenge and Mount Snowdon episodes, the verbal echoes between the two scenes seem less the result of coincidence or formulaic patterning, and more like a conscious attempt at imitation.

Geoffrey appears to have exploited contemporary curiosity about the construction of Stonehenge in order to add further glory to his creature Merlin Ambrose. The sources on which he drew when composing the Stonehenge episode, however, are quite mysterious.[79] Geoffrey is the first author to offer an explanation of the origin of the Stonehenge megaliths. His contemporary Henry of Huntingdon had similar antiquarian interest in the place. Henry describes the stones a bit more accurately than Geoffrey, but he admits that he does not know by what art they were built or for what purpose (Arnold, 1879, 12). This suggests that Geoffrey was the first who associated Merlin with Stonehenge's magical origins. In fact, because Geoffrey appears to have enjoyed his role as specialist in

fields unknown to Henry, Henry's professed ignorance on the subject
may have prompted Geoffrey to offer his own account of the raising of
the ancient monument and to make Merlin the hero of the piece.
Bearing in mind also that Alexander, bishop of Lincoln, patron of both
Geoffrey and Henry, took a particular interest in Merlin and his prophecies (see chapter 3), we may also sense in Geoffrey's Stonehenge episode
something of the writer's desire to impress his patron with his superior
knowledge. In any case, once he had conceived of Aurelius's construction
of Stonehenge as an antithesis to Vortigern's attempt to construct his
tower on Snowdon, Geoffrey at least had a dramatic framework on
which to build.

What more impressive site than Stonehenge was there for the burial
of the Britons massacred by Hengist at the monastery of Ambrius? Like
Dinas Emrys, the topography of Stonehenge itself tells a story. The presence of hundreds of Bronze Age barrows (burial mounds) in the vicinity
of Stonehenge was probably enough evidence for Geoffrey or his informants to interpret the monoliths as an ancient cemetery.[80] Moreover, not
having the benefits of modern petrographical analysis, he can hardly be
blamed for taking a Bronze Age monument for a Dark Age one. Once
he had conceived of Aurelius and Merlin as rebuilders of what Vortigern
had destroyed, Geoffrey did not have to look too far (only two miles)
from Amesbury, the putative site of the monastery of Ambrius, to discover a location worthy of their pious architectural program. Geoffrey
was not alone, after all, in thinking of prehistoric stone structures as
works of the Age of the Saints. Rhigyvarch claims that on the site where
Nonn, the mother of Saint David was raped by Sant, king of Ceredigion,
the earth threw up two stones, one at her feet and one at her head.[81]

The curative powers of the Stonehenge monoliths and their association with African Giants (they are called the Dance of the Giants, *Chorea
gigantum*) may easily have been derived by Geoffrey from common folk
belief about magical stones and the giants who were thought to have
inhabited early Britain. The twelfth-century Irish work *The Colloquy of
the Ancients* (*Agallamh na Seanórach*) traces the origins of Irish cairns,
tumuli, barrows, and pillar stones to the "huge Fiana" (Cross and Slover,
457–68). The transportation of the Stonehenge monoliths from Ireland
has been compared to the *Mabinogi* tales of the carrying of the talismat-
ic head of Bendigeifran back to Wales from Ireland and to the seizing of
the Cauldron of Regeneration by Llasar Llaes Gyfnewid. In other words,
the Welsh and Irish traditions have enough parallels to make it unlikely
that Geoffrey was either inventing the entire Stonehenge episode himself

or that, as Stuart Piggott tentatively hypothesized, he was in touch with Bronze Age traditions about the original patron and architect of Stonehenge (Piggott, 1941, 305–19).

The Story of Arthur's Conception

Geoffrey's final stroke in Merlin's portrait was to assign him a crucial role in bringing Arthur onto the stage of British history. Merlin had predicted Arthur's coming (under the name the Boar of Cornwall) as part of his elaborate prophetic outpouring before Vortigern on Mount Snowdon. Merlin's second prophetic anticipation of Arthur occurs at the time of Aurelius's death by poisoning at the hands of the Saxon Eopa, who has gained access to the British king by disguising himself as a British monk learned in medicine. Upon Aurelius's death, a star appears in the sky on three separate occasions causing widespread fear among the British. Proceeding from the star is a single beam at the end of which is a ball of fire in the shape of a dragon; from the dragon's mouth come two other beams, one of which stretches across Gaul, while the other reaches toward the Irish Sea and splits into seven smaller shafts of light. When commanded to explain the appearance of the star, Merlin calls up his prophetic spirit and interprets the portent to indicate the death of Aurelius. The star and the dragon, Merlin states, signify Uther, who must forthwith assume the kingship and engage the enemy in battle for victory will assuredly be his. The beam of light stretching across Gaul signifies Uther's very powerful son who will possess all the realms covered by the beam. The other beam signifies his daughter whose sons and grandsons will hold the kingdom of Britain successively (Thorpe, 201).

The portent in the sky was deemed necessary by Geoffrey in order to link Merlin directly to the Golden Age of British sovereignty under Arthur. He knew very well that great heroes are often heralded by natural phenomena. Some extraordinary display was required in the narrative itself as a foreshadowing of the coming of Arthur.

As far as we can tell, the dramatis personae of the legend of Arthur's conception are Geoffrey's invention: Uther, Gorlois, Ygerna, Ulfin, Jordan of Tintagel, and Britaelis. Some of these names Geoffrey took from saints' lives; others he probably invented for the occasion. Parallels to the story of the magical begetting of a hero are found in almost every culture. Indeed, tales of wooings (*tochmarca*), elopements (*aithid*), and conceptions and births (*coimperta*) were among the stock in trade of the Celtic storytellers. Efforts to identify Geoffrey's source for the story of

Uther's begetting Arthur on Ygerna, however, have not met with great success. Tatlock is inclined to downplay Geoffrey's debt to Welsh or Irish traditions (Tatlock, 1974, 315–16). For him, Jove's begetting of Hercules on Alcmena in the appearance of her husband Amphitryon is a close parallel that may have influenced Geoffrey. Tatlock also points out the similarity of Arthur's conception to that of Alexander in the popular Latin versions of the pseudo-Callisthenes's life of Alexander. Contemporary life may also have lent plausibility to Geoffrey's story of Arthur's begetting. Abducting the wife of a rival was not unknown in Geoffrey's day. Gruffydd ap Llywelyn defeated Howel in battle in 1039 and took Howel's wife for his own.[82] The abduction of Nesta, wife of Gerald of Windsor, a prominent Norman magnate in Pembrokeshire, by her cousin Owain ap Cadwgan in 1109 was a celebrated story in Geoffrey's time (Ithel, 82–96). Henry II's invasion of Ireland in 1172 was occasioned by an appeal from Diarmaid Mac Murchada, who was exiled from Leinster by Ua Ruaire, king of Meath, for having abducted Ua Ruaire's wife from confinement on an island in Meath while the king was away.[83] The Welsh law codes themselves recognize abduction as a crime and provide damages to be paid for it to the husband (T. Ellis, 1:347; Tatlock, 1974, 191, n. 58).

The parallels in Welsh and Irish literature are not to be dismissed. Not a few scholars have seen in the *Mabinogi* story of Pryderi's conception, the pattern of a terrestrial visitation by an otherworld god in order to beget a hero on an earthly mother.[84] Such a mythological substrata is evident in the conception and birth tales of Lug, Finn, CuChulainn, Conaire Mór, and Mongán among the Irish.[85] According to the *Destruction of Da Derga's Hostel,* Conaire Mór's father in the shape of a bird gained entrance to the prison where Mes Buachall was enclosed and made love to her (Rees and Rees, 214–15; Cross and Slover, 95–96). Later after she has been married to Eterscel, Mes Buachall's son Conaire is born to her. Conaire was blessed with three gifts: the gift of hearing, the gift of seeing, and the gift of judgment. In one of the conception tales of Mongán,[86] Manannán Mac Lir appears to the wife of Fiachna Finn, king of Ulster, in her husband's appearance, and begets the child Mongán upon her. In this instance, Mongán's conception is the result of a bargain between Manannán and Fiachna for allowing Manannán to beget a child on the king's wife.

Given such a pattern of otherworld fathers begetting heroes on noble women, it is not surprising that scholars have seen Geoffrey's story of Arthur's conception against this background. The fact that Ygerna is enclosed and closely defended in the Castle of Tintagel,[87] that Uther must assume the appearance of Gorlois in order to reach her, that Gorlois is away from the castle engaged in battle, and that the union of Uther and Ygerna results in the birth of the great warrior-king Arthur all point in this direction. The mysterious events surrounding the end of Arthur also suggest a return of the hero to his father's realm and reinforce the idea that his beginning also was by divine agency.

There can be little doubt that Geoffrey was capable of writing stories with overt mythological content. In fact, the parallels to Arthur's conception cited above apply equally well, if not better, to the legend of Merlin's birth. Merlin's mother is enclosed in a convent in the company of (guarded by?) nuns. She, too, is the daughter of a king. The creature who visits her comes in the disguise of a young man, appears without difficulty in her chamber, and has the power to remain invisible. Maugantius identifies him as one of the *incubi* (celestial beings who share the nature of man and god). Geoffrey used the conventions of divine conception stories, whatever his specific sources were, to lend authority, mystery, and dignity to the figure of Merlin. Merlin's prophetic, mechanical, and medicinal skills, we are to assume, derive in part from his preternatural origins. Arthur's case is rather different. If Arthur's conception has a mythological basis, it remains unstated, as it does in the case of Alexander. Uther's attraction for Ygerna is strictly sexual and passionate. Moreover, Merlin is persuaded to assist Uther in his seduction of Gorlois's wife not out of conviction that from this union a hero would be born, but rather out of pity for the suffering of the king: "Having discovered the anguish the king was suffering on account of her (Ygerna), Merlin was moved by such great love, and said to him, 'In order that you might have your will, you must use new arts unheard of in your day. I know how to bestow Gorlois's appearance on you with my medicines (*medicaminibus meis*), so that you will resemble him in all ways'" (Wright, 1984, 97; my translation).

The role that Merlin plays in this scene is that of a doctor called to minister to the suffering of a patient who also happens to be his lord and master. The language of the passage verges toward the terminology of *love-sickness* made familiar to the Middle Ages by Ovid and adapted later in the twelfth century into an elaborate system by Andreas Cappellanus and Chrétien de Troyes. Here in Geoffrey, however, the king's love is seen as a kind of irrepressible violence which can only be brought under control by sexual release. There is nothing *fin* about Uther's *amor*. Nor is there anything particularly divine about it. Geoffrey is not Chrétien de Troyes or

Wolfram von Eschenbach. We know nothing of Uther's internal torment. Geoffrey permits him no moment of eloquence to reveal to us the nobility of his suffering or the greatness of his endurance. His passion will out.[88]

By contrast with his story of Merlin's conception, Geoffrey's version of Arthur's begetting may appear sordid and undignified. But the two episodes both reveal a fundamental historic and moral issue that concerned Geoffrey throughout the *HRB,* namely, the ambiguity with which violence, passion, egoism, and cruelty express themselves in history. Vortigern's passion for Renwein has disastrous consequences for the British folk, hurling them not only into bloody conflict with the Saxons, but also setting into motion a spiral of reciprocal violence pitting Briton against Briton. Geoffrey makes no effort to disguise the destructiveness of Uther's passion. Quite the contrary, he seems deliberately to model the passage in which Uther falls in love with Ygerna after the earlier scene in which Vortigern's heart is filled with desire for Renwein. He portrays Uther's umbrage at Gorlois's sudden departure from the feast at London as a transparent pretext for the king to attack the duke, kill him, and take his wife. Geoffrey makes plain that Uther's sleeping with Ygerna was a combination of adultery and deception: "The king stayed that night with Ygerna and refreshed himself with his desired lovemaking. He deceived her with the false appearance he had assumed and also with false words he cleverly made up. He said that he left the besieged fortress secretly in order to see to her, his beloved, and to his castle. Believing all of this, she denied him nothing that he asked. On that very night she conceived Arthur, the most famous of men, who afterwards earned fame by his remarkable bravery" (Wright, 1984, 98; my translation).

To excuse Uther's adultery and deception is to turn a blind eye to Geoffrey's purpose and to miss the abrupt juxtaposition of Arthur's conception with its milieu in intrigue, lust, and deception. The last person to don a disguise in the *HRB* was Eopa, who posed as a doctor in order to gain access to Aurelius, whom he then poisoned to death with his "medicines" (Thorpe, 200). The begetting of Arthur takes place in circumstances of moral ambiguity, yet sometimes out of acts of violence and blind egoism come the great accomplishments of humanity. It is part of Geoffrey's greatness as a philosophical historian that he perceived this essential ambiguity in human affairs. He was not alone. Among his contemporaries, the hagiographers of the British saints also represented some of the most renowned and gifted holy men such as Saints David (James, 3–4, 30–31), Cynog,[89] and Kentigern[90] as the offspring of raped or deceived virgins.

Gone from such stories is the idea that the will of the gods is ineluctable and that man is powerless in the face of their desires. The focus of the legend of the conception of Arthur as well as that of David, Cynog, and Kentigern is on the human will as the chief agent in the historic process. Geoffrey and Jocelin of Furness, the author of the *Life of Saint Kentigern,* are eager to rationalize the conception legend of their heroes. Merlin administers newfangled medicines to give Uther the appearance of Gorlois. Kentigern's mother, in Jocelin's view, must have been drugged with letargion before being raped. In these efforts to downplay any suggestion of divine origin we can detect two motives: first, a desire to suppress impious analogies between the life of Christ and the careers of native heroes and saints, and second, a tendency to reflect the genuine complexity of human motivation involved in great historic change.

By placing Merlin at the threshold of the Golden Age of Arthur, Geoffrey has brought the prophet into a full cycle of death and life. Merlin enters the *HRB* at the nadir of British history in the reign of Vortigern and becomes the precipitating agent of that tyrant's demise. He plays a crucial role in the period of pious reconstruction under Aurelius, being uniquely responsible for erecting the memorial to the British dead at Stonehenge. Finally, he not only prophesies the coming of the Arthur (the Boar of Cornwall), but also arranges the liaison between Uther and Ygerna, at which time Arthur is conceived and Merlin's own prophecy fulfilled. Each of the three principal episodes of Merlin's career in the *HRB* is firmly rooted by Geoffrey in places rich in history (even if obscure history) and dramatic possibilities: Dinas Emrys, Stonehenge, and Tintagel. As far as we can tell, this tripartite structure of Merlin's career in the *HRB* is Geoffrey's own invention and reflects his interest as historian in imparting dramatic shape to the changing fortunes of British history. Piecing together the story of Merlin's career out of Nennius and a variety of other sources, Geoffrey created a character of imposing stature and lasting authority to stand behind the prophecies uttered to Vortigern as he sat on the bank of the drained pool at Dinas Emrys. It is to Geoffrey's credit as a man of letters that he bestowed such vitality on Merlin that his prophecies continued to be debated for the next 400 years and that his legend has lost none of its interest to the present day. Understanding something of the way Geoffrey assembled Merlin's legend and framed his predictions has been the purpose of the last section of this chapter. The prophecies themselves are the subject of the next chapter.

Chapter Three

The History of the Kings of Britain: The Prophecies of Merlin

The *Prophecies of Merlin* (*PM*) comprise book 7 of the *Historia Regum Britanniae* and occur about midway through the entire narrative. As we have seen in chapter 2, Geoffrey tells us that he had not yet reached the point in his history where Merlin exposes the ignorance of Vortigern's magi concerning the sinking of the king's tower, when he was urged on all sides by his contemporaries to publish (*edere*) the prophecies of Merlin, about whom there had been recent rumors (*de Merlino diuulgato rumore*). This chapter considers the content of the *PM*, their relationship to the rest of the *HRB* and to events of the twelfth century. Because the *PM* constitute such an extended and in many ways opaque digression from Geoffrey's narrative, we shall do well to begin by inquiring into Geoffrey's own account of their presence in his history.

The Genesis of the *Prophecies of Merlin, HRB* 7

Chief among those who pressed the task of translation on him, Geoffrey claims, was Alexander, bishop of Lincoln, a man of the highest religiousness and wisdom. Wishing to please Alexander, Geoffrey translated (*transtuli*) the prophecies and sent them to Alexander along with a prefatory letter, the text of which he includes along with his translation (Thorpe, 170–71; Wright, 1984, 73–74). In this prefatory letter (beginning *Coegit me, Alexander Lincolinensis*), Geoffrey confesses that he wanted to put off the task of translation for fear that if he embarked on it, he would never finish either it or his history of the deeds of the British kings. But out of admiration for Alexander and with assurance of the bishop's indulgence, he took up his rustic pipe and translated the prophecies into Latin from the British tongue, which was unknown to Alexander. Indeed, Alexander himself would have been the best man for the job had other business not occupied his time.[1]

Alexander's patronage of Henry of Huntingdon is evidence of his interest in history. What of his interest in prophecy? Salter and Gransden seem to think that Geoffrey's letter to Alexander is nothing more than an attempt to secure the patronage of the affluent bishop (Salter, 382–85; Gransden, 204). The various dedications Geoffrey penned to the *HRB* leave no doubt that he sought the favor of powerful men, as did William of Malmesbury (Robert, Earl of Gloucester), Henry of Huntingdon (Alexander, bishop of Lincoln), Gaimar (Ralph Fitz-Gilbert), Gerald of Wales (Henry II), and many other literary men of the day. In order to discount Alexander's interest in the *PM,* however, one would have to regard as a blatant fabrication, Geoffrey's claim that Alexander himself initiated the project. Such a claim was not likely to escape the notice of the bishop of Lincoln. We have to bear in mind that the learned men of Oxford and Lincoln formed a fairly tight group, often appearing together as signatories on official documents relating to the diocese of Lincoln in which the city of Oxford was located (see chapter 1). Ralph of Monmouth, a canon of Lincoln cathedral, appears on several charters with Geoffrey, his fellow townsman (Salter, 383–84). Robert of Chesney, a cosignatory with Geoffrey on another charter, was a secular canon along with Geoffrey at Saint George's college in Oxford before becoming bishop of Lincoln, upon Bishop Alexander's death in 1148 (Salter, 385). Geoffrey later dedicated his *VM* to Robert. Given such a milieu, Geoffrey probably would not have concocted the story of Bishop Alexander's urging him to provide a translation of the prophecies and then gone on to publish a dedicatory epistle containing such a lie. The same can be said, as demonstrated in chapter 2, for his claim that Walter the archdeacon gave him a "very ancient book in the British language."

The *PM* traveled quickly. They were in circulation by 1135 when they were first extensively quoted by Orderic Vitalis.[2] The history itself was in the possession of Robert of Torigni at Bec in 1139, some nine years before Bishop Alexander's death in 1148 (see chapter 2). Geoffrey's letter to Waleran, count of Meulan, is sufficient proof that when he wanted patronage he was not above openly asking for it and did not rely on elaborate and potentially dangerous pranks. In fact, sometime after Alexander's death, when the bishop's patronage was no longer a possibility, Geoffrey did revise his dedicatory epistle by deleting the fulsome praise of Alexander, but he let stand his original claim that it was Alexander himself who initiated the project (Faral, 3:189; Griscom, 96–98). This reinforces the view that the letter was indeed originally intended for Alexander's eyes and makes it highly unlikely that Geoffrey would have thus openly implicated the bishop in a literary hoax. Furthermore, every reader is struck by the abrupt manner in which Geoffrey breaks off his history in order to insert the book of prophecies. Indeed, book 7 strikes us as so intrusive precisely because Geoffrey, unlike many of his contemporaries, is not normally given to such ungainly digressions.

Therefore, unless we simply refuse to believe that sophisticated and worldly men of the twelfth century could be interested in the moonshine of political prophecy, a view that the evidence does not allow, we would do better to entertain the possibility that Alexander did indeed take a serious interest in Merlin and that Geoffrey could not resist the opportunity to satisfy the literary tastes of a potential patron. Moreover, a plausible rationale for Alexander's interest in Merlin is not lacking. To begin with, Anglo-Norman historians were interested in promulgating the view that their new possessions in England had a dignified and ancient past reaching far behind the Saxon plantation. Initiative for the great Cotton Vespasian collection of early British saints lives came from the Norman Benedictine monastery of Saint Peter's at Gloucester, and the manuscript itself was probably assembled at the Monmouth priory.[3] Belief in a legendary Trojan ancestry was shared by Normans and Britons alike and made the Conquest appear far less of a rupture of historic continuity than the Saxon and Danish invasions had been. The strong anti-Saxon bias of the Welsh Myrddin prophecies, or of the *Armes Prydein* (ca. 930) in which Myrddin figures as one of the principal prophetic authorities,[4] may well have reached the ears and aroused the curiosity of Bishop Alexander of Lincoln. Eadmer, Orderic, and William of Malmesbury all shared the view that the Norman Conquest was justified in part by the decayed state of the Anglo-Saxon Church and by the reforms instituted by Lanfranc and William I (Gransden, 173–74). Not purely by coincidence, however, in the *PM* does Geoffrey mentions two separate periods of violence against the Church and religion in the Anglo-Saxon period (Thorpe, 171–72). The advent of "the people dressed in wood and iron corslets" (the Normans) is presented in the *PM* as vengeance for the misrule and wickedness of the White Dragon, a view calculated, I believe, to conform to Norman justifications for the events of 1066. Also worth noting is the way the *PM* portrays the Norman Conquest as a partial restitution of British rights, thereby reinterpreting the ancient "hope of the British," the notion that we find in Nennius and the *Armes Prydein,* that one day the sovereignty of Britain will be returned to the "original" British folk.

Having included his letter to Bishop Alexander, Geoffrey resumed his narrative, with Vortigern sitting on the bank of the drained pool (*Sedente itaque Uortegirno*) from which the Red and the White Dragons emerge to fight. The White Dragon at first forces the Red Dragon to the edge of the pool, then the Red Dragon recovers and forces the White one back in turn. As they struggle, Vortigern commands Merlin to explain what the battle portends. Merlin breaks into tears, drinks in the spirit of prophecy (*spiritum hausit prophetie*), and predicts that the Red Dragon (the British folk) will be overwhelmed by the White Dragon (the Saxons) (Thorpe, 171).

As demonstrated in chapter 2, this tableau of the fighting dragons, as well as the interpretation given to it, derive from chapter 42 of Nennius's *Historia Brittonum*. In Nennius, of course, the scene ends when the Red Dragon victoriously pushes the White Dragon across the lake, whereupon the cloth vanishes. Ambrosius's interpretation of the scene in Nennius ends with the statement that "our people will arise, and will valiantly throw the English people across the sea" (Nennius, ed. J. Morris, 31).

Geoffrey brushes aside this optimistic denouement to the battle of the dragons. The history of England between the coming of the Saxons and Geoffrey's own day compelled him to revise this ancient "British hope." The Saxons were indeed to be crushed and the Britons to be restored after a fashion. But all this was to come about, according to *HRB* 7, through the agency of the Normans. Precisely at the place where Nennius's Ambrosius foresees the British "throwing the Saxons across the sea," Geoffrey's Merlin predicts merely a brief period of glory under Arthur (the Boar of Cornwall) to be followed by continued oppression at the hands of the Saxons and their allies. This period of renewed Saxon oppression, however, will end with the Decimation of Normandy (*decimatio Neustrie*), that is to say, with the coming of a new invader, "the people dressed in wood and iron corslets," who will reduce the Saxons to slavery and restore dwellings to the earlier inhabitants (Thorpe, 173; *pristinis incolis*).

If Alexander's informants told him that the Merlin prophecies foresaw that the Norman Conquest would bring long-needed reform to the Anglo-Saxon Church and restoration of the dignity (if not the sovereignty) of the British, understanding his desire to have these prophecies in a language he could comprehend is not difficult. Given the tightly knit circle of learned men who passed between Lincoln and Oxford at this time, Alexander probably had heard of Geoffrey's work and perhaps even that Geoffrey was currently writing about Merlin. Because Geoffrey seems to have enjoyed playing dog in the manger with regard to early British history, he was a likely choice for the translation Alexander had in mind. As we shall see later, the *PM* served more than one master, but there is little reason to doubt that the original stimulus for the collection came from the bishop of Lincoln, whose interest in prophecy was in all likelihood more than antiquarian.

The Role of the *Prophecies of Merlin* in Geoffrey's *Historia Regum Britanniae*

The prophecies in *HRB* 7 fall into the following three distinct parts.

Part 1. From the original Battle of the Red and White Dragons down to the resurgence of the White Dragon following the death of the Blessed King (Thorpe, 171–73). This first part extends historically from the advent of the Saxons down to the end of the *HRB* itself.

Part 2. From the crowning of the German Worm (*Germanicus uermis*) to the end of the career of the Lion of Justice (Thorpe, 173–74). This second part begins where the *HRB* itself ends and extends down to Geoffrey's own day and the reign of Henry I (the Lion of Justice).

Part 3. From the reign of the Lion of Justice to the cosmic disturbances that close the *PM* (Thorpe, 174–85). This third part covers events in the vague and distant future.

HRB Book 7: *Part 1*

The first set of prophecies apply for the most part to events within the *HRB*, and are, therefore, decoded by the later historic narrative itself. As we have seen, Merlin interprets the initial battle of the dragons as signifying the conflict of Britons (the Red Dragon) and Saxons (the White Dragon), thereby providing the first key to unlocking the obscure terminology and symbolism of the remaining prophecies. The interpretative task is henceforth passed on to the reader, who in turn should have little difficulty interpreting the prophecies of part one due to their close correspondence in content and language to the events described in the ensuing books of the history proper. The first prophecy to follow the tableau of the fighting dragons concerns the complete destruction of the cult of religion. Chronologically, the period represented by this prophecy is the reign of Vortigern in which the pagan Saxons enter the island of Britain and the king marries the pagan princess Renwein. We can scarcely miss the events to which this prophecy refers because Geoffrey has Ambrosius swear vengeance on Vortigern as the evil one responsible for the destruction of churches and the obliteration of Christianity in the land (Thorpe, 188). Later while on tour, Aurelius is grieved to find so many churches razed to the ground, and one of his first acts as king is to "restore the churches which the Saxon people has destroyed" at York and later at London (Thorpe, 189, 194).

Similarly, the career of the Boar of Cornwall, who comes next in sequence of prophecies, features an end to Saxon oppression, conquest of

the "island of the ocean" and the forests of Gaul, and striking dread into
the House of Romulus. The Boar's end will be uncertain (*exitus eius
dubius erit*), although he will be "celebrated in the mouths of the people,"
and his deeds will be "food for narrators" (Thorpe, 172). Given its place
in the sequence of prophecies, this clearly refers to the conquests of
Arthur, who according to the *HRB* was conceived at Tintagel in
Cornwall, hence the epithet, the Boar of Cornwall. The *HRB* tells of
Arthur's conquest of the islands of Ireland, Iceland, Gotland, and the
Orkneys and mentions that the young men of all the islands he conquered fought alongside him during his campaign in Gaul (Thorpe,
223). Lucius later accuses Arthur of laying hands on "all the islands of
the Ocean" whose kings used to pay tribute to Rome (Thorpe, 231). The
conquest of the "forests of Gaul" refers to Arthur's defeat of Frollo and
his subsequent pacification of Gaul, while his striking of dread into the
House of Romulus refers to his campaign against Lucius, which culmi-
nates in the victory of Saussy. After this, Arthur sets out to cross the
mountains and attack Rome itself, but he is deflected from his purpose
by the treachery of Mordred. The "uncertain end" that awaits the Boar
of Cornwall refers to the fate of Arthur following the Battle of Camblan,
where he is said to have been mortally wounded and then carried off to
the Isle of Avalon "so that his wounds might be attended to" (Thorpe,
261). No mention is made in the *HRB* of Arthur's career becoming "celebrated in the mouths of people," or serving as "food for narrators," but
we know from Herman of Tournai's report on the visit of the Laon
canons to Cornwall in 1113, that Arthur was on the lips of folk in
Cornwall.[5] His deeds were celebrated in Latin by Nennius and in Welsh
by the author of *Culhwch and Olwen*.

Most of the remaining prophecies in this first part are similarly decoded by the *HRB* itself. The Blessed King who fits out a navy and who
"will be numbered among the blessed in the hall of the twelve," is
Cadwallader. His father, Cadwallo, is the Man of Bronze of the *PM*, so
named for the bronze equestrian statue containing his embalmed body,
which the *HRB* tells us his followers raised to his honor on top of the
West Gate of London (Thorpe, 280). Following Cadwallo's entomb-
ment, the *PM* foretells that the Red Dragon will "struggle to tear itself
to pieces," that the "revenge of the Thunderer" will come, farmers' fields
will fail, death will come to all, and that those who survive this period of
destruction will flee their native soil. All these events come to pass in the
reign of Cadwallader toward the end of the *HRB*. Because of Cadwallader's illness, the Britons (the Red Dragon) lack strong leadership

and fall to feuding among themselves. Natural disasters (the revenge of the Thunderer) follow: crop failures, famine, and pestilence. Finally, the few who are left flee abroad to Brittany chanting Psalm 44:11, "Thou hast given us, O God, like sheep for meat, and hast scattered us among the Heathens."[6] Under the protection of Alan of Brittany, the Britons regain their numbers and prepare to return to their homeland under Cadwallader, who has assembled a powerful navy for the voyage. At the moment of departure, however, an angelic voice directs Cadwallader to abandon the expedition and to go instead to Rome ("the hall of the twelve [apostles]" in the *PM*) to do penance under Pope Sergius, where he would be "numbered among the blessed" (Thorpe, 282–83; *inter sanctos annumeraretur*). After sending his sons Yvor and Yni back to Britain to rule over those who remain, Cadwallader goes to Rome, where he is confirmed by Pope Sergius, dies in 689, and enters the hall of the Kingdom of Heaven.

Meanwhile, Yvor and Yni, having returned to Britain find only a handful of wretched Britons left. The island by this time has fallen so completely into the hands of the Saxons that the original inhabitants no longer even bear the name Britons, but instead are called Welsh. The Saxons, on the contrary, after suffering the consequences of the plague and famine, follow their usual custom and invite their fellow countrymen in Germany to reoccupy the deserted land. When word reaches them, a vast horde of men and women set forth together. Thus is fulfilled the last of the prophecies of part one of the *PM* concerned with the way the garden-island will be "stocked again with foreign seed" while the Red Dragon languishes at the far end of the pool (Thorpe, 173).

The prophecies of Merlin serve to lend veracity and dignity to the *HRB*. The book of prophecies supposedly derives from British antiquity, being the utterances Merlin made to Vortigern; they were supposedly passed down through the ages in the very language in which they were originally spoken. Geoffrey's pretended role was to serve once again as translator and transmitter of ancient tradition. The reader of the *PM* soon discovers that ancient British narrative and prophetic traditions both agree. The "very ancient book in the British language" and the book of prophecy (also in the British language) speak in different rhetorical voices, but agree on the basic outline of British history. Many readers of the *HRB,* baffled by the dense and enigmatic symbolism of the long third part tend to dismiss the prophetic book as a whole, thereby failing to see that Geoffrey conceived of the *HRB* and the *PM* as two interlocking and complementary ancient books translated from the

British language. The prophecies in this first part of the *PM* having been already "fulfilled," as it were, by the events recounted in the *HRB* itself, the two books intersect to reinforce the antiquity and veracity of Geoffrey's historic vision.

Further buttressing this concept of two separate but intersecting traditions is the presence in the first part of the *PM* of a few predictions that either contradict the *HRB* or plainly draw upon sources foreign to it. The prophecy that follows mention of the demise of the Boar of Cornwall (Arthur) for example, refers to six of the Boar's descendants before the advent of the Seawolf and the German Worm (Thorpe, 172). According to the *HRB*, however, the immediate successors of the Boar are only five in number: Constantine, Aurelius Conanus, Vortiporius, Malgo, and Keredic. During Keredic's rule Gormund (the Seawolf), with his "hundred and sixty thousand Africans," comes to the aid of the Saxons (the German Worm) in routing the Britons. After this, Geoffrey tells us that the British were "without sovereign power over their own land," fell into civil war and were "ruled by three tyrants instead of by a single king" (Thorpe, 265). Their next true king is Cadvan, but he comes on the scene long after Gormund's depredations. If he is to be counted sixth after Arthur, the chronology of the prophecy makes no sense because Gormund is supposed to arrive after the rule of six of the Boar's descendants. Moreover, Geoffrey later confirms the *HRB* version of Arthur's successors when he has Cadwallo tell Salomon that Malgo reigned fourth after Arthur (Thorpe, 274).

Another set of prophecies contrary to the *HRB* concerns the period in which the Seawolf will exalt the German Worm. During this time, the *PM* envisions several changes that will occur in the British Church. In one, the "sees of the primates will be moved to other places" and the high dignity of London will adorn Durobernia. In another, the "seventh pastor of York" will be visited in Armorica (Thorpe, 172).

As we have already seen, Geoffrey planned to write a separate book on the exile of the British clergy during the time of this persecution of the church under Gormund and the Saxons. The *HRB* tells of the flight of Archbishops Theonus of London and Tadioceus of York, the "primates" of the prophecy, along with their clergy and the relics of their saints. They take refuge at first in Wales, and later many of them set sail for Brittany, leaving the churches of the two provinces of Loegria (England) and Northumbria in ruin (Thorpe, 265). The *HRB* makes no mention of a pastor of York being visited in Armorica (Brittany). The commentators, however, confidently take this prophecy to refer to Samson of Dol, whom they sometimes identify with a Samson of York.[7] Geoffrey mentions a Samson being appointed archbishop of York by Aurelius and later mentions that Samson was driven from his see by the Saxons (Thorpe, 198, 221). He also knows of Samson of Dol and mentions that Tebaus (Teilo), a priest of Llandaff, succeeded Samson as the metropolitan of Dol (Thorpe, 230). Yet there is nothing in the *HRB* to indicate that Geoffrey thought of these two Samsons as the same person or that he knew of a "seventh" pastor of York who received visitors in Brittany.

There is little doubt, however, that this prophecy concerning the pastor of York is based on hagiographical traditions independent of Geoffrey. The *Life of Saint Teilo* in the *Book of Llandaff*, for example, tells of Teilo's voyage to Armorica where he meets Samson of Dol and sojourns there with him.[8] Also, the *Life of Saint Padarn* contains a story of Padarn's visit with Samson in Brittany.[9] Alanus states that Samson's seven brothers (*Sancti & magnifici, & magnarum virtutum viri*) accompanied him on his flight to Brittany, where they are still honored as the "seven saints of Britain" (Alanus, 27–30; *septem Britanniae Sanctos*). The reference in *HRB* 7 to a pastor of York being visited in Brittany probably alludes to such stories, if not these precise ones, which circulated about Samson and other great personages of the Age of the Saints.

As for Samson being called the "seventh pastor of York," no evidence for this title survives. Alcuin makes no mention of any bishop of York named Samson, nor do the lives of Samson of Dol connect him in any way with York.[10] Tatlock however, has shown that there was a cultus of Samson at York dating back to the eighth century and suggests that this Samson was traditionally identified with the Breton Samson of Dol (Tatlock, 1974, 244).

What we have said of the prophecy concerning the six successors of Arthur applies equally well to this one about the seventh pastor of York. What prevented Geoffrey from showing Teilo or Padarn or someone else visiting Samson in Brittany and hence "coding" this particular prophecy? Either he did not know the event to which the prophecy referred, or if he did know it, he chose to make no mention of it in his history. In either case, the impression left on the reader is that the book of prophecy and the book of kings are independent witnesses to the same history, even if they differ in minor details.

The same applies to the next prophecy concerning the "preacher of/for Ireland" (*predicator Hibernie*) who will be struck dumb by a child in the womb (Thorpe, 172). This might logically be taken to refer to Saint Patrick, whom Geoffrey mentions in *HRB* 8 as foretelling Saint David's birth and founding the monastery at Menevia (Thorpe, 262). In fact, the Welsh commentator on the *PM* in MS Peniarth 16 does take the preacher to be Patrick.[11] Yet the *HRB* itself makes no mention of Patrick's being struck dumb by a child in the womb. Geoffrey, however, was certainly not manufacturing the episode on which this prophecy is based. One of the most celebrated passages in Rhigyvarch's *Life of Saint David* (ca. 1095) concerns a preacher who is struck dumb in the middle of a sermon when Saint Nonn, who is carrying David in her womb, enters the church to offer alms for the child's birth. This is taken as a sign that Nonn's child will grow up to excel all the preachers of Britain in dignity, wisdom, and eloquence (James, 4 [Latin], 31 [English]).[12] The preacher goes unnamed in Rhigyvarch and in Ailbe's *Life of David*,[13] as well as in the *HRB*.

The epithet *predicator Hibernie* in Geoffrey's day could apply equally well to Gildas as to Patrick. Caradoc of Llancarfan's *Life of Gildas*,[14] the Vespasian redaction of the *Life of Saint David*, David's *vita* composed by Giraldus Cambrensis,[15] and the Welsh *Buchedd Dewi* (*The Life of David*)[16] all identify the preacher as Gildas. Caradoc's *Life of Gildas* states that after being struck dumb by the presence of the pregnant Nonn, Gildas (the *sanctissimus praedicator*) left Britain for Ireland, where he converted innumerable folk to the Catholic faith (Mommsen, 107–10).

How did Geoffrey understand the prophecy? Did he along with Caradoc think of Gildas as the preacher from Ireland who "will be struck dumb by a child in the womb"? Or did he have Patrick in mind? Did he know only Rhigyvarch and was therefore unable to "key" the prophecy with a specific person in the *HRB*? If Geoffrey used Rhigyvarch's *Life of David*, he took great liberties with it. In Rhigyvarch, Patrick comes to Rosina Vallis in Dyfed, the future site of the monastery of Menevia, intending to serve God there, but is advised by an angel that his place has been reserved for one who is to come 30 years hence. The angel then assures Patrick that God has a special plan for him as missionary to the people of Ireland (James, 2–3 [Latin], 30 [English]). Geoffrey has a rather unique version of these events in the *HRB*, claiming that Patrick actually founded Menevia and that he, rather than the angel, prophesied David's birth (Thorpe, 262). Geoffrey was certainly capable of rearranging his sources to fit his needs. He could have easily worked in the legend of an anonymous preacher into the proper chronology of *HRB* 8. Had he understood the preacher from Ireland to be Patrick, he could have made mention of this in the *HRB* when speaking of Patrick's sojourn in Dyfed. If he knew that the prophecy referred to Gildas, why did he not work in a suitable reference to him when mentioning the career of Saint David in book 8 of the *HRB*? The lack of conformity between the *HRB* and the *Book of Prophecies* in this case and in the other two cases we have examined suggests that the two "ancient books" derived from very different sources. This is particularly true when, as we have seen, so many other prophecies in part one are "fulfilled" by events described in books 8–12 of the *HRB;* that is to say, they show evidence of having been carefully arranged by Geoffrey to correspond to events in the *HRB*.

Because Geoffrey usually took such pains, as we have seen, to "code" the *PM* with his history, his decision to admit contradictory prophecies seems deliberate. Of course, one might postulate that Geoffrey cleverly composed certain prophecies that contradicted his history in order to give *HRB* 7 the appearance of deriving from independent sources, but a simpler explanation is that many of the prophecies in *HRB* 7 were not Geoffrey's own concoctions, but were useful to him precisely because of their obviously independent character. They vary from the *HRB* in relatively minor ways, in any event, and do not undermine its authority. On the contrary, they tend to corroborate Geoffrey's claim in his letter to Alexander of Lincoln that he left off the history to gather Merlin's prophecies, presumably from sources other than those he used for the *HRB*. And in spite of that, the *Book of Prophecies* so closely corroborates the *Book of Kings!*

The two other prophecies in this section of *HRB* 7 are also at variance with the *HRB*'s view of the administrative structure of the early British Church. As far as the *HRB* is concerned, London remains, along with York and Caerleon, one of the three metropolitan cities of Britain. Its "high dignity" is never transferred to Canterbury (Durobernia). No mention is made of the pallium of Caerleon being transported to Saint David's. On David's visit to Menevia in *HRB* 8, when such a transfer might have been described, Geoffrey specifically mentions that David remained archbishop of Caerleon until his sudden death at his beloved monastery of Menevia (Thorpe, 262).

These two prophecies concerning the transfer of ecclesiastical authority from London to Canterbury and from Caerleon to Saint David's reflect controversies over these churches in Geoffrey's own day and arise out of complex play for power among the bishops and archbishops of England and Wales during the first three decades of the twelfth century. Because the claims and counterclaims of various parties could only be settled by plausible documentation establishing the antiquity of various practices, this period witnessed a lively flurry of literary "research," out

of which arose the "Canterbury forgeries," the *Book of Llandaff*, the letter
of Saint David's to Pope Honorius II, and the prophecies of Merlin that
we have been discussing.[17] The traditions of the early Church in Britain
and the Roman administrative structure on which they were presumed
to have been based provided the key for the church of Saint David's
claim to metropolitan status. Moreover, the Vespasian lives of the early
British saints and the lives and charters of the *Book of Llandaff* show how
important the preservation of the traditions of the early Celtic Church
had become at a time when Norman reorganization of the Church in
Wales was reaching a critical stage. In view of this activity, Geoffrey's
HRB takes on special importance because it claimed to provide what no
one else had ever dared, a continuous history of the British people from
the time of Brutus down to Cadwallader.

The ecclesiastical prophecies of *HRB* 7 stress that a fundamental
break with British Church history took place in the post-Arthurian period. According to the *HRB*, Caerleon was both the military and ecclesiastical center of Britain during the Golden Age of Arthur. But in the
turbulence that came after Arthur's demise, the pallium of the ancient
Roman legionary fortress of Caerleon would pass, according to the
prophecy, to Menevia. This prophecy must have been intended to lend
support to Saint David's claim to metropolitan dignity, priority in its dispute with Llandaff, and independence from Canterbury. On the other
hand, it undercut the authority of the Church of Saint David's assertion
that the pallium had been in her possession since the time of Pope
Eleutherius, A.D. 140 (J. Davies, 1, 249). The prophecy insists, on the
contrary, that Saint David's received the pallium as a result of the
breakup of Roman-Christian order and the general decline in Britain
from the greatness of the Golden Age of Arthur, although it is not specific as to when the transfer of Caerleon's dignity actually took place.

The situation is the same for Canterbury. Everyone who read Bede
knew that Augustine settled in Canterbury because it was the chief city
of King Ethelbert of Kent. Merlin's prophecy insists that Canterbury's
primatial dignity was derived in some unspecified manner from London,
the principal Roman city of southeastern Britain. In making this argument, the prophecy views Canterbury's status as a departure from the
most ancient Christian traditions in the island, thereby undermining her
pretensions to superiority over all other churches in the land. It might
also lend support to the view of Bernard and the Church of Saint David's
that Augustine had no power to alienate the ancient privileges of the
British Church.

If most of the prophecies of part one of *HRB* 7 function, as I have suggested, to buttress the authority of Geoffrey's own view of early British history, the prophecies concerning Caerleon, York, and London demonstrate the relevance of the *HRB* to contemporary (that is, twelfth-century) history.

Whether these prophecies were originally contrived by partisans of Saint David's and London prior to Geoffrey is difficult to determine, but if such were the case, they would be the sort of utterance to set off "rumors" among contemporary churchmen and to attract the attention of prominent bishops such as Alexander of Lincoln. Apart from the *HRB* itself, the Canterbury forgeries, and to a lesser extent the *Book of Llandaff*, demonstrate that the line we draw between historic documentation and literary composition was a good deal less sharp to the eyes of twelfth-century writers. The "uncoded" status of these prophecies vis-à-vis the *HRB* suggests an origin independent of Geoffrey, but the exalted position of Caerleon as a primatial see in one of the prophecies indicates that Geoffrey, Caerleon's most avid booster, probably had a hand in its composition. And, of course, the moderate view of the other prophecy in regard to the antiquity of Saint David's pallium points away from Bernard and his colleagues. This suggests the likelihood that Geoffrey mingled the task of editor with that of "translator" in passing along prophecies he found attributed to Merlin.

It should be evident that the first part of *HRB* 7 plays an integral role in validating Geoffrey's view of the character of early Britain and serves to highlight or underscore those passages in his history that stress the discontinuities of British history and the ultimate break up of Roman and Roman-Christian culture wrought by the Saxon invasions. Written at a time when Welsh churches were coming under increasing Norman control and were engaged in the task of assembling evidence of their ancient privileges and traditions, these prophecies stand as a voice of moderation between the rival claims of the partisans of Saint David's and Canterbury. As the later history of the *PM* demonstrates, prophecy was a powerful tool in the pursuit and exercise of power during the Middle Ages. Some of the prophecies of this part of *HRB* 7, aroused the interest, passion, and scorn of eminent men of the twelfth and early thirteenth centuries, and may well have reached the ears of the pope and the Roman Curia.[18]

The second part of the *PM,* which relates principally to Norman governance of England, enjoyed an equally varied history, as demonstrated in the following section.

HRB Book 7: *Part 2*

The pining away of the Red Dragon at the far end of the pool refers to the closing events of Geoffrey's history, to the period in the *HRB* following Cadwallader's death in Rome, when Yvor and Yni rule over the wretched remnant of the British population, now called the Welsh, who have taken refuge in the depths of the woods of Wales. Part 2 of the *PM* foretells events to occur from the eighth through the twelfth centuries; that is, from the end of the period covered by the *HRB* to Geoffrey's own day. Unlike the early British history that formed the matter of the *HRB,* the Saxon, Danish, and Norman periods were relatively well-known to Geoffrey's audience. *HRB* 8–12 was necessary to decode much of the first part of the *PM,* but only a cursory knowledge of the history of the Anglo-Saxons, Danes, and Normans in England was required to interpret part 2 of the prophecies. By this time, however, the underlying destiny of the garden of Britain had been established, and had been revealed jointly by the two "ancient books in the British language," *HRB* and *PM.* Part 2 simply demonstrates that the same destiny continued to play itself out in the more recent and familiar history of the island-garden. We have already seen how this interplay between early British history and contemporary events functions in the three "ecclesiastical prophecies" of part 1. Part 2 of the prophecies takes this connection as its main object and shows the signs in recent history that point inexorably to the fate of the native and the alien seed.

The second part of the *PM* begins with the German Worm's tearing down the Prince of Brass, the British apotropaic statue containing the embalmed body of Cadwallader, which was to have struck terror into the hearts of the Saxons. A term had been set, however, for the career of the German Worm itself. It would "remain in restlessness and subjection for a hundred and fifty years," and would hold possession for 300 years (Thorpe, 173). Geoffrey borrowed this prophecy from chapter 23 of Gildas who implies that it came from a Saxon augury taken when the three original "keels" departed their homeland for Britain at the request of the "proud tyrant" (Winterbottom, 26).[19] Along with the tableau of the fighting dragons and the interpretation given to it, Gildas's prophecy is another example of Geoffrey's use of preexisting vaticinal material in composing the *PM.* How much importance to attach to the figure of 300 and 150 years in Gildas and Geoffrey is difficult to know. The number three and its multiples are commonplace figures. Perhaps both Gildas and Geoffrey simply intend us to understand the prophecy to mean that Saxon dominance will end one day in the not too distant future.[20] In any case, the prophecy foresees that the final demise of the Saxons will occur in two phases: first, the North Wind will take away the flowers that the West Wind made to bloom in the Saxon garden. Although there will be some gilding of the temples during this period, the sword "will not cease its work." The German Dragon will scarcely be able to take refuge in its caverns when vengeance for its betrayal will overtake it. Then, although its strength will be renewed for a short period, the "decimation of Normandy" (*decimatio Neustrie*) by "a people dressed in wood and in iron corslets" will do it grave harm on account of its wickedness. This people will "restore the original inhabitants" (*restaurabit pristinis incolis*), and the destruction of foreigners will be evident to all. Later Merlin foresees that the "seed of the White Dragon" will be uprooted from "our little gardens," and its surviving progeny will be decimated (Thorpe, 173).

In these prophecies, Geoffrey has made Merlin play the role of a Second Isaiah, reinterpreting the content and significance of ancient prophecy in the light of recent intervening events. The end of Saxon domination had long been anticipated in Welsh prophecy such as the *Armes Prydein*. In place of the alliance of Celtic armies under Cynan and Cadwallader, which according to the *Armes Prydein* will drive the Saxons across the sea and reclaim the island of Britain, Merlin foresees the Danish and Norman people as the new instruments of *ultio* and *restauratio*, vengeance (or punishment) and restoration. Geoffrey preserves the idea of punishment for the Saxon and restoration of the dignity of the British folk, but his view of how this will be accomplished owes more to his reflections on the history of England since 1066 than it does to any specific prophetic scenario. We have already seen how the Normans themselves rationalized their occupation of England on legal and moral grounds. William's invasion was justified because Earl Harold had perjured himself in refusing to abide by his promise to allow William to take the throne upon Edward the Confessor's death (d. 1066).[21] Osbern regarded the Norman Conquest as punishment in particular for the sins of King Ethelred, especially for his supposed role in the murder of Edward the Martyr (d. 978). He saw both the Danish invasions and the Norman Conquest as fulfilling Saint Dunstan's prophecy of the evils to befall the English for their sins.[22] Eadmer followed Osbern in these opinions and added that the decayed state of the English monasteries as a result of the Danish incursions justified the Norman Conquest.[23] This general view of things is reflected in Merlin's statement that although there will be gilding in the temples, the sword "will not cease its work," and vengeance for the German Dragon's treason will ultimately overtake it. The North Wind (the Danes), and the "people dressed in wood and iron corslets" (the Normans), will root up the alien seed, decimate the remainder of its progeny and yoke them in perpetual slavery. Even the ancient theme of the restoration of the dwellings of the "original inhabitants" had to be refashioned to reflect post-Conquest Norman settlement strategies. As is well-known, William brought with him from Normandy, a contingent of Breton auxiliaries under Alain Fergant whom he settled in strategic locations in England and Wales.[24] Indeed, the ruling family he established in Monmouth under Wihenoc (or Gueithenauc) in 1075 was of Breton origin, and it may be from this folk that Geoffrey traced his British heritage (Lloyd, 1942, 466–67; Lloyd, 1939, 2:523–24; Ditmas, 451–56).

We can well imagine, therefore, that Geoffrey's Anglo-Norman audience might have been flattered by the role that Merlin predicted for them up to this point in *HRB* 7 because that role closely paralleled their own view of their place in recent history. The section following, however, offered less comfort. *HRB* 7 does not mention William the Conqueror specifically, but alludes to William Rufus and Robert Curthose as the two dragons to follow the decimation of Normandy. The death of Rufus (1087–1100), killed by an arrow shot by Walter Tirel while hunting in the New Forest (2 August 1100), is said to have been brought about by the "arrow of envy" (*inuidie spiculo*), while Curthose is said to return "under the shadow of a name" (Thorpe, 173–74). Neither of these statements is easy to interpret in detail, but they both suggest rancor and divisiveness within the Anglo-Norman ruling aristocracy and were so interpreted by the earliest commentators on *HRB* 7. The first allusion implies that Rufus was deliberately murdered with an arrow out of a motive of envy or hatred (*inuidia*). This contrasts with the view of historians closest to the event such as Eadmer, the *Anglo-Saxon Chronicle,* Orderic, Suger, and William of Malmesbury, none of whom indict Tirel or anyone else for intentionally killing the king.[25] Alanus states that the opinion of nearly everyone was that Tirel acted unknowingly and by accident (*inscium & casu*) when he shot Rufus (Alanus, 69). He is right, however, when he goes on to observe that Merlin's prophecy urges us to believe otherwise (Alanus, 69).[26] Nevertheless, Alanus is not inclined to fix the blame on Tirel and contents himself with the vague observation that Rufus was "hated by heaven and earth" (*"invissus esset coelo & terrae"*) for his overbearing ways and corrupt life (Alanus, 68). Given this attitude on the part of his contemporaries, therefore, Geoffrey's decision to include (compose?) the *inuidie spiculo* prophecy as Merlin's only comment on the reign of Rufus is remarkable. Geoffrey was quite possibly not himself the author of this prophecy because William Rufus's death was often interpreted by contemporaries as a demonstration of God's justice in history. Many people claimed *post eventum* to have foreseen the king's end (Hollister, 640–42). Orderic even tells us that Abbot Fulchred of Shrewesbury predicted in a sermon on 1 August 1100 that the land would soon be freed from iniquity by the "bow of divine vengeance," and that "the arrow was out of its quiver, ready to wound" (Orderic, ed. Chibnall, 5, 287–89).[27] On the very day of his death, Rufus was warned about the portents and visions of his end, but scornfully dismissed them as the dreams of snoring monks (Orderic, ed. Chibnall, 4, 85–86). Imagining Geoffrey or someone else before him inserting his own favorite prophet, Merlin, into the list of dignitaries who foresaw the king's end is not difficult.

Whether the *inuidia* of the prophecy is God's or man's is difficult to know, but Rufus's murder assumes significance with its presence in the *HRB* 7 as a meaningful rather than a random event, revealing a pattern familiar to readers of Geoffrey's history, namely, the ineluctable downfall of great men and great civilizations and the unexpected reversals of history. The allusion to Robert Curthose's returning "under the shadow of a name" is usually taken by the commentaries on *HRB* 7 to refer to Robert's inability upon return from his crusade to seize the throne of England from his younger brother Henry I, his defeat by Henry at Tinchebrai (1106) and his subsequent imprisonment and death at Cardiff Castle (Hammer, 1949, 115; Alanus, 71; Orderic, 6, 387).[28] The *HRB* 7 pairs the demise of these two brothers and sons of the Conqueror and suggests that their ambitions were cut short by family rivalry and hatred. Their appearance on the stage is brief, and the major events of their lives, apart from their exemplary downfalls, go unnoticed by the selective eye of the prophet.

The main concern of the prophecy at this point is with the reign of Henry I (1100–35), who is styled the Lion of Justice (*leo iusticie*). The reader should bear in mind that the *PM* was originally written while Henry still ruled and would have been read by contemporaries with the greatest sense of immediacy and recognition. Orderic Vitalis states that anyone knowledgeable in history can interpret the prophecies of Merlin and see that they have consistently come to pass right down to the reigns of Henry I and Gruffydd ap Cynan (d. 1137), who still await the future that has been ordained for them by God (Orderic, ed. Chibnall, 6, 387). The earliest commentators on *HRB* 7 generally agree about the events alluded to in the reign of the Lion of Justice, showing that what strikes us perhaps as veiled and obscure in the language of prophecy was not necessarily so to its intended audience. The use of animal symbolism was so familiar to medieval readers through its use in the prophetic books of the Bible that it would have been taken as a natural mode of the elevated and suggestive discourse of prophecy.

Henry's honorific title, *leo iusticie,* fittingly captures the quality of his reign as envisioned in Merlin's prophecy concerning him. The title *Lion of Justice* implies rule, mastery, and vigilance, as well as violence and ruthlessness in the pursuit of justice. The characterization of Henry's reign in the *HRB* 7 shows that he lived up to the ambivalence of the sobriquet bestowed upon him by Merlin. On the one hand, we might count the king's protracted military campaigns in Normandy and France, and his success against his Welsh adversaries ("At his roar the towers of Gaul shall shake and the island Dragons tremble" [Thorpe, 174]). His reform of the currency in order to suppress forgery and physical mutilation of coins ("The surface of the coinage will be cleft, the half [penny] will be round" [my translation, cf. Thorpe, 174]) was praised by contemporaries, as was the stern justice that befell robbers, highwaymen, and marauders during Henry's rule ("kites will lose their ravenous hunger and the teeth of wolves will be blunted" [Thorpe, 174]). The punishment meted out to counterfeiters, castration and loss of the right hand, strikes us as an example of the king's cruelty. More typical of the opinion of his contemporaries on this subject, however, is the comment in the *Anglo-Saxon Chronicle,* which takes the punishment as an example of the king's justice against men who had conspired to ruin their country (Whitelock, 1961, 191 [anno 1125]).[29] The death of three of Henry's children ("The Lion's cubs will be transformed into salt-water fishes," [Thorpe, 174]), including his only legitimate son, William, in the sinking of the White Ship (25 November 1120), was a personal and political calamity that evoked sympathy for the king. The commentators usually take the prophecy concerning the nesting of the Eagle of Mount Aravia to refer to the marriage of Henry's daughter Matilda to Henry V (1114), or to her subsequent marriage to Geoffrey of Anjou (1128) (Hammer, 1935, 16; Hammer, 1942–43, 599; Hammer, 1948, 116; Alanus, 79–80). If this identification is correct, the marriage would form a pair of family events along with the episode of the White Ship. Any political bias in this prophecy, if it indeed does refer to Matilda, is difficult to perceive.

The other events referred to in Merlin's prophecies on the reign of Henry, however, do not reflect equally as well on the king's administration or the mores of his court. Henry's policy of taxing married clergy ("In the days of this Lion gold shall be squeezed from the lily-flower" [Thorpe, 174], and so on) was seen by some contemporaries more as an example of the king's greed than as a sign of his reforming zeal (Alanus, 77). Preachers frequently inveighed against the foppish dress and effeminate hair styles of the members of Henry's court.[30] Merlin's prophecy on this topic ("Those who have had their hair waved shall dress in woollen stuffs of many colours, and the outer garment shall be a fair index of the thoughts within") shares the view of Bishop Serlo of Séez, who scolded the king and his men for their modishness in a sermon at Carentan in 1105 (Orderic, 6, 65).

As for the prophecy concerning Henry's administration of the forests ("The feet of those who bark will be cut off" [Thorpe, 174]), there can be little doubt that it expressed the widespread resentment of many against the draconian measures taken by agents of the crown to protect deer and other game from poachers. The practice referred to in the prophecy was known as "lawing" (Freeman, 5, 163–64), and consisted of amputating or mutilating one paw from all dogs in the vicinity who might menace the king's fauna (Hammer, 1935, 15; 1940, 417; Alanus, 77–78). Orderic writes: Henry "appropriated to himself hunting rights over beasts everywhere in England; he ordered that the paws of dogs dwelling near the forests be partially cut off, and allowed only a few nobles and employees the privilege of hunting on his lands" (Orderic, 2, 4). Alanus paraphrases the prophecy as follows, "It says that while beasts will have peace, mankind will suffer punishment," although he takes the second part to refer to Rufus's cruel suppression of rebellion (Alanus, 78).

Finally, this second part of *HRB* 7 closes with a sequence of interrelated prophecies having to do with bloody conflicts in various parts of Britain, which presumably are to precede or accompany the end of the reign of the Lion of Justice. The first of these simply states, "Venedotia [North Wales] will be red with maternal blood" (Thorpe, 174). Of the many bloody family disputes in North Wales in the early part of the twelfth century, one appears to have particularly shocked contemporaries and to have found its way into one of Merlin's prophecies. In 1125, Cadwallon, son of Gruffydd ap Cynan, slew three of his maternal uncles, Goronwy, Rhiddid, and Meilyr of the cantref of Dyffryn Clwyd. Eight years later in 1132, Cadwallon himself was murdered near Llangollen by two of his own cousins, Einion ab Owain and Cadwgan, son of Goronwy, in revenge for Cadwallon's killing of Goronwy (T. Jones, 1955, 108–11, 113). The Exeter commentator on *HRB* 7, a man with detailed knowledge of Welsh affairs, takes this prophecy to refer to Cadwallon's slaying of his uncles, but makes no mention of Einion and Cadwgan's later act of vengeance (Hammer, 1949, 116). The prophecy that follows this one ("The house of Corineus will slay six brothers" [Thorpe, 174]) commemorates another act of vengeance committed in Cornwall ("The house of Corineus") some years before 1130. In this episode, Frewin, the sheriff of Cornwall, and six other Cornishmen took vengeance by slaying the six sons of Toki, all apparently of Norman ancestry, ostensibly for their role in the death of a Cornishman named Osulf. This anti-Norman reprisal in Cornwall must have been something of a cause célèbre because it was recorded not only in the Pipe Rolls for 1130, which list the fines imposed on Frewin and his accomplices, but also in a Gloucestershire tax account more than 100 years later. The Pipe Rolls call Frewin's fine an "old debt" (*de veteri debito suo*), indicating that the murder of Toki's sons occurred sometime before 1130, perhaps quite a bit earlier (Padel, 1984, 26–27).[31]

Geoffrey apparently used these two fairly recent events as models to project the kind of disorder that would follow the anticipated death of Henry I. These two prophecies lead to a general lament on the mournful condition foreseen for the island at this time. ("The island will lie sodden with the tears of the night-time," and so on [Thorpe, 174].) As far as I can tell, the prophecies concerning Venedotia and the house of Corineus are the last prophecies in the *PM* based on actual events. Everything that follows is truly visionary.

Henry I died at his hunting lodge, the castle of Lyon-la-Forêt in Normandy on 1 December 1135. His body was taken to Rouen and embalmed. His entrails, brains, and eyes were removed and interred in the church of Notre Dame de Pré in Emendreville, while his body was carried to Reading and there buried according to his own instructions, early in 1136. At some time following the death of the king, someone, perhaps Geoffrey himself, added a prophecy immediately after the one beginning "The island will lie sodden . . . ," alluding to the dissection of Henry's corpse. This prophecy runs: "Woe to you, Normandy, since the brain of the lion will be spilled out upon you, and when his limbs have been scattered, he will be sent away from his native soil" (Griscom, 387, n. h, 46–47; also Hammer, 1951, 126, n. 88; Wright, 1984, xi; *"Ue tibi neustria quoniam in te cerebrum leonis effundetur & dissipatis menbris a natiuo solo eliminabitur"*). We do not know when this prophecy was added to the

PM. Orderic quoted extensively from *HRB* 7 in his *Ecclesiastical History,* book 12, chapter 47, but his copy of the prophecies seems not to have included *"Ue, tibi, neustria"* (Orderic, ed. Chibnall, 6, 380–89). Chibnall suggests that Orderic composed chapter 47 shortly before Henry's death, but incorporated it into his history not earlier than 1136, making this the earliest reference we have to Geoffrey's *PM* (Orderic, ed. Chibnall, 6, xviii). The *HRB* itself, however, is usually thought to have been finished by Geoffrey between 1136 and 1138. Orderic, therefore, may have been quoting from a copy of *HRB* 7, which was circulating as a pamphlet separate from the complete *Historia Regum Britanniae,* and without allusion to Henry's corpse (Tatlock, 1974, 418–21; Chambers, 28–29; Fletcher, 464–69).[32]

There is nothing implausible in this. As we have seen, the *PM* has the look of a separate book, complete with prefatory letter explaining how Geoffrey grudgingly left aside his history to work on the book of prophecies that Bishop Alexander of Lincoln, requested of him. Geoffrey does not state that Alexander wished to see a book of Merlin's prophecies included as part of a larger history, but simply that the bishop wanted the prophecies themselves. Internal evidence suggests, as we have seen, that Cadwallon's murder of his uncles in 1125 is the last reasonably secure event alluded to in *HRB* 7, but that we might possibly push this date forward to 1132, the year in which Cadwallon himself was killed by Goronwy. Neither of these dates precludes the possibility that an original *libellum* containing the prophecies of Merlin, without the *"Ue, tibi, neustria"* prophecy, circulated in Normandy before Henry's death, and was the *Merlini libellum* from which Orderic says he took a "short extract" (*lectiuncula*). Apart from the prophecies of Merlin, Orderic does not appear to have been influenced by the work of Geoffrey of Monmouth. The *"Ue, tibi, neustria"* prophecy turns up in the earliest surviving commentary on *HRB* 7 (British Library MS Cotton Claudius B vii ff., 224r–233v; Hammer, 1940, 145), written probably between 1147 and 1154, that is, within Geoffrey's own lifetime (d. 1155).[33] Because Geoffrey revised his dedicatory letter to Alexander following the bishop's death in 1148, there is reason to think that he did not regard the original text of *HRB* 7 as above improvement as circumstances changed, although apart from the *"Ue, tibi, neustria"* interpolation, the text of *HRB* 7 was very stable and shows no significant signs of updating by successive redactors.

Proving that Geoffrey himself inserted the *"Ue, tibi, neustria"* prophecy into the *PM* is impossible. The evidence does establish, however, that some person living close to the time when the *Historia Regum Britanniae* was composed saw that this was the proper place in the text of the *PM* to record the death of Henry I. In any case, it probably did not take prophetic inspiration on Geoffrey's part to foresee that upon Henry's death, the tensions that he held in check by his forceful and ruthless character were likely to break out into violent conflict. Others apart from Geoffrey of Monmouth sensed a turn for the worse would follow the king's death. Gerald claims that the Flemings of South Wales, anticipating reprisals that would befall them after Henry's reign, sold what they had and departed Wales a year to six months before the king's actual death (Gerald of Wales, trans. Thorpe, 147). The killing of Toki's sons appears to have been a political act, the vengeance of native Cornishmen against their Norman rulers (Padel, 1984, 26). In its present context in the *PM,* the reprisal of Frewin and his fellow Cornishmen is a prelude to a general decline in Norman fortunes in Britain, and it may have figured as such in political verse before Geoffrey wrote *HRB* 7. Henry's death was, indeed, the spark that ignited a long-anticipated conflagration in Wales in 1136, as well as a civil war in England. In these closing prophecies of part 2 of the *PM,* Geoffrey looked beyond Henry even to the end of Norman rule that would occur under a "She-lynx" who would follow Sextus ("the Sixth"), conqueror of Ireland (Thorpe, 175).

Part 2 of *HRB* 7 recapitulates, therefore, the concept of the rise and fall of an alien seed in the garden of Britain. The Norman plantation undergoes the same cycle of dominance and decline in part 2 that the Saxon seed experienced in part 1. The sad plight of England during the war between Matilda and Stephen seemed to fulfill the dire predictions of the *PM* concerning the era immediately following Henry I: bloodshed and reprisal in Scotland, and slaughter for those who oppose the marauding "cubs of the lion" (Thorpe, 175). The brief period of tranquillity under Sextus, who will renew holy places, endow the churches and clergy, and "throw down the walls of Ireland," appeared a true prophecy of the reign of Henry II ("he shall be crowned with the head of the lion"), who conquered Ireland in 1171 (Thorpe, 175). Little wonder that twelfth-century readers of Geoffrey found *HRB* 7 an accurate revelation of the course of their history. But Merlin unequivocally foresees an end to Norman domination of Britain during the reign of the "She-lynx." ("Normandy will lose both its isles and be deprived of its former dignity" [Thorpe, 175].) The prophecies of Merlin envision the Normans ultimately as yet another alien seed that will flourish briefly and then be swept away forever from the island garden.

HRB 7: Part 3

The last and longest section of *HRB* 7 has proven to be a source of frustration to readers. The prophecies of the previous two parts at least were anchored in concrete historic events and showed, albeit often obscurely, the same concern for the shaping events of history that is evident in the rest of Geoffrey's *HRB*. Even some of Geoffrey's warmest admirers, however, have thrown up their hands in distress over the rambling jumble of prophecies in part 3 of the *PM*. Faral admits that the normally controlled Geoffrey here abandons himself "au délire le plus échevelé," while Tatlock speaks of the "mysterious vaporing" that hangs about *HRB* 7 and calls the interpretation of Geoffrey's prophecies a "Serbonian bog" (Faral, 2:65; Tatlock, 1974, 405, 403). Christopher Brooke perhaps best summarizes the sentiments of generations of readers when he states that this part of the *PM* simply trails off into "complete gibberish" (Grierson and Brooke, 288).

Attempts to identify the sources of Geoffrey's intoxication have pointed in diverse directions. Faral detects echoes of the Sybilline Books, the prophetic books of the Old Testament (particularly Isaiah and Ezechiel), the Book of Revelation, Lactantius, Saint Augustine, and Adso's *Libellus de Antichristo* (Faral, 2:49–53). He thinks also that Geoffrey may have drawn more proximately on the *Prophecy of Saint Berchan,* Gildas, and the *Life of Saint Edward the Confessor,* but denies that he had any knowledge whatsoever of Welsh prophecy. Tatlock, on the other hand, doubted that Geoffrey knew much in particular about the Sibylline prophecies, but argued that the Bible and Welsh vaticination could have provided him with the technique he needed to spin out his web of prophecy (Tatlock, 403–21). Tatlock was led to this conclusion by the existence of numerous pre-Geoffrey Irish prophecies, as well as by prophecies attributed to Merlin, but betraying no debt to Geoffrey, in Gerald of Wales and in the *History of Gruffydd ap Cynan.* Tatlock also accepted Rydberg's conclusion that Geoffrey drew on Lucan's *Pharsalia* 1, 649–72, for the astral predictions that conclude the *PM* (Tatlock, 1974, 405–6). More recent studies of animal symbolism in *HRB* 7 have led scholars such as Doris Edel and myself to conclude that Geoffrey may have drawn on the rich stock of animal epithets reserved for famous warriors in early Welsh heroic poetry and in the medieval Welsh genealogies.[34] All of these studies tend to confirm the opinion of the twelfth-century historian William of Newburgh that Geoffrey compiled *HRB* 7 by mingling prophecies of his own invention along with those of Merlin (Hamilton, 1:5). The *PM* stands as the quintessential conjuring act by Geoffrey, showing him to be a master at disguising the mechanism of his art.

Yet we should not be so blinded, baffled, or exasperated by the vast stretches of skimble-skamble stuff in the third part of the *PM* as to miss its main thrust. The underlying theme of the prophecies, the brevity of the dominion of foreigners in Britain, is reiterated simply and eloquently in part 3 by the comparative scale of the prophecies concerned with the period following the restoration of native rule. The Saxon/Danish and Norman segments (that is, what has been labeled parts 1 and 2) of the *PM* occupy but a small fraction of the vast future Merlin foresees for the garden-island. To be more precise, of the 10 pages of prophecies comprising the *PM* in Wright's edition (74–84), a scant one and a half pages are dedicated to the Saxon and Danish periods (74–75), while the entire Norman presence from the historic "decimation of Normandy" down to the anticipated loss of sovereignty under the "She-lynx" occupies but another one and a half pages (75–77). The rest (77–84) comprises the period of restoration of British rule beginning with the return of the island's inhabitants, the diversion of the Periron River by the old, white-haired man on a white horse, and the alliance of Cadwallader and Cynan with Scotland.

Geoffrey undoubtedly derived a portion of this scenario from Welsh sources. As we have seen in chapter 2, the *Armes Prydein,* foretold two centuries earlier that the island of Britain would be returned to its rightful rulers when Cadwallader and Cynan joined together to defeat the "stewards of the Great King" (Athelstan) at Aber Peryddon (Geoffrey's Periron). The same Welsh poem predicted that an alliance of warriors from Ireland (including apparently the Danes of Dublin), Scotland, Strathclyde, Angelsey (or the Isle of Man?), Cornwall, and Brittany would join with the Welsh to drive the Saxons across the sea and to reclaim the inheritance lost by Vortigern. According to the *Armes Prydein* and Geoffrey, this restoration of British sovereignty will be of no short duration, but will last until Judgment day (*hyt vrawt*).

The identity of Cadwallader and Cynan, the promised redeemers of the *Armes Prydein,* is not entirely clear. Bromwich thinks that the first of these is the Cadwallader who was king of Gwynedd in the seventh century and who died in the great plague of 664 (Bromwich, 1978, 292–93; Bede, trans. Sherley-Price, 279–81; Nennius, ch. 64). His great fame as one of the two saviors of the British people may derive from confusion of his name with that of his more warlike father Cadwallo, who overthrew the English Northumbrian dynasty in 633–34. In any case,

Cadwallader and Cynan's exalted stature in the *Armes Prydein* shows that they played the part of "sons of prophecy" among the Welsh for over two centuries before Geoffrey's *HRB*. In the *HRB*, as we have seen, Cadwallader, son of Cadwallo, is stayed from returning to Britain by the voice of an angel who commands him to travel to Rome in order to do penance before Pope Sergius. Cadwallader dies in the holy city in 689. But the angelic voice promises that the British will once again take possession of the island "when the moment should come which Merlin had prophesied to Arthur" (Thorpe, 282). He goes on to state that the moment of restoration would arrive when the relics that once belonged to the Britons had been carried from Rome to Britain.(Thorpe, 283). Cynan of the *Armes Prydein* may be the same Conan Meriodocus who in Geoffrey is the ancestor of the kings of Brittany and an ally of Maximian, who rewarded him with the territory of Brittany for his help in Maximian's conquest of Gaul. Conan's death is presumed in two passages in the *HRB* (Thorpe, 149, 272).[35]

Once again we are drawn back to the conclusion that the *PM* draw on very different traditions from, and are rather imperfectly integrated into, the *HRB*. The *PM* makes no mention of the return of the relics of the British saints. Yet, this is the condition required, according to the voice of the angel in the *HRB*, before the promised restoration of British dignity can take place. Moreover, the *PM* specifies that Cadwallader and Conan will lead the alliance of Celtic people against the foreigners, which will inaugurate the long-hoped-for day of Restoration. Are we to assume that they will return from the dead to play this role? The *HRB* leaves no doubt about their deaths. But what of Arthur? He is the only one about whose death there is at least some measure of ambiguity in the *HRB*. If Geoffrey were serious about integrating the prophecies of Merlin into his history, he would have made Arthur the promised redeemer in the *PM* instead of Cadwallader and Conan, or at least have anticipated such a role for these latter two warriors in the body of his history. The evidence points in the other direction. The scenario of Restoration as we find it in the *PM* is not of Geoffrey's invention, but derives from a Welsh source such as the *Armes Prydein* or something very similar to it, which Geoffrey left much as he found it.

Tatlock and Rydberg were probably right to detect the influence of Lucan's *Pharsalia* in the astral disturbances that end *HRB* 7. The suggestion for such a denouement, however, was already in the *Armes Prydein*'s insistence that the Restoration of British sovereignty would last "until Judgement day." The plethora of predictions that intervenes between the Restoration and the end of *HRB* 7 owes something to the language and imagery of the Bible and the bestiaries, but seems to be largely of Geoffrey's own invention. In place of the orderly sequence of rulers who gave shape to the prophecies up to this point, the predictions that stretch ever onward after the Restoration follow no readily apparent chronology and certainly offer no breezy prospect of a golden age of peace and prosperity. They are, however, not without plan and purpose: they simply foresee, one might even say they imitate, a long period of native British sovereignty uninterrupted by foreign invasion and domination. I take this to be the main point of part 3 of *HRB* 7. By contrast with the previous two parts, the scope of the prophecies in part 3 implies a finality and duration to the Restoration that sets it apart from all other periods in the history of Britain. The theme of the alien seed dominated the rapid sequence of prophecies in parts 1 and 2; the Restoration in part 3 brings about a corresponding slackening of the pace and the promise of a long age of British rule. This was a deliberate, if risky, rhetorical strategy on Geoffrey's part. Admittedly, his readers on the whole, unlike Melville's, have not been quick to see the poetry in the blubber.

Conclusion

This chapter has attempted to bridge the gulf separating the modern reader from one type of literature and historic thought during the Middle Ages. Political prophecy, like epithalamium and panegyric, is today a dead literary genre. We tend to regard its appearance in the works of respected medieval authors such as Dante and Geoffrey of Monmouth as an unfortunate blemish. We puzzle over the eagerness of a sophisticated and worldly Norman administrator such as Bishop Alexander of Lincoln to possess a collection of Merlin's prophecies. It helps to see Alexander's curiosity about Merlin against the larger pattern of Norman interest in pre-Saxon Britain and to understand how the anti-Saxon biases of Welsh prophecy might have served Norman purposes. It also helps to know how the *PM* function within Geoffrey's *HRB* itself and how they resonate against the politics of a rapidly changing society.

If we are to understand something of the role that political prophecy played in medieval historic judgment in general, however, we have to go a step further and grasp the peculiar epistemology of prophecy. Viewing political prophecy as exclusively concerned with the future is wrong. As book 7 of Geoffrey's *HRB* shows, prophecy is principally about continuity, about the search for a common thread, a meaning that links past, present, and future. Prophecy is unlike history in its extreme selectivity. Only those events that point the way and reveal the underlying pattern and direction of history are of interest to the prophet. He seeks permanence and meaning in a world of constant change. A firm understanding of God's ancient covenant with Israel was all that Isaiah or Ezechiel needed in order to discern where their present course would lead. Prophecy, in other words, justifies history. How else can the underlying pattern be revealed except by a scrupulous meditation on what has been?

Prophecy's quest for permanence also determines the character of its vocabulary: to the prophet, Henry I is the Lion of Justice, not simply an individual bound to time and place, but an abstraction, a grammatical ambiguity, a figure of nature, a sign. Far from being a source of irritation, the symbolic language of prophecy was for medieval readers rather a mark of dignity and seriousness, as well as a goad to the imagination. The two ancient books Geoffrey welded together to make the *HRB,* the *Book of Kings,* and the *Book of Prophecies,* confronted the same philosophical issues of change, decline, suffering, betrayal, and recovery. The *Book of Kings* documented the recovery of Trojan fortunes on the shores of Britain following the burning of Troy, the steady growth of the British folk, and the gradual loss of their independence. The *Book of Prophecies* in its turn accepted that loss of independence as a historic fact, but went on to reveal the essential structure and meaning of British history whose logic ineluctably pointed forward to recovery, to a period of restored native sovereignty free from alien domination. It is a great credit to Geoffrey's genius that his two books endured as the essential version of British history and destiny for some 400 years. Understanding the role that prophecy played in shaping that vision has been the purpose of this chapter.

Chapter Four
The *History of the Kings of Britain:* Arthur and His Successors

The culmination of the *HRB* is Geoffrey's account of the magnificent career of Arthur, son of Utherpendragon and Ygerna, which occupies about 20 percent of the entire *HRB*. Geoffrey could count on his audience's knowing something of Arthur, but the details of the British warrior's life as preserved in the sources, Nennius, the Welsh Annals, and Welsh literary and oral traditions were conveniently vague and contradictory enough to allow Geoffrey to exercise his customary independence and to give free rein to his fertile imagination.

Although Geoffrey does not tell us that people in his day were actively discussing Arthur, a claim he does make for Merlin, we know that this was the case. William of Malmesbury, when describing in his *Gesta Regum* (1125), how Arthur helped Ambrosius to overcome the Saxons, adds, "This is the Arthur about whom the trifles of the Britons (*Britonum nugae*) rage even today; clearly he was a worthy man about whom genuine histories, rather than the dreams of lying fables, ought to speak (*non fallaces somniarent fabulae, sed veraces praedicarent historiae*)." Later in this same work, William comments that because Arthur's tomb has never been discovered, the old popular songs (*antiquitas naeniarum*) still tell that he will one day return (Chambers, 250).[1] Earlier in the twelfth century, in 1113, a group of canons from Laon while traveling from Exeter to Bodmin in Cornwall were shown the "chair and oven of King Arthur, famed in the fables of the Britons." In Bodmin, a local man with a withered hand began an altercation with one of the group named Hagenellus, apparently by claiming that Arthur was still alive. Herman of Tournai, who recollected this episode in his *De Miraculis S. Mariae Laudunensis* (1146), claims that had the confrontation not been halted by armed men, blood would have been spilled. He also notes that this incident resembles the way the Bretons are accustomed to dispute with the French over King Arthur.[2]

Because Geoffrey was particularly adept at providing his audience with information unavailable to his colleagues in the field of history, the

Arthurian section of the *HRB* could be seen as a response to William of Malmesbury's claim about the absence of *veraces historiae* concerning Arthur. As we might expect, however, Geoffrey's Arthur was probably not entirely what William had in mind. And while Geoffrey does not overtly endorse the idea of Arthur's return, his account of the British king's exploits was, nevertheless, destined to provoke many a controversy, although no bloodshed, as far as I know, among generations of readers.

Arthur's career in the *HRB* falls into several distinct periods: (1) the reconquest of Britain and neighboring islands; (2) the campaigns in Norway, Denmark, and Gaul; (3) Arthur's Plenary Court at Pentecost; (4) victory over the Romans in Gaul; and (5) the Battle of Camblan.

The Reconquest of Britain and the Neighboring Islands

One of Geoffrey's most daring strokes in writing the *HRB* was to claim that through the military leadership of Arthur the Britons not only recovered their strength following the death of Utherpendragon, but even drove the Saxons out of Britain entirely. In Nennius, Arthur aids the British kings in their conflicts with the Saxons in his capacity as *dux bellorum*.[3] Geoffrey, however, promotes Arthur to the rank of sole reigning king of Britain. He strategically reduces Nennius's list of Arthur's 12 battles to three principal ones, and associates each of these vaguely with the three regions of Britain where the Saxons historically had been dominant (Northumbria, Mercia, and the general region of Southeastern Britain). It is noteworthy that Henry of Huntingdon, Geoffrey's contemporary, claims in his *History of the English* that the locations of Arthur's 12 battles can no longer be determined (Arnold, 1879, 49). Ever eager to supply information that Henry and William of Malmesbury did not have, Geoffrey confidently identifies the locales of three of Arthur's battles. The first of his conflicts with the Saxons takes place on the Douglas River, which Geoffrey situates in the vicinity of York; the second in the Caledonian Wood, near the town of Kaerluideoit, identified by Geoffrey as Lincoln; the last on a hill near Bath.

Arthur first traps Colgrin in York, but is forced to withdraw to London to consult with his advisors when Saxon reinforcements arrive under Baldulf, Colgrin's brother. Hoel of Brittany and 15,000 men soon join their British comrades, and their combined force first decimates the Saxons at Lincoln and then traps them within the Caledonian Wood, where they nearly starve to death. Arthur, however, allows the pagans to depart in their ships after they deliver hostages and agree to pay tribute thereafter to the British. The Saxons leave but have a change of heart on their voyage back to Germany and return to Britain, putting ashore at Totnes. Harried constantly by Arthur, they take refuge on a hill near Bath, where Colgrin, Baldulf, and thousands of others are killed. Finally, while Arthur goes back north to aid Hoel in his fight against the Scots and Picts, Cador, Duke of Cornwall, pursues the remaining Saxons under Cheldric to the Isle of Thanet. There he kills Cheldric and forces "the remaining Saxons to surrender."

Geoffrey leaves the impression, in other words, that the Saxons were routed from their traditional kingdoms and utterly expelled from Britain during the early years of the young Arthur's reign. They would not return again until the traitorous Mordred sought their help in his attempt to usurp the throne, dated by Geoffrey in the year 542. Needless to say, this account differs considerably from the view of the Saxon settlements as found in Gildas, Bede, Nennius, and in Geoffrey's contemporaries, Henry of Huntingdon and William of Malmesbury, none of whom assign any such momentous role to the Battle of Bath.

The idea that the British during this time were allowed a respite from Saxon depredations and a period of peace comes originally from Gildas and was repeated on Gildas's authority by Bede and Nennius and many later authorities (Winterbottom, 28). Gildas attributes this respite to British success at the Battle of Badon Hill, which he states occurred in the year of his birth, 44 years and one month before the time in which he was writing.[4] Although he lived and wrote in this peaceful hiatus, Gildas nevertheless bitterly denounced the vices peace brought and excoriated the tyranny of Britain's contemporary rulers (Winterbottom, 28–36). Geoffrey, on the other hand, interprets the post-Badon period not merely as a respite, but as the Golden Age of Arthur (about whom Gildas says nothing) in which the British enjoyed their regained sovereignty over the entire island.[5] Indeed, Geoffrey takes special pains to stress the importance of the Battle of Bath as the climactic moment in the British reconquest of the island. He has Archbishop Dubricius give a bracing speech before the battle, portraying it as a holy crusade, and he pauses to describe the ceremony of Arthur's donning his armor, including his shield Pridwen with its "likeness of the Blessed Mary, Mother of God, which forced him to be thinking perpetually of her" (Thorpe, 217).

Arthur's campaigns against the Picts and the Scots following the expulsion of the Saxons serve as a bridge to his international conquests and may have been suggested to Geoffrey by the picture of Arthur as

leader of an international band of warriors in Welsh narrative tradition,
particularly in the prose tale *Culhwch and Olwen,* although how he would
have come to know this tradition is not clear. It is likely, too, that
Geoffrey's depiction of Arthur's northern campaigns were largely a
duplication of his earlier battles against the Saxons. Just as the Saxons
took refuge from Arthur in the Caledonian Wood, where they would
have died of starvation had Arthur not taken pity on them, so, too, the
Picts and Scots flee the king's fury, taking refuge on the 60 islands of
Loch Lomond (borrowed from the *mirabilia* of chapter 67 of the *Historia
Brittonum*) where they, too, would have perished of starvation had not
Arthur shown them mercy in response to the pleading of their bishops.
Their fortunes are momentarily raised by the arrival of Gilmaurius, king
of the Irish, just as Colgrin is relieved at the siege of York by Baldulf's
coming to his aid from Germany. Again, where the Saxons are permitted
to return to their homeland as tribute-paying subjects of the British, the
Picts and the Scots are allowed to possess "some small tract of land of
their own, seeing that they were in any case going to bear the yoke of
servitude" (Thorpe, 219–20). Arthur's rebuilding of churches destroyed
in the Saxon depredations recalls Aurelius Ambrosius's great reconstruction of British churches following his execution of Hengist and grant of
pardon to Octa and Eosa (Thorpe, 193–95). Arthur's restoration of
churches and his appointment of his chaplain Priamus as metropolitan of
York is part of Geoffrey's effort to construct Arthur as the *rex pius,* the
opposite of the role the king plays in many Welsh saints' lives.[6] The
power that he has to invest his own nominee in a vacant metropolitan
see would have been the envy of Henry I, who was forced by threat of
excommunication in 1105 to surrender his right to invest the prelates of
England.

    As a symbol of the peace that the reconquest brings to the island at
this time, Arthur marries Guinevere, the most beautiful woman in the
country. Geoffrey found Guinevere along with Kay and Bedevere among
Arthur's entourage in Welsh tradition (she appears in *Culhwch and Olwen*
as Arthur's Queen Gwenhvyuar or Gwenhwyuar), and promoted her to
new status. In the *HRB* Guinevere is not only a beautiful woman, but
also a descendant of a noble Roman family and has been brought up in
the household of Duke Cador of Cornwall (Thorpe, 221).

    Arthur's conquests of Ireland, Iceland, Gotland, and the Orkneys are
swiftly accomplished in the course of the next summer. This brief section
of the *HRB* reveals once again that one of Geoffrey's principal strategies
in inflating Arthur's career to epic proportions was to present him as

both the epitome and the apex of previous British accomplishments. He repeats the deeds of his predecessors, but on a larger scale. Utherpendragon, Arthur's father, had defeated Gillomannius the Irishman, and had taken away the Giants' Ring from Mount Killaraus; Arthur defeats Gilmaurius (an obvious duplicate of Gillomannius) and takes possession of the entire island of Ireland. Brennius had earlier in the *HRB* voyaged to Norway and married the daughter of Elsingius, king of the Norwegians, while his brother Belinus captured Ginchtalacus, king of the Danes, releasing him only on condition that the Danes pay tribute to Britain. Geoffrey has Arthur recapitulate these achievements of his predecessors by subjecting both Norway and Denmark to his rule and placing his brother-in-law Loth on the throne of Norway. Geoffrey's remark that the British army in Norway and Denmark "scattered the rural population and continued to give full license to their savagery" until the two countries submitted to Arthur (Thorpe, 223), recalls the "unheard-of savagery" Brennius vented on the folk of Italy following the sack of Rome (Thorpe, 99).

Arthur's later conquest of Gaul and defeat of the Romans can easily be seen as a reiteration of Brennius's rise to become king of the Allobroges and his subsequent conquest of Rome. Again, we recall that Arthur is crowned at Silchester by Dubricius, archbishop of the City of the Legions, just as Constantine, his grandfather, was crowned in the same city by Guithelinus, archbishop of London. The young king's distribution of all his possessions following his coronation recalls the manner in which Brennius secured the allegiance of the Allobroges by distributing his father-in-law's treasury (Thorpe, 95). Mimeticism is Arthur's ruling humor.

Geoffrey also attempts to construct Arthur's epic stature by providing the British king with the accouterments of ancient and medieval heroes familiar to a Norman audience. Thus, Arthur's arms have impressive-sounding names: Pridwen (his shield), Ron (his spear), Caliburn (his sword). The first two of these probably came down to Geoffrey from Welsh traditions. In *Culhwch and Olwen,* for example, Arthur voyages in his ship *Prydwen,* and swears oaths on his weapons, which include not only Rhongomiant, his spear, but also Wynebgwrthucher, his shield, Carnwennan, his knife, and Caledfwlch, his sword. He also has a steed named Llamrei and, amusingly, a dog named Horse (Cafall). Why Geoffrey decided to rename Arthur's sword is unclear, but perhaps he was eager to combine classical as well as native traditions in naming the British king's weapons. He tells us that Caliburn was forged in the Isle of Avalon (Thorpe, 217). This would certainly call to mind for Geoffrey's audience the forging of Aeneas's arms by the Cyclops in the fiery caves of Vulcan on the Isle of Lipari (*Aeneid,* 8:416 ff., 615–25).[7] Virgil speaks of the Cyclops's hammering out the "iron bars of the Chalybes" (*stricturae Chalybum*), and the word *Chalybes* may have suggested the name Caliburn to Geoffrey. As if to signal the admixture of native and classical traditions in the naming of Arthur's weapons, Geoffrey described the spear Ron in a sentence in which a Latin hexameter with internal rhyme was embedded: *hec erat ardua lataque lancea, cladibus apta* (Thorpe, 217; "long, broad in the blade and thirsty for slaughter").

It is instructive to recall that in the *Song of Roland,* the oldest surviving copy of which was written in England around the time when Geoffrey was composing the *HRB,* Charlemagne similarly has his sword Joyeuse, his horse Tencendur; and Roland has his horn Olifant, his horse Veillantif, and his sword Durendal. The sword Durendal also has a mystical provenance, Charlemagne having been instructed by an angel to deliver it to Roland (laisse 172). In its hilt are sacred relics: Saint Peter's tooth, the blood of Saint Basil, a lock of Saint Denis's hair, and a piece of the Virgin Mary's robe. Arthur's Caliburn is similarly endowed with a mysterious and numinous origin though Geoffrey avoids bestowing explicitly Christian sacral qualities upon it.

On the other hand, Geoffrey chose not to suppress the idea that came to him in a confused form from Nennius that Arthur carried the picture of the Virgin Mary on his shield,[8] and that he, too, was one of the illustrious *miles Christi* doing battle against pagans. The speech given by Archbishop Dubricius on the eve of the Battle of Bath, in fact, puts the approaching conflict in terms of a holy war, an idea familiar to an audience living in the aftermath of the First Crusade. Dubricius speaks of the British forces under Arthur being "marked with the cross of the Christian faith" and tells the troops assembled before him that to die for their brothers in defense of their fatherland is to follow in Christ's footsteps. He concludes, "if any one of you shall suffer death in this war, that death shall be to him as a penance and an absolution for all his sins, given always that he goes to meet it unflinchingly" (Thorpe, 216). The idea of blood martyrdom was given special redefinition by Pope Urban II in preaching the First Crusade (November 1095) some 40 years earlier than the *HRB* when, according to Fulcher of Chartres, he promised the *milites Christi* that those who died in the siege of Jerusalem would be considered martyrs and that their souls would go to heaven.[9] The same idea was repeated in the *Song of Roland* (laisse 89) by Archbishop Turpin who promised the French that if they died in battle against the Saracen, their martyrdom would guarantee them a place in Paradise. While Turpin takes the precaution of having the French formally confess before making such assurances, Dubricius apparently maintains that death itself in such circumstances represents *penitentia et ablutio* (Wright, 1984, 103) as long as "one goes to meet it unflinchingly." It must have been of some comfort to Geoffrey's audience to know that Arthur shared their own crusading ideology.

Finally, Geoffrey is at pains to place his own narrative stamp on the depiction of the early career of Arthur. To Nennius's description of Loch Lomond's 60 islands, each with a lofty crag on top of which stands an eagle's nest, Geoffrey adds the original idea that the birds gathered there each year to predict important events about to occur in the kingdom. Pähler has pointed out how Geoffrey's adaptation of this passage converts it into one of the many structural markers linking the parts of the *HRB*.[10] In this case, the description of the marvelous islands with their prophetic birds is a link in a chain of prophetic utterances in the *HRB*, beginning with Diana's prophecy to Brutus, through the prophecies of the Eagle of Shaftesbury, Merlin's prophecies, and Alan, king of Brittany's consultation of various prophetic books in the closing episodes of the *HRB*.

The Campaigns in Norway, Denmark, and Gaul

The second Arthurian section of the *HRB* is marked by Arthur's resumption of military campaigning after a period of peace lasting 12 years. The Gildasian information about the post-Badon respite is thus segmented in the *HRB* into alternating periods of peace and war. This second section is essentially a prelude to Arthur's later confrontation with the Romans in Gaul, but it also initiates the centrifugal trajectory of his career away from Britain toward imperial ventures on the continent. The last phase of this trajectory is cut short when Arthur is compelled to return to Britain to face Mordred at the fatal Battle of Camblan.

Geoffrey begins by informing us that Arthur and his court by this time had become paragons of civilized behavior and that the king's reputation for "generosity and bravery spread to the very ends of the earth." Arthur had invited "distinguished men from far distant kingdoms" to join him, while imitation of the dress and arms of the court became the rage of the day (Thorpe, 222). Geoffrey implies, however, that this projection of the king's charisma had another side: Britain's power inspired fear and defensive preparations among other nations, even those quite far away. Geoffrey does not elaborate on this idea in the passage under discussion, but he later gives us a clue to its significance. At the outset of Arthur's campaign against Frollo in Gaul, Geoffrey remarks that although Frollo was resolved to put up stiff resistance against Arthur, he could really do little because "the young men of all the islands (*iuuentus omnium insularum*) which Arthur had subdued were there to fight at his side," and that "the better part of the army of the Gauls was already in Arthur's service, for he had bought them over by the gifts (*sua largitate*) which he had given them" (Thorpe, 223). Little wonder kings such as Frollo and emperors such as Leo had cause to fear and oppose Arthur. Geoffrey seems at pains to emphasize that Arthur's growing power was based on his ability to undermine his opponents by draining their lands of their fighting men, whose loyalty he secured by munificent distribution of the spoils of victories. Arthur's conquests make possible the distribution of vast spoils of war to the young men of the islands that have fallen under his sway, but incessant conquest is the condition for maintaining his might. The continual search for more disposable booty to purchase the loyalty of his international army is thus the basis of the king's political might.

This naturally calls to mind the career of Brennius (see chapter 2), who as the younger brother under the "Trojan" system of primogeniture, was compelled to seek his fortune in foreign conquests in order to achieve economic and political parity with his older brother Belinus. Tonuuenna, the brothers' mother, reminds Brennius that the chief salutary effect of the system of primogeniture in his case was that it forced him to amass power and wealth through his own enterprising spirit. Arthur's international legions gathered around him presumably for the same reason. The combination of the king's generosity and power yields rich dividends for the young men who attach themselves to Arthur's court.

This may explain why defensive preparations among the yet unconquered nations provoke Arthur to action. His continental campaigns are made to appear as preemptive attacks intended to keep open the resources that guarantee his following. The conquest of Norway is undertaken in order to install Arthur's brother-in-law Loth on the Norwegian throne. Loth's claim is based on his being left the kingdom by his uncle Sichel, the recently deceased king of Norway, although the people of the country raise their own ruler, Riculf, to the throne. Arthur's savage reduction of Norway and Denmark is followed immediately by his attack upon Frollo, "Tribune" of the province of Gaul. As has been noted above, however, the youth of Gaul are by this time in the pay of Arthur, and Frollo's army quickly collapses and takes refuge in Paris where, besieged by Arthur's superior forces, they begin to starve to death.

Rather than see his people gradually die of hunger, Frollo challenges Arthur to single combat on an island outside Paris. In the ensuing bitter fight, Arthur finally gains the victory by delivering a lethal blow with his sword: Arthur "raised Caliburn in the air with all his strength and brought it down through Frollo's helmet and so on to his head, which he cut into two halves" (Thorpe, 225). The city immediately surrenders, and Arthur is free to finish his campaign in Gaul by dividing his army with his cousin (or nephew?) Hoel of Brittany. The conquest of Aquitaine, Gascony, and all of Gaul is achieved within the next nine years. Arthur then celebrates with an assembly in Paris, where he divides up the regions of Gaul among his closest lieutenants: Neustria (Normandy) to Bedevere, his Cup-bearer, Anjou to Kay, his Seneschal, and "a number of other provinces to the noblemen who had served him" (Thorpe, 225). He then returns to Britain.

Geoffrey attempts to cast the conflict between Arthur and Frollo in epic terms. The meeting in single combat on an island as a means to decide the outcome of a dispute recalls numerous places in classical literature and the Bible in which conflicts were decided by champions chosen from either side (Tatlock, 1974, 345–46). It might also have had contemporary resonances. William of Malmesbury states that William the Conqueror proposed that he and Harold decide the right to the crown of England by single combat (Giles, 276). Henry of Huntingdon reports that Edmund Ironsides and Cnute met on the (island) of Olney in Gloucestershire in single combat to decide their contest for control of England (Arnold, 1879, 185). Henry recounts that when Edmund's blows had overcome Cnute, Cnute cried out that they should divide the kingdom between them. Unlike Arthur, Edmund agreed to the division, and the two leaders exchanged the kiss of peace. The kingdom of Wessex went to Edmund, Mercia to Cnute.[11]

Again, the mention of Arthur sending Hoel off to attack Guitard and the Poitevins in Aquitania recalls the conquest of Brutus and Corineus over Goffar and the subsequent devastation of Aquitaine, while the blow Frollo received from Caliburn recalls the stroke delivered by Corineus against the Poitevin leader, Suhard: Corineus "struck Suhard on the crest of his helmet and at the spot where he made contact slit him in two halves from top to bottom" (Thorpe, 68). The echoes of the earlier Trojan battles in Gaul at this point in the *HRB* serve to remind us that

Brutus and Corineus were traveling westward as exiles under Diana's instructions in search of a promised land. While Diana's prophecy that Britain would subject the whole world never comes to pass, Arthur does have four "imperial" precursors, Brennius/Belinus, Constantine, and Maximianus. Hoel observes that the Sybilline Books predict that three Britons will seize the Roman Empire (Thorpe, 234). Arthur's conquests echo those of his Trojan ancestors in order to remind us of the differences. His imperial campaigns take him away from the center (Britain) toward the periphery (Gaul). He wages war in order to gain tribute from conquered nations and to distribute booty, land, and offices to his young warriors in order to keep them in his service. In this he resembles both Brennius and Belinus, but also the Romans, the archimperialists of the *HRB* whose rapacity Arthur comes increasingly to imitate. The campaigns against Scandinavia and Gaul, then, seem to set the stage for decline from the Golden Age of Arthur. While setting out to meet the Roman challenge, which he has deliberately provoked by his invasion and division of Gaul, Arthur sets the stage for his own betrayal by Mordred. With this perspective in mind, it is difficult to see Arthur's adventures on the continent as Stephen Knight does as Geoffrey's propagandizing for Norman conquests in England and elsewhere.

Arthur's Plenary Court at Pentecost

The description of Arthur's plenary court held at Pentecost following his return to Britain is one of Geoffrey's most colorful passages in the *HRB*. The choice of Caerleon-on-Usk as the site of this display of culture and sophistication was Geoffrey's own. Geoffrey held the town of Caerleon-on-Usk in high esteem, and bestowed a number of honors upon it throughout the *HRB*. From Nennius (chapter 56) he probably learned that one of Arthur's 12 battles was fought in the City of the Legions (Nennius, ed. J. Morris, 76; *in urbe Legionis*). In lieu of a battle, however, Geoffrey placed Arthur's most splendid and important crown-wearing assembly in this city.[12] According to the *HRB*, Caerleon-on-Usk was founded by Belinus, became the seat of a Roman archflamen, and subsequently of an archbishopric, an office occupied in Arthur's day by the saintly Dubricius. The ruins of the town's Roman baths, walls, temples and amphitheater, today magnificently restored, were still much in evidence during the twelfth century, and attracted the admiration of Gerald of Wales when he traveled through the town in 1188 (Gerald of Wales, trans. Thorpe, 114–115). Geoffrey states that the town was taken over by the Romans as their winter quarters, and thereupon the name changed from Caerusk ("Citadel on the Usk") to Caerleon ("The Citadel of the Legions"). As demonstrated in chapter 2, Geoffrey was eager to dignify the region of his birth with a glorious past. He relocated the scene of Vortigern's death from his fortress on the Teifi River to Mount Doartius (Cloartius) near Monmouth. In the Pentecost episode, Geoffrey provides additional evidence of Caerleon's greatness by claiming that the city housed a college of 200 men learned in astronomy who foretold to Arthur "any prodigies due at that time" (Thorpe, 227). He accurately describes Caerleon's lovely location on the banks of the Usk, surrounded by woods and meadows and proclaims its buildings and palaces with their gold-painted gables "a match for Rome." Moreover, the place was sanctified by the blood of two early martyrs, Julius and Aaron, in whose honor two churches were established, the former for "most lovely virgins dedicated to God," the latter for a monastery of canons (Winterbottom, 19; Bede, trans. Sherley-Price, 1, 7; Tatlock, 1974, 235). If Geoffrey knew of Welsh traditions, as represented by *Culhwch and Olwen,* situating Arthur's court at Celli Wic in Cornwall (Bromwich, 1978, 3; Padel, in Bromwich, 1991, 234–38), he chose to ignore them in favor of a location closer to his own home in Monmouth. The impressive Roman remains of Caerleon were, in any case, far more in keeping with Geoffrey's view of Arthur's court as a sophisticated international center, than was the hill-fortress of Celli Wic (modern Castle Killibury) in Cornwall (Ditmas, 1973, 520).

The pageantry of the crown-wearing ceremony in Caerleon with its august assembly of international guests and its stately procession is designed perhaps more than any other passage in the *HRB* to Normanize the British past. This public representation of the power, splendor, and solidarity of the British during the Arthurian period would be familiar to the aristocratic audience of the *HRB*. It clearly has little to do with the reality of Dark Age Britain or with the image of Arthur's court as depicted in the Welsh *Culhwch and Olwen.* Following a practice familiar to the Norman kings of England, Arthur's assembly takes place at the time of one of the three yearly councils customarily held in Anglo-Norman England, the other two being Easter and Candlemas (2 February). Henry I, for example, discussed with his barons the betrothal of his seven-year-old daughter to the future Emperor Henry V at his Whitsuntide (Pentecost) court in 1108.[13] Conversely, the historic resonances of Pentecost (the Feast of the Descent of the Holy Spirit upon the Apostles), provided Geoffrey yet another opportunity to exploit the associations of sacred events for secular purposes. On Pentecost, 12 tongues of fire descended on the apostles as they were gathered in the upper room (Acts 2:1–4). Similarly, into the gilded court of Caerleon on Pentecost in the *HRB,* march 12 Roman legates, "men of mature years and respectable appearance" (Thorpe, 230). They have not come to bestow gifts of the Holy Spirit, but rather to demand tribute. Pentecost's celebration of human speech, as symbolized by the apostles' charism of tongues, is represented in the Pentecost episode in the *HRB* by the "Ciceronian eloquence" of Arthur's reply to Lucius's demand for tribute (Thorpe, 233).

Like the Norman kings, Arthur issues a formal writ of summons to his court, which is held for the same general purpose in order to "renew pacts of peace with his chieftains" (Thorpe, 226). Building solidarity and forestalling the threat of revolt were among the chief aims of the councils of the Norman monarchs of England. At the 1131 council in Northampton, for example, Henry had all the barons of the realm who had not already sworn fealty to Matilda do so at this time (William of Malmesbury, trans. Giles, 487). The projection of the king's might and the aura of his kingship was further underscored by the close and harmonious alliance of the church and the crown. Hence, Bishop Dubricius, chief among the three metropolitan prelates present at Arthur's crowning, presides over the ceremony, and celebrates the mass. Stately processions, the chanting of "exquisite harmonies" by the companies of clerics, and the presence of the four kings from Albany, Cornwall, Demetia (South Wales), and Venedotia (North Wales), who proceed the king and bear four golden swords, further symbolize the support given by the ecclesiastical and secular magnates to their king. The division of male and female (an ancient Trojan practice, Geoffrey confidently assures us) is strictly observed; the Queen is led with her four consorts to her own crowning in the church of Saint Julius dedicated to the ideal of holy virginity.

The pageantry of the first part of the Pentecost ceremony is designed to impress the eye and the mind with the degree of solidarity enjoyed by the British under King Arthur. This was a utopian fantasy, of course, which bore little resemblance to the reality of Geoffrey's day. As in the picture of the fraternal harmony that came to exist between Belinus and Brennius, the Caerleon idyll projects an image of social unanimity, benevolent monarchical hegemony, conciliar consensus politics, a static social hierarchy, and solidarity between secular and ecclesiastical powers, all of this founded on the king's distribution of lands and titles to the deserving members of his court. For this brief moment in the pastoral setting of Caerleon, all rivalries, tensions, and personal ambitions, are dissolved in a golden moment of peace and concord. Geoffrey claims that he must resist the urge to describe the event at too great length, but he must content himself with the observation that Britain at this time had attained "such a level of dignity, that it excelled other kingdoms in abundance of wealth, the richness of its ornamentation, and the urbanity of its inhabitants."[14]

Pageantry is followed by games. Like pageantry, games are also a public proclamation of the court's self-image, this time in the fields outside the city rather than inside the city itself. In order to show the court of Arthur to have been a pacesetter in fashionable behavior, Geoffrey composed a remarkable scene of imitation battle (Wright, 1984, 112; *simulacrum prelii*). As the women watch the jousting matches from atop the walls of Caerleon, "they kindle [in the men] the raging flames of love as though it were a game."[15] Women wore the colors of their favorites in the contests and "scorned to accept the love of any man unless he had been tested three times in battle. Thus, the women became chaste and more virtuous (*caste et meliores*) and the knights more worthy (*probiores*) for love of them" (my translation; cf. Thorpe, 229). This passage may have been partly inspired by the story of the tasks that Culhwch had to accomplish in order to gain the hand of Olwen, but it certainly owes much also to the growing vogue for the doctrine of *fin amor*, which was taking shape particularly in the South of France, but which had not quite yet become the rage in England in Geoffrey's day. The passage demonstrates Geoffrey's awareness of the latest literary trends and is designed to show the court of Arthur as the pinnacle of sophisticated behavior. The passage is especially remarkable because Geoffrey does not elsewhere in the *HRB* display much interest in such courtly amusements. The association of eroticism and violence in the scene is paralleled in a number of passages elsewhere in the *HRB,* particularly in the passion of Uther for Ygerna, and later in the attempted rape of Hoel's niece by the giant of Mont-Saint-Michel. Geoffrey is quick to point out, however, that in Caerleon, the game of "imitation [of] battle" promulgates womanly chastity and masculine worthiness.

The first part of this scene ends with Arthur's distribution of a "personal grant of cities, castles, archbishoprics, bishoprics, and other landed possessions" to those who had done him service, demonstrating the ideal of monarchical hegemony with the king possessing the power to distribute lay and ecclesiastical benefices without opposition or outbursts of rivalry.

Arthur appoints men to various ecclesiastical offices, particularly his uncle David to the archbishopric of Caerleon upon Dubricius's decision to take up the hermetical life, and, after consulting Hoel of Brittany, Tebaus of Llandaff as successor to Samson as archbishop at Dol.

The scene of the Pentecost crownings in the *HRB* in many respects contrasts sharply with the reality of life and politics in the days of Henry I. Stephen Knight has stressed (rather too single-mindedly) how this and other passages in the *HRB* are "mystifications" and "euphemizations" of the ruthless exercise of power by the Norman kings. A reading of the *Brut y Tywysogyon* for the years 1100–35, would also dispel any doubt that in the minds of contemporary annalists, the reign of Henry I in Wales, where Caerleon is located, was a series of revolts, burnings, assaults, cattle rustlings, hangings, dismemberments, abductions, fratricides, broken alliances, ethnic rivalries, gougings, and acts of mutilation and castration. But Geoffrey was no slavish propagandist. The Pentecost scene only lulls the senses momentarily. Taken within its larger dramatic context, it is far from comforting. Geoffrey is about to shatter this delicate image by showing the results of immoderate pride and reckless adventurism at the court of King Arthur. What better way to drive his lesson home to members of his immediate audience than by weaving their own image into the tapestry? The greatness of Arthur intensifies his fall, while his dominating personality, once removed from the scene, will render Britain weak and vulnerable.

The utopian fantasy of Caerleon is interrupted by the sudden entry of 12 envoys of Lucius, Procurator of the Roman Republic in Gaul. They bear Lucius's pompous and boorish letter commanding Arthur to appear in Rome by mid-August to answer for his "criminal behavior" in withholding the annual British tribute to Rome and for seizing Gaul and the Islands of the Ocean. The leading men of the court withdraw with the king to a large tower to discuss their response to the Roman legates. During Arthur's consultation with his chieftains, Cador expresses the view that this summons is God's plan to call them away from such courtly follies as "burning up their strength with women" (*mulierum inflammationes*), and to direct them back to their real work, warfare (Thorpe, 232).

Arthur's reflections carry Cador's reasoning a step further. He argues that Caesar's conquest of Britain was only made possible by the internal disunity of the Britons of the day, and he goes on to enunciate the high-minded principle that "nothing that is acquired by force and violence can ever be held legally by anyone" (Thorpe, 232). Ironically, however, he urges that the disagreement between the Britons and the Romans, itself be decided by force, "let him who comes out on top carry off what he has made up his mind to take" (Thorpe, 233). He concludes that because Belinus and Brennius sacked Rome, and Constantine and Maximianus were elevated to the throne of Roman emperor, history favors the British. Rome, he asserts, owes tribute to Britain. This vigorous statement of the principle that might makes right is roundly praised by Hoel, who adds that the Sybilline *Books of Prophecies* foretell that "for a third time someone born of British blood shall seize the Empire of Rome" (Thorpe, 234). In Hoel's view, the hand of God holds out to Arthur a prize "ripe for the conquering." Anguselus adds that he thirsts for the blood of the Romans "as if I had been prevented from drinking for three whole days." When all the other allies had spoken and pledged their support for retaliation against the Romans, Arthur counted his army at 183,300 men, excluding foot soldiers (Thorpe, 235).

When these pledges were received, the various allies were sent away to muster their troops to meet the Romans in August. Upon receiving the British challenge, the Roman legates returned home. Lucius then assembled an exotic international force led by men whose names would have had particularly strong emotional force for an audience imbued with a zeal for crusading and whose literary tastes held anti-Muslim literature, such as the *Song of Roland,* in high regard: Mustensar, king of the Africans; Ali Fatima, king of Spain; Pandrasus, king of Egypt, and so on. In August, when news of their approach reaches Arthur, he sets out from Southampton to meet them, leaving the defense of Britain to his nephew Mordred and his queen Guinevere.

The response of the British to the Roman challenge reveals their enterprising and restless spirit, their taste for adventure, and their love of liberty. At the same time, however, their appetite for risky ventures and their reliance on force as the decisive factor in determining right are the very principles that will unravel the fabric of Arthur's empire. Under such an ideology, what is to prevent a Mordred from seizing a prize "ripe for the conquering"? Where a decisive blow struck against the king will leave the throne open to the strongest, who would hesitate? And where war and sexuality are closely allied, the usurper (such as Uther, Arthur's father) enters the bedchamber as well as the field of battle. Loyalties in the Arthurian milieu are often founded on the distribution of spoils, and personal glory is measured by the extent of one's dominions. Arthur's departure from Britain with 183,300 troops is Mordred's golden opportunity for self-realization.

Victory over the Romans in Gaul

As a transition from the ceremony at Caerleon to the confrontation between the armies of Arthur and Lucius, Geoffrey constructed two prefatory scenes. In the first of these, Arthur has a dream on board ship as his fleet approaches the coast of Gaul. He envisions a bear flying through the air and causing the surrounding lands to quake at its roar. Suddenly, out of the west approaches a terrifying dragon whose eyes light up the countryside. In the battle between the two animals, the dragon bests the bear and hurls its scorched body to the ground. Arthur's companions cheerfully interpret his dream to signify that the king, symbolized by the dragon, is about to defeat some formidable giant, represented by the bear. Arthur, however, feels that the dream has some other significance having to do with his approaching confrontation with the Emperor (Thorpe, 237).

The dream is part of Geoffrey's dramatic strategy for this final phase of Arthur's career, which will see the British ruler raised to the status of a world conqueror. It slows the pace of the narrative and, as a familiar device in ancient and medieval epic tradition, it adds dignity to the story and contributes a heightened sense of anticipation to the approaching conflict. Geoffrey signals its symbolic complexity by having the king propose an interpretation at variance with the one given by his lieutenants.

Both interpretations have merit. As the son of Utherpendragon arriving in France from Britain, Arthur might logically be represented by a dragon from the west. In the symbolic battle between the two dragons on Mount Snowdon, Merlin interprets the Red Dragon to stand for the British folk. But Arthur was also represented by the beam of light projecting from the fiery dragon that appeared in the sky shortly before the death of King Aurelius (Thorpe, 200–1). He was also known in the *PM* as the Boar of Cornwall, presumably because of his conception at the Castle of Tintagel. Hence the king's suspicion that his dream may be interpreted from more than one perspective raises the possibility of additional levels of meaning. Because the Welsh *arth* means "bear," Arthur himself might plausibly be seen as the bear who will be defeated by a *draig* (Welsh for both "dragon" and "leader") from the west, namely Mordred, the leader left behind to defend Britain in the king's absence. Geoffrey leaves open the possibility, in other words, that the dream foreshadows at the outset of Arthur's Roman campaign, the tragic end of his career at the Battle of Camblan.

The second prefatory scene is Arthur's slaying the giant from Spain who has taken to terrorizing the coast of Brittany from his dwelling atop Mont-Saint-Michel. This episode itself appears as an anticipation of Arthur's defeat of the Romans, the other rapacious interlopers in Gaul. The battle against the giant of Mont-Saint-Michel is an interlude in the larger framework of the *HRB,* taking place while Arthur is awaiting the arrival of the remainder of his army. The whole scene has its own carefully constructed plot, with introductory exploratory adventures by Kay and Bedevere, who meet the bereaved nurse of Helena, who forewarns them of the giant's nightly visitations. Hearing the report of the giant's foul murder of Helen, the niece of King Hoel of Brittany, Arthur himself proceeds to confront the enemy and slay him in single combat. The episode is rich in visual details such as the fires burning high up on the mountains as Arthur's men approach at night in their boats, the view that Arthur has of the giant illuminated by the light of his fire, his mouth blood-smeared with the gore of raw pig flesh, the scene of Arthur's men that night back at camp staring in awe at the giant's severed head that lies on the earth before them. Whether Geoffrey himself invented this story or elaborated a preexisting local legend is impossible to determine, but the carefully constructed structure of the Mont-Saint-Michel episode has all the marks of Geoffrey's genius for contriving vivid and dramatically rich narratives.

The Mont-Saint-Michel interlude also looks back within the *HRB* itself to the giant-slaying activities of Brutus's companion Corineus and suggests that Arthur epitomizes the glory of his Trojan ancestors. It also has unmistakable signs of the grotesque exuberance of Celtic giant-slaying stories, such as Goreu's slaying of Ysbadaddan Chief Giant, and the plucking of Dillus Farfawg's beard by Kay and Bedevere, both of these in *Culhwch and Olwen.* Geoffrey's knowledge of some such tales involving the taking of an adversary's beard is evidenced in Arthur's recollection of his earlier battle against Retho, the giant of Mount Aravia (= Mount Snowdon), to which he compares his encounter with the unnamed giant of Mont-Saint-Michel. This allusion is especially noteworthy because Geoffrey seems at such pains elsewhere in the *HRB* to ignore the Welsh version of Arthur as a typical Celtic chieftain, in favor of his own view of the king as a powerful European monarch.

There are also clear reminiscences, even exact verbal echoes, of Virgil's *Aeneid,* which associate Arthur's defeat of the giant of Mont-Saint-Michel with Ulysses's mutilation of the Cyclops (Faral, 2:286–87). Knowledge of this story would have come to Geoffrey through the third book of the *Aeneid* (lines 588–654), in which Archaemenides, one of Ulysses's men, tells of his experiences when left behind by his companions in the cave of the Cyclops. The Mont-Saint-Michel interlude in the *HRB* thus represents an amalgamation of native and classical lore concerning a hero's encounter with giants[16] and elevates the British Arthur to the status of a rival to the great heroes of antiquity. Knight's reading of this scene as an exorcising of Henry I's "castration anxiety" over the "phallic aggression" of his older brothers seems far-fetched, to say the least.[17]

Curiosity about Mont-Saint-Michel in Geoffrey's day was probably aroused by the plans of Abbot Bernard to construct a new church for this popular place of pilgrimage.[18] Mont-Saint-Michel and the nearby island of Tumbellana (Tumbelana, Tumbelania, Tumbalenia, and so on) were known locally as "the two rocks" (*duae tumbae*), but the names must have suggested to Geoffrey that the smaller of them, Tumbellana, was a "tomb" commemorating a woman named Elena. This offered to Geoffrey an opportunity to engage in one of his favorite pastimes of inventing a colorful tale to account for a place name. He was, after all, attracted to romantic landscapes, such as Stonehenge, Tintagel, Loch Lomond, and Caerleon, for each of which he conjured up memorable stories. Hence, following the defeat of the giant of Mont-Saint-Michel, the *HRB* states that Hoel had a chapel built over her grave on the mountain where she was slain: "The peak took its name from the girl's burial-place and to this very day it is called Helena's Tomb" (Thorpe, 241; *Tumba Helene*). The pathetic story of Helen's fate at the hands of the giant of Mont-Saint-Michel appears to have been Geoffrey's own eponymous creation, but in the period after the publication of the *HRB*, it became a standard feature of the legendary history of the place.[19] With his army now fully assembled, Arthur set forth to encounter the Roman army at Autun.

Geoffrey dedicated about one-third of his entire account of Arthur's career to the battle in Gaul between the British and the Romans (Thorpe, 241–57). Although critics such as Tatlock and Faral have faulted this whole episode for its hazy sense of geography and its amateurish grasp of military tactics, Geoffrey clearly took great relish in it (Tatlock, 1974, 102; Faral, 2:289–95). His overall purpose of elevating the British of the Arthurian Age to the status of a great imperial power on a par with the Romans has never been in doubt.

The dramatic pace of the episode builds slowly from initial challenges exchanged between the two forces, and a set of minor skirmishes, retreats, and reformations, to the final encounter of the two great armies in the valley of Siesia, the actual conflict being preceded by high-flown speeches by Arthur and Lucius to their respective troops. Arthur's entry into the battle at a decisive moment tips the balance against the Roman forces, who flee before the British. The episode ends with a description of the aftermath of the battle, including the burial of the dead.

In addition to pacing the dramatic action carefully, Geoffrey did his best to embellish the encounter with all the literary conventions of the classical and medieval epics (*Aeneid, Pharsalia, Waltharius,* and so on) and the various chansons de gestes of the period. Warriors boast before their adversaries and curse the souls of their slain foes to hell, the fallen "drum the earth with their heels" and "vomit forth their lives with their life-blood," and so on; some of these passages contain very close verbal echoes of the *Aeneid,* as we might expect.[20] Geoffrey's Roman army comprises characters with plausible sounding names, such as the Senator Petreius Cocta, Hyderus, son of Nu, Gaius Quintillianus (Lucius's nephew), and Evander, king of Syria. The encouraging prebattle exhortations delivered by Arthur and Lucius also have an authentic ring to them and read like a page out of Livy, Caesar, or Suetonius. Even the nuances of the addresses by Arthur and Lucius are dramatically fitting. Arthur praises his men for maintaining their manly valor in spite of enjoying a life of ease for the past five years; he appeals to their love of liberty and their racial pride. Most significantly, perhaps, he holds before them the promise of vast plunder to be had after they have routed the enemy and sacked the city of Rome: "yours shall be its gold, silver, palaces, towers, castles, cities and all the other riches of the vanquished" (Thorpe, 249). Lucius, on the other hand, prepares his troops for battle by recalling the grand deeds of their ancestors as models for their progeny; he traces the growth of the Republic to the valor of the early Romans and ends by promising his men that if they stand firm they will win. All of this is nicely suited to the character and strategic position of the two forces, the British army being motivated by mercenary considerations, the Romans by pride of ancestry. That Geoffrey could imitate so well the tone and verbal texture of the classical battle speech is a tribute to his Latin learning.

Arthur enters the fray at a moment of reversal for his men, flinging himself on the Romans and cutting down horse or rider with a single blow with his "wonderful sword Caliburn." His intervention is decisive. Emboldened by the king's display of fury, the British overcome the Romans. Lucius and many thousands of his troops are killed, the rest flee before the British onslaught.

The British victory over the Romans produces the rather uncharacteristic remark from Geoffrey that this was all ordained by "divine might" (*divina potentia*). This passage is missing from the Variant Version of the *HRB* as are other authorial reflections on the narrative (Wright, 1988, 171). While the theme of the rise and fall of various people and their leaders has been clearly and repeatedly articulated by this point in Geoffrey's history, the invocation of divine power as the agency for change is at rather sharp odds with Geoffrey's efforts elsewhere in the *HRB* to focus on human agency in the history and to avoid appeals to divine causality. Perhaps Robert Hanning is right when he states that Geoffrey's principal concern in this passage is with the historic pattern of the rise and fall of nations on the wheel of fortune.[21]

As usual in the Arthurian section of the *HRB,* Geoffrey seems at pains to Normanize his Britons. Thus, he tells us that after the battle at Siesia, the body of Bedevere was born by the Neustrians (the ancient name for the inhabitants of Normandy) to Bayeux, a city which his grandfather, Bedevere I, had founded; Bedevere was buried there "in a cemetery in the southern quarter of the city" (Thorpe, 257). This may refer to the monastery of Saint Vigor, whose nearby cemetery in the twelfth century still contained tombs and cinerary urns dating back to Roman times, or perhaps to the cathedral of Bayeux, whose bishop in Geoffrey's day was Richard, illegitimate son of Robert of Gloucester, one of Geoffrey's patrons, and a dedicatee of the *HRB* (Tatlock, 1974, 89–90).[22] Kay the Seneschal is buried in Chinon, a city in Anjou that he founded. These two members of Arthur's entourage are drawn out of Welsh Arthurian tradition and have been promoted by Geoffrey to the status of founders of venerable Norman and Angevin cities. Throughout the encounter with the Romans also, the Breton forces under Hoel and the Cornishmen under Cador perform particularly well. Geoffrey even manages to work into his account of the fate of a man from the Monmouth area, Prince Hyrelglas of Periron, who dies in an early skirmish against the Romans.

Finally, there is the question of why Geoffrey chose to depict Arthur at the pinnacle of his career outside of Britain fighting the Romans in Burgundy. If Ashe is correct in believing that Geoffrey was merely setting down the military exploits of the historic British King Riothamus in sixth-century Gaul, the problem of his locating the battle would be resolved (Ashe, 1981, 301–23). Riothamus is last heard of in the historic record retreating from the Goths in the direction of Burgundy. But the identification of Riothamus with Arthur raises a host of other problems concerning the supposed floruits of the two "kings," Arthur in the fifth century and Riothamus in the sixth century, their different names (Arthur/Riothamus), the identity of their adversaries (Riothamus fought for, Arthur against, the Romans), and the question of how Geoffrey would have learned of the career of Riothamus, which is preserved only in fragmentary allusions in Jordanes, Gregory of Tours, and Sidonius Apollinaris.

Taking up a suggestion made by Faral, Keller proposed that Geoffrey located the final encounter between the Romans and the British in Siesia (which Keller identified with the Val-Suzon near Autun in Burgundy[23] because it was near, and sounds similar to Alesia, the site of Caesar's crushing defeat of the Gauls under Vercingetorix (Faral, 2:291; Keller, 693–98). Geoffrey might have learned of Siesia from pilgrims traveling from England to Rome via the popular Paris-Dijon-Lyon route, who may have visited the church dedicated to Saint Reine in Alise-Seint-Reine (= Alesia). Information on the siege of Alesia may have been conveyed to travelers by local monks eager to extol the town's illustrious past. The battle at Siesia would, therefore, be yet another example of Geoffrey's revisionism: British forces and their allies under Arthur vanquish the Romans on the very location where the Gaulish army under Vercingetorix succumbed to the Romans centuries earlier.

The Battle of Camblan

Arthur passes the winter following his defeat of the Romans in the same region and has time also to subdue the Allobroges. When summer comes, he sets off intending to capture Rome, but as he is passing through the mountains, word reaches him that his nephew Mordred has placed the crown of Britain on his head, and Guinevere "having broken her earlier marriage vows had been joined to him in forbidden sexual love" (my translation; cf. Thorpe, 257). Addressing himself to a "noble duke" (*consul auguste*), Geoffrey observes that he will not remain silent on this subject for he "found it in the aforementioned [book] in the British language and heard it from Walter of Oxford, a man most learned in various histories" (Wright, 1984, 129; *ut in prefato Britannico sermone inuenit et a Gwaltero Oxenefordensi in multis historiis peritissimo uiro audiuit*). Geoffrey then goes on to say that the infamous traitor Mordred had allied himself with the Saxon leader Chelric, who, at Mordred's command, had brought more than 800 ships of Saxon pagans. In exchange for their support, Mordred had promised the Saxons the land between the Humber and Scotland, as well as "all that Hengist and Horsa had

held in Kent in Vortigern's day" (Thorpe, 258). He also allied himself
with Britain's archenemies, the Scots, Picts, and Irish.

Arthur puts ashore at Richborough, where Caesar landed centuries
before on his third invasion of Britain, and drives Mordred's forces inland
after bitter fighting in which two of Arthur's trusted lieutenants,
Auguselus, king of Albany, and Gawain, Arthur's nephew, are slain.
Mordred first takes refuge in Winchester, but is soon driven from there
to Cornwall, which he reaches by ship. Learning of Mordred's defeat,
Guinevere flees from York to Caerleon where she takes vows among the
nuns in the Church of Julius the Martyr, "promising to lead a chaste life"
(Thorpe, 259). This is the last we hear of Queen Guinevere in the *HRB*.
Meanwhile, Arthur pursues Mordred to the River Camblan in Cornwall
where their armies meet in bloody conflict. In an attack led by Arthur,
Mordred is killed; soon after the Saxon Chelric and many Irish, Scots,
and Picts are also slain. Arthur himself is mortally wounded and is "carried off to the Isle of Avalon, so that his wounds might be attended to"
(Thorpe, 261). Before departing, he hands the crown over to his cousin
Constantine, son of Cador, duke of Cornwall. All of this occurred according to the *HRB* in the year 542 after the Lord's Incarnation.

While the Battle of Camblan (or Camlann) was not listed by Nennius
among Arthur's 12 battles, the event was not entirely Geoffrey's own
creation. His expressed reluctance to describe Mordred's betrayal and
forbidden sexual love with Guinevere must give way, he tells us, to the
historic record: both the "British book" and his learned friend Walter
attested to the unhappy truth. One senses in these remarks a genuine
sense of regret on Geoffrey's part that his role as historian compels him
to enter upon a subject he would rather avoid. This is not to deny, of
course, that the rhetorical effect of an author's expression of scruple over
his material is often to stimulate the reader's desire to know, but this
effect may simply be the by-product of the author's real sentiments. In
any case, Geoffrey is usually thought to have known the *Annales
Cambriae*, which mention the "gueith Camlann" under the year 537 and
claim that Arthur and Medraut both fell (*corruerunt*) in that encounter
(Nennius, ed. J. Morris, 85). The *Annales*'s use of the term *gueith,* which
can mean "work" or "battle" in Welsh, would appear to indicate a Welsh
source for the Camblan entry in the text, and indeed, the Battle of
Camblan is usually taken as a genuine historic event. Its character and
location, however, are far from clear. The *Annales Cambriae,* for example,
do not specify that Camblan was a river, nor do they overtly state that
Arthur and Medraut were opponents in the conflict. Locating the proba-

ble site of the battle, has also been problematic; one of the most often championed locations is Camboglanna, present-day Birdoswald, a fort situated on Hadrian's Wall in the border region of Scotland (Jones, 1964, 6; Bromwich, 1975–76, 173).[24] The territory of northern Britain is frequently proposed as the home of the historic Arthur's activities. If Geoffrey knew anything about this, he deliberately transferred the location of the battle to the River Camblan (presumably the Camel River) in Cornwall, a region he may have once visited (Ditmas, 1973, 512–13, 521–22). In doing so, he ignored the improbability of the geography of this part of Cornwall, where there is no suitable port of disembarkation to receive a fleet carrying a large army such as the *HRB* claims accompanied Mordred. On the other hand, Geoffrey may simply have been following local Cornish tradition that had appropriated to its own region the site of Arthur's last battle. Dramatic considerations, as usual, may also have been paramount in Geoffrey's mind. In situating Arthur's fatal battle against Mordred in Cornwall, Geoffrey was bringing his hero, the Boar of Cornwall, back to the land of his conception. The king's beginning (at the Castle of Tintagel) and end are also parallel in that they are both shrouded in magic associated with medicine, and with mysterious, if not mythical, persons: Merlin, whose transformative medicines were indispensable to Arthur's being conceived, and the unnamed residents of the Isle of Avalon, who will cure the king's wounds.

Mordred may also be an amalgamation of tradition and Geoffrey's own imagination. If the tradition behind the *Annales Cambriae*'s entry on the Battle of Camblan was that Arthur and Mordred fought against one another, it would have played nicely into Geoffrey's concept of British history. Mordred's betrayal of Arthur is abruptly announced in the *HRB* without explanation of his motives. On the contrary, in order to account for Mordred's actions, the reader is forced to reflect on the nature of betrayal as revealed elsewhere in Geoffrey's history. What he discovers is that Mordred stands at the head of a long line of traitors in the *HRB* stretching back to Assaracus, the young man of mixed Trojan and Greek blood who goes over to Brutus's side out of fear of the cruelty of his Greek half-brother (Thorpe, 56). The British prince Androgeus, who joins Caesar's army just before its third invasion of his homeland, provides decisive help that allows the Romans to win the Battle of Durobernia and force Cassivelaunus to render tribute to Rome (Thorpe, 116–19). Assaracus's betrayal is reiterated in Brennius's revolt against his brother Belinus, king of Britain, although this dispute ends happily (Thorpe, 90–99). The conjoining of political and sexual betrayal appears in Locrinus's passion for Estrildis, daughter of the king of Germany, which leads to Locrinus's death in battle against his own wife Gwendolen (Thorpe, 75–77). Geoffrey rightly associates Mordred with Vortigern (Thorpe, 258). Both turned to the Saxons, Picts, Scots, and Irish, traditional enemies of their people, to mount their revolt. Perhaps most important, however, is the similarity of Vortigern's passion for the Saxon princess Renwein to Mordred's sexual liaison with Guinevere. In both of these cases, as in the depiction of Uther's passion for Ygerna, the wife of one of his lieutenants, Geoffrey describes sexual passion in blunt and almost clinical language, leaving no doubt about its destructive power and its capacity to subvert established political order. Once Guinevere knows that Mordred's bid for the throne has been checked, she wastes no time in abandoning him to his fate and seeking refuge and a reformed life among the nuns of the church of Julius the Martyr in Caerleon. The quest for personal glory and wealth in risky adventurism is what brought Arthur to challenge the Romans in Gaul and to dare to march on Rome itself. Seen within its larger context, Mordred's revolt is thus part of a long and unhappy pattern in the *HRB* of individuals pursuing their own personal gratifications at the expense of communal welfare. The reiteration of the theme of betrayal throughout the *HRB* seems to be part of Geoffrey's larger strategy of exposing the tragic consequences of the human proclivity toward personal aggrandizement, sexual gratification, and grandiose ambition. Unfortunately, Mordred's ambitions will precipitate a state of unprecedented military weakness among the Britons and will cause the final loss of their cherished liberties.

What did Geoffrey understand about the *insula Avallonis* in the *HRB*? Did he take the second element to be the name of a person, "the isle of Avallo," as Faral thought (Faral, 2:299–301)? He lists an Aballac as one of the 20 daughters of King Ebraucus, apparently deriving the name from the Welsh genealogies, where Aballac appears as the son of the mythical Beli Mawr, ancestor of various north Welsh dynasties (Thorpe, 79; Bromwich, 1978, 266). Did his knowledge of Welsh inform him that *afal* meant *apple,* and hence that the Isle of Avalon was the "isle of apples"? He certainly made this connection by the time of the *VM* where he calls the place *insula pommorum* ("island of apples") rather than *insula Avallonis.* How much did he know about the association of apples with the Celtic otherworld? The *HRB* is conspicuously silent on all of this. Geoffrey's spelling of Avalon with two ll's may indicate that he was thinking of Avallon, a town in Burgundy, whose name originates in

Gaulish Aballone or Avallone, "place of apples" (Bromwich, 1978, 267). Ashe has recently suggested that Avallon may have been on Geoffrey's mind because it is situated in the vicinity of France where we last hear of Riothamus (Ashe, 1981, 315–16).[25]

Geoffrey assumes a cautious attitude in the HRB toward the concept of Arthur as the "undying hero." As we have already seen, this idea was current in Cornwall and Brittany long before Geoffrey composed the HRB, and it was referred to explicitly by William of Malmesbury a decade before Geoffrey completed his history. Even apart from Arthur, the idea of the "undying hero" must have been familiar enough. Geoffrey probably knew from Suetonius that long after Nero's death, some thought that the emperor still lived and would one day return; starting around the year 1000 the notion circulated that Charlemagne was yet alive. Clearly, Geoffrey was aware that Cadwallader and Cynan were cherished in Welsh prophetic poetry as revenant redeemers, for he casts them, rather than Arthur, in this role in the PM (see chapter 3). The "undying hero" motive may have become associated with Arthur in Wales in connection with the assertion in the "Stanzas of the Graves" that the grave of Arthur was a "wonder" or "among the difficult things to find in the world" (Jones, 1964, 18). The idea, as applied to Arthur, probably reached Geoffrey from Cornwall and Brittany. It is tempting to look ahead to the VM (see chapter 5) in order to supplement Geoffrey's terse comment in the HRB on Arthur's being transported to the Isle of Avalon to be cured of his wounds. In the later poem (lines 908–40), Geoffrey elaborates on the Island of Apples or the Fortunate Island, as it is called in the VM where Taliesin and Barinthus take Arthur to be cared for by Morgen and her sisters. But this scenario is neither present nor implied in the HRB. The only other information the HRB supplies in regard to the Isle of Avalon is that Arthur's sword Caliburn was forged there (Thorpe, 217). This vaguely hints at Arthur's departure to the island as a return to a place with which he already had at least some connection. We might also notice that in the HRB Geoffrey provided no information on Merlin's end. Following his assumption of the appearance of Britaelis, Uther's companion, we simply hear no more of Merlin in Geoffrey's history.

Geoffrey's silence on Arthur's return in the HRB may have been due to the inflammatory potential of such an idea at a time of insurrection in Wales. He continued to refuse to endorse the idea of Arthur as a future redeemer in the VM. In the poem (lines 959–75) Merlin rejects Taliesin's call to bring Arthur back if he has been cured of his wounds. Instead,

Merlin envisions the Restoration of British sovereignty to be accomplished by Conan and Cadwallader. Finally, the Bern MS of the *HRB* (Wright, 1984, 132) adds the words "May his soul rest in peace" (*Anima eius in pace quiescat*) rather awkwardly after the dating of the Battle of Camblan rather than following the information on Arthur's being carried to Avalon. These words have the look of a later interpolation, but their sentiment is not entirely out of keeping with Geoffrey's own hesitations over Arthur as a future redeemer.

Arthur's Successors

Following his dazzling and unique portrait of Arthur's career, Geoffrey returned to a narrative of events with which his readers had at least a measure of familiarity. His brief account of events from the mysterious end of Arthur down to the final loss of British sovereignty is derived principally from Gildas and Bede. The manner in which Geoffrey deals with the subject of the passage of dominion over the island of Britain, however, reveals his determination to reconstruct the dismal portrait of British leaders that he found in Gildas and to unmask the prejudices and biases of Bede's influential *History of the English Church and People*.

The names of the four kings who immediately follow Arthur in the *HRB* (Constantine, Aurelius Conanus, Vortipore, and Malgo) are taken from chapters 28–33 of Gildas, containing the famous denunciation of the vices of the five tyrants who ruled Britain in Gildas's own day (Winterbottom, 29–33). Geoffrey passes over Gildas's fourth tyrant, Cuneglasus, perhaps finding his career too sordid for redemption. The fifth successor to Arthur in the *HRB,* Keredic, under whom the Britons lose control over a considerable part of the island, appears to have been Geoffrey's own invention. In order to establish that British sovereignty over Britain survived well beyond the rule of King Arthur, Geoffrey converts Gildas's tyrants into successive, rather than simultaneous rulers. He also brushes aside most of Gildas's scathing denunciations of the moral shortcomings of these men, and elaborates instead on their supposed political and military accomplishments.

Concerning Arthur's immediate successor, Constantine, for example, Gildas states that "from the bitter vine of the men of Sodom, he had planted a slip of unbelieving folly in the soil of his heart," and that he was guilty of "the stench of frequent and successive adulteries." Gildas also denounces Constantine for having torn two "royal youths" from the bosoms of their mothers and having put them to death, along with their guardians, as "their arms were stretched out . . . to God and the altar" (Winterbottom, 29). Geoffrey completely ignores these fulminations of Gildas against Constantine's Sodomite follies and frequent adulteries (Thorpe, 262). As for the two royal youths who were so piteously torn from the bosom of their mothers, Geoffrey reveals them to have been no innocent babes at all, but rather the rebellious sons of Mordred who are slain only after their revolt fails and they seek sanctuary; one before the altar of Saint Amphibalus in Winchester, the other within a monastery of friars in London. Constantine's violation of the venerable British law of sanctuary, rather than his sexual sins, results in his being "struck down by the vengeance of God." His followers in the *HRB,* however, give him a dignified burial by the side of Utherpendragon at Stonehenge.

Geoffrey's treatment of Gildas's other tyrants follows the same revisionist strategy. Gildas accuses Aurelius Conanus of being even a worse sinner than Constantine. Aurelius is engulfed in parricide, fornications, adulteries, and a love of civil strife. Geoffrey's Aurelius Conanus, Constantine's nephew, is no angel either. He comes to the throne in the *HRB* by imprisoning his own uncle, who should have succeeded Constantine, and murdering this man's sons. But Geoffrey ignores Gildas's catalogue of Aurelius's private sins, and claims that he would have been worthy of the crown were it not for his delight in civil war. His successor, Vortiporius, denounced by Gildas for murder, adultery, and the "rape of a shameless daughter," becomes in the *HRB* an able warrior, who defeats the Saxons and their allies, and rules "frugally and peacefully." Malgo succeeds Vortiporius in the *HRB,* but we hear nothing of his scandalous behavior as recorded by Gildas (murdering his uncle, usurping the crown, committing sodomy, and breaking his monastic vows). Geoffrey chooses to stress Malgo's handsome appearance, bravery, generosity, and the mildness of his rule.

Equally as important as the *HRB*'s favorable (although not uncritical) version of these successors to Arthur is the extent of their political authority. Geoffrey takes pains to indicate that each of them exerted dominance over the Saxons and ruled the entire island. Especially important in this regard are the achievements of Vortiporius and Malgo. Vortiporius crushes a Saxon army that has been augmented by allies brought over from Germany. Malgo uses the hegemony established by his predecessors at home to reestablish British rule over the six neighboring islands first conquered by Arthur. Thus the Golden Age of Arthur lives on to a considerable degree in the four capable, if imperfect, leaders who rule the land after the greatest British king.

Yet, while Geoffrey was able to postpone the inevitable, he was not able to ignore it entirely. A significant portion of Britain is lost under the weak rule of Keredic, fifth in succession following Arthur. Significantly, however, Geoffrey denies the Saxons a critical role in the downfall of Britain. The African king Gormund must be called over from Ireland with his 160,000 Africans to overthrow Keredic. Even the mighty Gormund, however, is unable to conquer Britain without first allying himself with the Saxons and then receiving help from Isembard, the apostate nephew of Louis, king of the Franks.[26] As a result of this alliance, a substantial portion of Britain (Loegria) falls under the sway of Gormund and the Saxons. The monasteries of the "two provinces" of Northumbria and Loegria have to be abandoned. The archbishops of London and York flee with the relics of the saints to Wales and Cornwall, while many other British clergy seek refuge in Brittany. Even in this wretched condition, however, Geoffrey claims that the Britons continued to harry the enemy with attacks out of Cornwall and Wales, the only territories remaining thoroughly under British dominion.

For the closing episodes of the *HRB* Geoffrey turned to Bede's *History of the English Church and People*. Unlike the scrappy chapters on the post-Arthurian England in Nennius's *Historia Brittonum,* Bede's history offered Geoffrey a detailed and continuous narrative of the period in which British sovereignty waned and was finally extinguished. As the recognized authority on the establishment and evolution of the Germanic kingdoms in England and their subsequent conversion to Christianity, Bede was thus unavoidable. Moreover, the logic of Geoffrey's own *HRB* required a confrontation with Bede's anti-British biases. One might even say that in having supplied a sympathetic, circumstantial, and more or less plausible account of British history up to this point, Geoffrey had already gone a long way toward decentering Bede's history. As a parallel account of the early history of the island of Britain, the *HRB* exposes the narrowness of the ecclesiastical focus of Bede's *History of the English Church and People.* For Bede the history of Britain essentially begins with the subjection of the nation to Roman authority. The later pre-Saxon history of the island is a sorry record of a people plagued by inveterate civil discord, prone to heretical belief, in constant need of militant missionary expeditions from Gaul to force them back to the path of orthodoxy, weak, vulnerable, and fatally reliant on Roman protection against their more robust neighbors and capable of effective resistance to aggression only when led by men of Roman ancestry such as Aurelius. In Bede, there is no mention of the Trojan settlement under Brutus, no record of British cultural achievements (for example, cities, laws, roads, ecclesiastical and civil institutions, and conquests), and no knowledge of the Golden Age of Arthur.

More important perhaps for the final pages of Geoffrey's *HRB* was Bede's view that the mission of Augustine was made necessary by the low moral condition into which the Britons had sunk in spite of the best efforts of Germanus and his colleagues to restrain their vices. In the *HRB*, however, the mission of Germanus and Lupus takes place, as shown in chapter 2, during the reign of the tyrant Vortigern, long before Augustine's arrival, with which it has no organic connection. It is successful, moreover, in stamping out heresy. Geoffrey states flatly: "the religion of the true faith was restored to them [the Britons] by the preaching of these saintly men" (Thorpe, 160). Bede introduces the advent of Augustine following his description of the second campaign of Germanus, this time accompanied by Severus (no mention of this second visitation in the *HRB*) against the British Pelagians and thus implies that the two events were closely linked in time. When the efforts of Germanus and Severus proved inadequate to the task of deracinating the unruly heretical tendencies of the British, Bede claims, Pope Gregory called on Augustine. Thus the Augustinian mission, according to the *History of the English Church and People,* had a twofold aim, first to evangelize the English and second to recall the Celtic Church, which had stubbornly refused to evangelize their English neighbors back to the lap of Roman orthodoxy.

The *HRB* puts into context the British clergy's refusal to Christianize the English by clearly laying blame on the English themselves for the destruction of the Christian Church in Britain: "This Augustine was to preach the word of God to the Angles, who, blinded by their pagan superstition, had done away with Christianity entirely in the part of the island which they controlled" (Thorpe, 160). The British refusal to aid Augustine in his mission to the English is expressed in the *HRB*, as it is in Bede's history, by Dinoot, abbot of the monastery at Bangor. The *History of the English Church and People,* however, shows Augustine meeting twice with the British clergy. At the first of these meetings he bests the British priests in a show of holiness by curing a man whom the British priests were unable to cure. In the second meeting, the British clergy childishly refuse to comply with Augustine's demands after taking umbrage at his neglect to rise in show of respect as they enter the monastery for their conference. For their refusal, Augustine prophesies that they will "suffer the penalty of death." In the *HRB* there is but one meeting, at which the learned Dinoot, abbot of a monastery of well in excess of 2,000 monks, excoriates the Saxons for their role in depriving the British of their fatherland (Thorpe, 266). Consequently, the British owe the Saxons no allegiance whatsoever, Dinoot concludes, and have about as much in common with them as they do with dogs! Naturally, Geoffrey passes over in silence Bede's obsession with the Celtic Church's noncanonical date for celebrating Easter.

And so it goes with the rest of Geoffrey's recasting of Bede's *History of the English Church and People*. The Battle of Chester according to Bede's *History* was a divinely sanctioned "slaughter of faithless Britons" in fulfillment of Augustine's prophecy. To Geoffrey, however, it was a reprisal by the "Saxon tyrant," Ethelfrid of Northumbria, for Dinoot's rebuff to Augustine. Whereas Bede claims that the monks of Bangor assembled near the field of battle to pray for a British victory, Geoffrey places them as refugees from Ethelfrid's fury inside the city of Leicester.[27] Their slaughter wins them a "crown of martyrdom" in the *HRB*. The British leader Brocmail in the *History of the English Church and People* callously abandons the monks to their fate, whereas Geoffrey has him defending Leicester and inflicting "enormous losses" on the enemy before being forced to flee.

Bede's version of Edwin's career is similarly undermined by Geoffrey. In the *History of the English Church and People* Edwin takes refuge from Ethelfrid's hatred (which goes unexplained) at the court of Redwald, king of the Angles, where he receives instructions from an angel who assures him of his future greatness. With the aid of Redwald, Edwin overthrows Ethelfrid, assumes the crown of Northumbria, and later leads his people to embrace the Christian faith.

Geoffrey has a rather different view of the great Northumbrian king. In the *HRB* the pregnant wife of Ethelfrid flees her husband, who wishes to put her aside for another woman. She takes refuge in the court of the British king Cadvan, where her son Edwin is born. Edwin is later raised with Cadvan's son Cadwallo, and is taught knightly ways at the court of Salomon, king of Brittany. Far from having the capacity to seize the throne of Northumbria by military force, Edwin, according to the *HRB*, must request Cadwallo's permission to wear a crown. Warned by his loyal servant Brian that history has shown the Saxons to be a people without honor or faith, Cadwallo refuses Edwin's request for a crown on the grounds that it was customary that there should be but one king in all of Britain. Angered at his friend's response, Edwin returns to Northumbria and wages war against Cadwallo. Amusingly, Geoffrey has

Edwin rely for guidance, not on an angelic visitor, as in Bede's *History of the English Church and People,* but rather on a Spanish magician named Pellitus, who is endowed with extraordinary powers of interpreting the course of the stars and the flight of birds! With Pellitus's help, Edwin drives Cadwallo into exile, first to Ireland, then to the court of King Salomon of Brittany.

Salomon and Cadwallo jointly bemoan the sad condition of Britain. Though shamed by Salomon's observation on the feebleness of the Britons's resistance to the Angles, Cadwallo nevertheless agrees with the king on the cause of the fallen condition of his countrymen, namely, the depletion of Britain's most valorous and noble citizens during the migration to Brittany of Maximianus and Conanus. Brittany preserved the flower of the noble descendants of Brutus, while Britain was left with the baser element; as might be expected from a nation of low-born citizens, the Britons soon fell into the vices of their kind: pride, sexual excesses, a scorn for truth, viciousness, tyranny, violence, and rebellion (Thorpe, 273). The speeches of Salomon and Cadwallo are part of the mystique of Brittany that permeates the *HRB,* and perhaps reveal that Geoffrey's so-called racial sympathies lay with the Breton (Tatlock, 1974, 396–402). The speeches also function, however, to belittle the Saxon achievement. The Saxons managed to subdue only a small percentage of the island's degenerate and feckless population, even with the help of the fierce Gormund.

The same subversive strategy underlies Geoffrey's rewriting of Bede's account of the death of Edwin at the Battle of Hedfield (Haethfelth in Bede). In the *HRB* Edwin's fortunes begin to change when Cadwallo's faithful servant Brian returns to Britain in disguise and assassinates Edwin's Spanish astrologer Pellitus. Cadwallo invades Britain with auxiliaries supplied to him by Salomon and defeats Peanda of Mercia with whom he then allies. He goes on to defeat Edwin and cruelly decimate the Angles with a view to wiping out their entire race (deeds forecast in the *PM* as the bloody achievements of the Man of Bronze). The alliance with Peanda, which is so critical to Cadwalla's success in Bede, is of only incidental importance to Geoffrey's Cadwallo. The British victory in the *HRB* is due in large measure to the help supplied by their allies from Brittany.

Geoffrey is no less aggressive toward Bede's Caedwalla, the king of the West Saxons or Gewissae, who abdicates his throne after only two years in order to travel to Rome to be baptized. He dies in Rome in 689. Out of admiration for the pious Saxon king, Pope Sergius has the king's body interred in Saint Peter's and directs that an epitaph be inscribed on his tomb commemorating his holiness.

Geoffrey confiscates Bede's version of Caedwalla's career and turns it to his own purposes. By openly reminding the reader that his Cadwallader is the same as Bede's Caedwalla, Geoffrey invites the reader to witness his challenge to his English predecessor. Wright correctly observes that this mention of Bede removes the possibility that Geoffrey simply mistook a Saxon for a Britton.[28] In the *HRB* Geoffrey consistently interprets the Gewissae as the people of Gwent (South East Wales).[29] He leaves us to conclude that the holy man praised by Bede, and celebrated by Pope Sergius was a Briton, not a Saxon.

While the British lose their grasp on the island during the reign of Cadwallader, Geoffrey is careful to point out that their dispersal and exile were brought about not by Saxon might, but because of a series of natural disasters (plague and famine) sent their way by God. The plague was suggested to Geoffrey by Bede, who mentions the occurrence of a plague in the chapter before the one describing Cadwalla's career (Bede, trans. Sherley-Price, 229–30). But the language in which Geoffrey describes the plague is taken not from Bede, but from Gildas. And for good reason. Gildas had denounced the British for their vices and had interpreted the foreign invasions as the scourge of God. Geoffrey's plan was to undermine Bede's exaltation of the Saxons by showing that their conquest of the island was due not to their own virtues but to the British loss of their covenant with God. For this purpose Gildas was the more serviceable authority.

Thus as the British leave the ravaged island behind them, they chant, as they do in chapter 25 of Gildas, a verse from Psalm 43 (44):11–12, "Thou hast made us, O God, like sheep for slaughter, and hast scattered us among the nations" (Winterbottom, 28). The parallelism between the fates of the British and the Hebrews elevates the dignity and tragic tone of the British exile from their promised land. As they depart, Cadwallader interprets their fate for them by insisting that their exile was sent by God as punishment for their transgressions, crimes, and folly. In the words of the *PM*, which foresee this event, the Britons suffered "the Revenge of the Thunderer." Furthermore, subtly interwoven into Cadwallader's denunciation of the British is his insistence that no human agent was able to deprive them of their land. He ends by inviting the inveterate enemies of the British to occupy the deserted island: "Come back you Romans! Return, Scots and Picts! And you too, Ambrones and Saxons! The door to Britain now lies wide open before you. The island which you could never capture stands empty now through the wrath of God. It is not your valor which is forcing us to leave but the power of the Supreme King, whom we have never ceased to provoke" (Thorpe, 281).

The *HRB* begins and ends with the occupation of Britain, but no two events could be more dissimilar. The garden-island, which was once held out in pristine condition to the noble race of Trojans, has now been wasted by the wrath of God. It is reoccupied by an "odious race" (*nefandus populus*) who come across in multitudes from Germany and meet insignificant resistance from the few pathetic Britons inhabiting the remote woods of Wales. The Saxons rush to occupy the waste land under divine wrath like vultures descending on a dead carcass.

After Cadwallader has spent some time in exile in Brittany, he secures the help of King Alan in assembling a fleet with which to invade Britain, but an angelic voice (confiscated from the spirit who adresses Edwin in Bede's *History of the English Church and People*) speaking to him out of the thunder admonishes him that he must abandon this enterprise and travel to Rome to visit Pope Sergius. The voice adds that the Britons would not return again to their native land until the relics of their saints had been transported from Rome back to Britain (Thorpe, 283). Thus, just as Geoffrey had portrayed the Trojans following the prophecy of Diana toward their destined homeland on the empty island in the sea beyond Gaul, so, too, here in the closing passages of his history he depicts the British diaspora in Brittany receiving divine promise of a new beginning. It is difficult to miss the angelic voice's allusion to the opening lines of the *Aeneid* in which Aeneas and his Trojans are said to have carried their household gods away from Troy to Latium (*inferretque deos Latio*).[30]

Typical of Geoffrey's secular viewpoint, however, he has Alan compare the angel's prophecy to Cadwallader with the written prophecies of the Eagle of Shaftesbury, the Sybil, and Merlin. Only after satisfying himself that the sacred and profane utterances agree on the fate of Britain does Alan advise Cadwallader to follow the angel's commands. Cadwallader journeys to Rome, is confirmed by Pope Sergius, and dies in the holy city in 689.

The fractious and degenerate Britons remaining in their homeland gradually decline in power in spite of being led by Cadwallader's son Yvor and his nephew Yni and are overwhelmed at last by their Saxon foes. Along with their ancient valor, they also lose their very identity, being hereafter called Welsh instead of Britons.[31] Conversely, once British sovereignty has been extinguished, the Saxons grow into a people worthy to possess the land. They acquire the same marks of civilized behavior that Brutus and his Trojans brought to Britain so many centuries before, by maintaining peace among themselves, cultivating the land, building cities and fortifications, and agreeing to be ruled by a single king, Adelstan (Athelstan).

Thus, Geoffrey of Monmouth ends his history of the careers of 99 kings of Britain by showing the passage of dominion over the island from the Britons to the Saxons. Yet by postponing Saxon hegemony until the reign of Adelstan, who ruled during the tenth century, Geoffrey denies the Germanic peoples of Britain the preeminence accorded them by their own histories, particularly the *Anglo-Saxon Chronicle* and Bede's *History of the English Church and People*. Subsequent historians, seeking to incorporate Geoffrey's *HRB* into a general survey of Insular history, faced the difficult, if not impossible, task of reconciling the established English authorities who placed the passage of dominion centuries earlier, typically during the sixth century, with Geoffrey's relentlessly British perspective on the periodization of the island's history.[32]

Finally, several manuscripts of the *HRB* contain an epilogue in which Geoffrey bequeaths to his contemporary Caradoc of Llancarfan the task of continuing the history of the Welsh kings from Cadwallader onward and leaves to William of Malmesbury and Henry of Huntingdon the job of composing the history of the Saxon kings. He warns the latter two historians, however, to say nothing of the British kings because they are not in possession of the book in the British language that Walter of Oxford brought back from Brittany. How seriously to take these remarks is difficult to know. Valerie Flint is right to see in Geoffrey's epilogue the culmination of a series of rebuffs that he directed throughout the *HRB* at his three colleagues in the field of history. The rhetorical tradition of the author boasting over his accomplishments, however, is at least as old as Horace's *Odes* and often takes the form of commanding rivals, ancient or contemporary, to fall silent (the *taceat*-formula) or to yield place (the *cedat*-formula) to the superior merits of the current writer.[33] Such pride of authorship would even lead Dante (*Inferno*, 25, 94–102) to command both Lucan and Ovid to fall silent before his superior poetic merits. Geoffrey's self-assertion may spring also from a genuine sense of individual accomplishment at having supplied his readers with something entirely new, a more or less plausible continuous history of early Britain, where before him there had been only fragments and lacunae. Then, too, the epilogue to the *HRB* can be compared to Marie de France's bristly comments in the epilogue to her *Fables*, both texts reflecting a growing proprietary consciousness among twelfth-century authors toward their literary labor and a fear that it might be alienated from them.

Chapter Five

The Life of Merlin

With the *PM* and the *HRB* behind him, Geoffrey turned once again to the figure of Merlin in the last of his works, the *Vita Merlini* (*Life of Merlin* or *VM*), a poem in 1,529 Latin hexameters. Along with the *PM* and the *HRB,* the *VM* demonstrates Geoffrey's career-long interest in Merlin, who, like Arthur, figured prominently in all of his works. The fact that Geoffrey dropped Merlin from the *HRB* with such uncharacteristic abruptness may possibly indicate that he already anticipated continuing the prophet's saga in some future work. In any event, the last we hear of Merlin in the *HRB* is during the reign of Utherpendragon, whom Merlin transforms into the shape of Gorlois by the administration of certain medicines whose magical virtues are known to him. Assuming the appearance of Gorlois, Uther sleeps with Ygerna, who that night conceives Arthur. Merlin himself takes the appearance of a person named Britaelis, and we hear no more of him in the *HRB*.

Summary of the *Vita Merlini*

The prologue announces the subject of the poem to be the madness of the prophetic bard, which is to be sung through the playful muse. Geoffrey asks the dedicatee of the poem, Robert, "glory of the bishops," to display more favor to the author than did his predecessor.

Merlin, the lawgiver and prophet of Demetia (South Wales), goes mad and takes to the woods following a battle in which three brothers of Peredur are killed. He is accompanied in his wilderness life by an old wolf. Merlin's madness is cured one day by listening to music played in the forest by one of King Rodarch's men. When brought back to Rodarch's court, where Merlin's wife Gwendolen lives along with his sister Ganieda, Rodarch's queen, Merlin's madness returns, and he is imprisoned by the king. After revealing Ganieda's adultery and proclaiming Gwendolen free to marry again, Merlin is released from prison and returns to the wilderness. Hearing of Gwendolen's approaching marriage, Merlin rides to court on the back of a stag, leading a troop of does and she-goats. Ridiculed by the bridegroom, Merlin hurls the stag's antlers at him, killing him. Ganieda builds a house with 70 doors and windows for Merlin in the forest and begins to visit him there. Here Merlin prophesies (*O rabiem Britonum*) the misfortunes to befall Britain. When Rodarch dies, Ganieda joins her brother in his wilderness house, as does Taliesin, who has recently returned from study with Gildas in Brittany. Taliesin discourses on the wonders of nature, including the Island of Apples (*insula pomorum*), where Taliesin and Barinthus took Arthur after the Battle of Camblan to be cured by Morgen, who rules the island along with her six sisters. Merlin laments the condition of Britain in his own day under Conan, murderer of Constantine. He foresees deliverance some day by another Conan who will come from Brittany to ally with Cadwallader. Merlin's insanity is then relieved by the waters of a spring that suddenly appears, and Taliesin speaks about the special powers of water. Asked by the leaders of the country to resume his public life, Merlin refuses, claiming that no riches could draw him away from his beloved Calidon retreat. He discourses on the special nature God has bestowed on birds. Later, he discovers in the woods a man named Maeldin, one of his former companions, who was driven mad after eating apples originally intended for Merlin. Maeldin's sanity is restored by spring water. Merlin, Taliesin, Maeldin, and Ganieda (who has led a chaste life since Rodarch's death) form a community in Merlin's woodland house. One day, Ganieda prophesies while gazing on the windows radiating with sunlight. She foresees events to occur in Oxford, Lincoln, Winchester, Wales, and Scotland and calls upon the Normans to cease their violence in the kingdom. Merlin declares an end to his own prophetic career; henceforth, Ganieda would prophesy with Merlin's authority.

In the epilogue Geoffrey of Monmouth calls on the British to bestow the laurel crown upon him for having sung their battles; he is the one who composed the book now called the *Deeds of the Britons* (*Gesta Britonum*), which has been proclaimed throughout the world.

The Date of the Poem

The date of the *VM* can be fixed with confidence between 1148 and 1155 (*Vita Merlini,* ed. Clarke, 40–42; Chambers, 48; Faral, 2:29–36).[1] In the preface to the poem, Geoffrey asks Robert to guide his work and to show greater favor to its author than did his predecessor in the see to which Robert had recently succeeded. These remarks clearly refer to Robert of Chesney, who succeeded Bishop Alexander, the dedicatee of the *PM,* as fourth bishop of Lincoln in December 1148. As a former canon of Saint

George's in Oxford, Robert was known to Geoffrey. The two men were also cosignatories on a grant of land in Knolle in 1151 (see chapter 1). If the dedication were written quite recently after Robert assumed office in Lincoln, the *VM* might have been begun a year or so earlier in 1146 or 1147. It was obviously completed before Geoffrey's death in 1155.

Attempts to assign a precise date to the *VM* have not met with much success. Parry argued, for example, that the battle between two stars and wild beasts alluded to in Ganieda's prophecy in lines 1498 ff., took place in the year 1150 at Consyllt (Coleshill) in Flintshire in North Wales.[2] He noted that Ganieda refers to this battle as taking place "under the hill of Urien," where the Deirians and Gewissi formerly met during the reign of Coel. Parry took this to be Geoffrey's recollection of the sixth-century battle at Argoed Llwyfain alluded to in one of the Taliesin poems. In that battle, Urien, chief of Rheged, routed Fflamddwyn (Flamebearer), chief of the Angles of Bernicia. Taliesin's Argoed Llwyfain was located in the north of Britain, but there was apparently a place of the same name in Geoffrey's day in the district of North Wales where Consyllt was located. The battle of Consyllt pitted the forces of Madog ap Maredudd, king of Powys, and Ranulf, earl of Chester, against the Welsh chieftain Owain Gwynedd. Geoffrey would have taken an interest in this encounter because Owain's decisive victory over Madog and Ranulf halted Norman expansion into North Wales, and made a visit by Geoffrey to Saint Asaph, to which he was elected bishop in 1151, a very dangerous, perhaps even impossible, undertaking.

Perry's dating of this prophecy did not convince Faral, who found the reference to "wounds inflicted on foreigners" in Ganieda's prophecy inapplicable to the troops of Madog and Ranulf (Faral, 2:29–36). He interpreted Ganieda's prediction as a whole to refer to events between the siege of Oxford in June 1139 and the Battle of Wilton in 1143 and the depredations which followed. On the other hand, Faral could offer no evidence to show that Wilton or its environs was ever known as "the hill of Urien."

Efforts by nineteenth-century scholars such as Thomas Wright and San-Marte to date the poem during the thirteenth century are no longer given serious attention.

Manuscripts. The *VM* survives complete in only one manuscript, dating from the latter part of the thirteenth century: British Library MS Cotton Vespasian E.iv. ff. 112v–138v, on which all editions of the poem have been based. Substantial extracts covering about half the total number of lines of the poem were inserted between the years 525 and 533 in three manuscripts of Ralph Higden's *Polychronicon* dating from the fourteenth and fifteenth centuries (BL MSS Harley 655, Royal 13.E.i., and Cotton

Julius E.viii.). Another fifteenth-century manuscript in the British Library, Cotton Titus A.xix., also contains extracts of the *VM* taken out of a copy of the *Polychronicon,* as well as the two Lailoken Fragments, which will be discussed below. Fragments from the prophecies of the *VM* are contained in two other manuscripts, BL MSS Cotton Cleopatra C.iv. of the late fifteenth century, and Harley 6148 of the early seventeenth century (Parry, 21–22; *Vita Merlini,* ed. Clarke, 43–44).

Editions: The *VM* was first edited in 1830 by William Henry Black for the Roxburghe Club.[3] A second edition of the *VM* was published in Paris in 1837 by Francisque Michel with an introduction by Thomas Wright.[4]

The first modern critical edition of the *VM* was that of John Jay Parry in 1925. Parry based his edition on MS Cotton Vespasian E.iv. and a thorough collation of all the other surviving manuscripts. Parry provided a faithful prose translation on the page facing the Latin text and included translations of some of the Welsh Myrddin poems. He securely established Geoffrey as the author of the *VM,* Robert of Chesney as the dedicatee, and the date around 1150, rather than the early thirteenth century, as had been proposed previously.

The *VM* was edited once again four years later by Edmond Faral as one of the documents in his three-volume study of the Arthurian legends, *La Légende arthurienne.* Faral's edition (in classicized spelling) was based on MS Cotton Vespasian E.iv.

Basil Clarke's 1973 edition of the *VM* for the University of Wales Press was essentially a revision of Parry's text with some new textual emendations, but offered a fresh prose translation and a complete introduction covering questions of date, sources, literary relationships, manuscripts, and previous editions. Clarke's edition also had copious notes, amounting in many cases to brief essays, on all the names in the poem. Clarke also exploited advances since Faral's and Parry's day in the study of the *HRB,* twelfth-century literature, historiography and hagiography, and the Welsh Myrddin and Taliesin poems. In appendices to his edition Clarke also included translations of the Lailoken Fragments and selected stanzas of the *Afallennau.*

Sources of the *Life of Merlin*

As shown chapter 2, the Merlin of the *HRB* was created by Geoffrey largely out of the character of Ambrosius in Nennius's *Historia Brittonum.* Merlin Calidonius of the *VM,* according to the fiction of the poem, is the same person as the prophet of the *HRB,* but living at a later date and involved in new experiences. For the material of these later adventures of Merlin, Geoffrey turned to traditions concerning the North British wild man figure known in the literary sources as Lailoken and also to a body of Welsh prophetic poetry associated with a character named Myrddin, or Myrddin Gwyllt, "Myrddin the Wild."

The Lailoken Fragments. The story of the North British wild man known as Lailoken probably reached Geoffrey through some version of the life of Saint Kentigern, the patron saint of Glasgow. According to a tradition current about the time Geoffrey was writing the *VM,* Kentigern, while wandering in exile, founded a church on the banks of the Elwy River in North Wales and left it under the care of a monk called Asaph, after whom it later took its name (Jackson, 1958, 313 ff.). Geoffrey's appointment as bishop of Saint Asaph's sometime around 1150 may have been the occasion that brought him into contact with the legends concerning Kentigern and Lailoken. British Library MS Cotton Titus A.xix. preserves an incomplete life of Saint Kentigern and two fragments concerning Lailoken, known to scholars as Fragment A and Fragment B.[5] The manuscript in which these stories are contained dates from the fifteenth century, and Fragment B shows the influence of Geoffrey by tentatively identifying Lailoken with Merlin (a name Geoffrey himself invented). Cotton Titus's identification of Lailoken and Merlin shows that the copyist of the fragment (or of its lost exemplar) recognized the similarity between the Lailoken material and the *VM.* He must be counted, therefore, among the earliest scholars to reflect on the source of Geoffrey's poem.

Fragment A tells of Kentigern's chancing on the wild man Lailoken in the forest one day. Asked by the saint to explain his presence there, Lailoken tells how he was driven into the wilderness by a voice that came to him from the sky during a battle and that blamed him for the carnage on the field that day. The story relates the deep sympathy that Kentigern felt for Lailoken in his harsh life in the wilderness; it also contains a version of the motif of the threefold death, which Lailoken predicts for himself (to be killed by stones and clubs, pierced by a sharp stake, and drowned in water), and which comes true when he is set upon by the shepherds of King Meldred. He also predicts the death within a year of the king of Britain, the most holy of bishops, and the most noble of lords.

Fragment B does not specifically mention Kentigern, but concerns Lailoken's capture and detention in Dunmeller at the court of King Meldred who holds Lailoken until the prophet reveals his reason for laughing over the leaf he discovered attached to the queen's shawl. Lailoken also foretells a threefold death for himself. The queen's shepherds later kill Lailoken "as it is recorded above" (a clear reference to Fragment A), and the prophet is buried 30 miles from Glasgow near the place where he used to live.

From this material, or something similar, Geoffrey derived the idea of a man being driven to the wilderness by a voice from the sky during the carnage of battle.[6] In the *VM*, however, Merlin's flight to the woods is brought about by his own grief over the death of Peredur's three brothers, a motive more in keeping with the poem's theme of personal responsibility and voluntary withdrawal from the evils of the world. Rodarch's sympathy for Merlin in the *VM* may also owe something to Kentigern's kindly attitude toward Lailoken. The motif of the threefold death is, of course, common to the Lailoken fragments and the *VM*, but in the latter Geoffrey has intricately woven it into the story of the queen's infidelity and the prophet's laugh at the sight of an incriminating leaf in her hair, both of which details occur in Fragment B.[7] Lailoken's action explains the queen's implacable hatred toward him and his death at the hands of her (or the king's) shepherds. Geoffrey, on the other hand, never adequately explains Ganieda's rather improbable fidelity to Merlin in spite of his revelation of her adultery. Perhaps in attempting to fuse the Lailoken story with its Welsh analog in the Myrddin poems, he simply failed to provide an account of the reconciliation of brother and sister. In the Welsh poem, *Cyfoesi Myrddin ac Ei Chwaer Gwenddydd* (*Dialogue between Myrddin and His Sister Gwenddydd*), Myrddin's sister Gwenddydd converses with her brother and urges him to prophesy.[8] Geoffrey may have known a now lost collateral tradition connected with the *Cyfoesi* whereby Myrddin and Gwenddydd lived together harmoniously. If so, this would have run counter to the Lailoken Fragment B, which has the prophet dying at the hands of the queen's shepherds. Gwenddydd addresses Myrddin as *llallogan,* a term whose meaning and evolution is still unclear.[9] If *llallogan* does derive from the name Lailoken, however, this would at least show that the Welsh and Scottish variants of the wild man legend were assimilated at some point. Whether this occurred before or after Geoffrey's *VM* is a matter of conjecture. In any case, the *VM* never resolves the problem. Merlin exposes his sister's adultery, yet she builds a house for him in the woods and after Rodarch's death takes refuge with him there. The idea of Merlin securing his freedom in exchange for explaining his laughter to Rodarch may have been suggested to Geoffrey by the same episode in the Lailoken Fragment B tradition.

Finally, in both fragments, Lailoken possesses the power of prophecy; in Fragment A he foretells the death of the king, just as Merlin knows in the *VM* (ostensibly without being informed by a court source) that Rodarch has died, although he does not actually predict his death.

The Welsh Myrddin Poems. The *VM* derives in part also from Welsh traditions concerning Myrddin, sometimes known as Myrddin Wyllt (Myrddin the Mad) (Tolstoy; Bollard, 13–54),[10] who is said to have fought at the Battle of Arfderydd.[11] Discerning precisely what Geoffrey knew of the traditions concerning Myrddin is difficult, partly because of his tendency to turn his sources to his own literary purposes and partly because of the incomplete knowledge we have concerning the Battle of Arfderydd and its participants; partly, too, because the highly allusive Welsh poems concerning Myrddin assume much knowledge on the part of the listener and are themselves fluid and sometimes contradictory.

Among the Welsh Myrddin poems, Geoffrey surely drew upon the *Armes Prydein,* a tenth-century Welsh prophetic poem in which Myrddin figures as a prophetic authority. The *Armes Prydein* also furnishes Geoffrey with the scenario of the restoration of British sovereignty under the joint leadership of Cynan (Conan) and Cadwallader. He reused this material from the *PM* in the Arthurian section of the *VM,* as demonstrated in chapter 3.

From Welsh sources, too, comes the *VM*'s association of Merlin with Taliesin. These two are interlocutors in *The Dialogue of Merlin and Taliesin* (1050–1100),[12] which alludes to the many fallen men at the Battle of Arfderydd and to seven score of nobles who became madmen (*ygwllon*) and died in the Forest of Celidon (*Yg coed keliton*).

Myrddin also mentions his prophecy (*vy darogan*) in the *Dialogue,* although he does not actually utter a prophecy. This poem, therefore, establishes the association of Myrddin and Taliesin in a poem alluding to the events of Arfderydd at least 50 years before the *VM*. The *Dialogue,* being essentially a lament by the two speakers over the destructiveness of battle, may have played some part in suggesting to Geoffrey that his Merlin should retreat from the world into the wilderness. Welsh Triad 44 implies that Peredur and Gwrgi were the opponents of Gwenddolau at Arfderydd. A note added to a late version of the *Annales Cambriae* claims that Merlin went mad at the Battle of Arfderydd in 573 (*Merlinus insanus effectus est*); the Latin form of the name (*Merlinus*) indicates Geoffrey's influence here (Winterbottom, 85).

The portrait of Taliesin's vast knowledge in the *VM* is also derived from Welsh traditions. Taliesin was held in high esteem by the Welsh as one of their earliest poets (the *cynfeirth*) and is mentioned by Nennius as one of the poets "famed in British verse" (Winterbottom, 37, ch. 62). Many of the poems in the *Book of Taliesin* are prophecies and imply a kind of omniscience on Taliesin's part, as does the *Hanes Taliesin;* both of these works survive in versions later than Geoffrey, but Taliesin's reputation for omniscience and prophecy were evidently established in Welsh before Geoffrey. This tradition probably could not have been entirely Geoffrey's doing, although some influence on Welsh legends about Taliesin by Geoffrey is not inconceivable.

Similarly, Gwennolous, the ruler of Scotland in the *VM,* against whom Peredur and Rodarch fight, is Gwenddolau whom Welsh Triad 29 and the *Annales Cambriae* claim died at Arfderydd. In the Welsh Myrddin poems, particularly, *Afallennau, Oianau,* and *Cyfoesi* (Bromwich, 1978, 57; Winterbottom, 85)[13] Myrddin appears to have been under the protection of Gwenddolau and laments his patron's death. His flight to the forest may have been necessitated by Gwenddolau's demise. Oddly, in the Myrddin poems it is Rhydderch and his steward Gwasog whom Myrddin most fears in his hiding place under (in?) the apple tree in the Forest of Celidon. For some reason, however, Geoffrey reversed the roles of the *dramatis personae* of the Battle of Arfderydd. In the *VM,* Merlin fights on the side of Peredur and Rodarch against Gwennolous.

The chronology of the Battle of Arfderydd and the traditional dates of the participants would have proved an inconvenience for Geoffrey, assuming he knew about them. The Battle of Arfderydd, for example, in which Myrddin was ostensibly driven mad according to Welsh tradition, is dated 573 by the *Annales Cambriae.* This date is some 27 years later than the onset of Merlin's madness according to the chronology of the *VM* (*Vita Merlini,* ed. Clarke, 140, n. to line 431 ff.). Jocelin's *Life of Kentigern,* may reflect native traditions in claiming that the deaths of Rhydderch (Geoffrey's Rodarch) and Kentigern occurred in the same year (612, according to the *Annales Cambriae*) (Forbes, 241). But Merlin mentions Rodarch's death in his *O rabiem Britonnum* speech (lines 596–98), which would place it at least 60 years earlier. These contradictions simply demonstrate the difficulty Geoffrey confronted in fusing the traditions of his own creation, Merlin Ambrosius of the *HRB,* with those of Myrddin of the Welsh. The fact that he does not name the conflict between Peredur and Gwenddolau in the *VM* as the Battle of Arfderydd, perhaps reflects his desire to keep matters a little hazy on this point. Perhaps he also thought that such problems would only nag the overly scrupulous. Later readers such as Gerald of Wales, however, often insisted on distinguishing between two Merlins: Merlin Ambrosius of the *HRB*, and Merlin Calidonius of the *VM*, in spite of Geoffrey's efforts in the *VM* to show that they were the same person.[14]

The Welsh poem, *Afallennau*, the earliest copy of which is found in the *Black Book of Carmarthen* alludes to Myrddin's remorse over the death of his sister's son (or son and daughter). Although the poem does not specifically connect these deaths with the Battle of Arfderydd and Myrddin's retreat into Coed Celyddon, perhaps this was assumed knowledge on the audience's part. The theme of a man fleeing to the wilderness specifically as a penance after mistakenly killing his sister's son in battle is present elsewhere among works Geoffrey may have known. It occurs in the Breton *Life of Saint Gurthiern* (= Vortigern), sometimes cited as the source for Geoffrey's Latinized form of Gwenddolau's name, Guennolous (Saint Guennoleius's relics are mentioned in this life).[15] Geoffrey's Merlin, however, is initially overcome by grief (*tantus dolor*) over the death of Peredur's three brothers (*VM*, 71). No comfort that is offered him can draw him out of this condition, and he finally succumbs to madness (*VM*, 71; *furias*). Geoffrey's poem in this regard does not seem to follow its sources and analogs in exploring a state of madness occasioned by guilt, but focuses rather on the psychological consequences of the destructiveness of warfare. It is noteworthy, too, that in both the *Afallennau* and the *Oianau*, Myrddin laments his fallen condition and isolation from the pleasures of court life, whereas Geoffrey's Merlin resists all attempts to draw him back to courtly vanities. Indeed, as an indictment of the follies of court society and a celebration of the life of withdrawal, contemplation, learning, and friendship, the *VM* departs markedly from the narrative point of view of the Welsh poems.

The *Afallennau* also refers to Rhydderch, by his traditional Welsh epithet, *Hael*, "the Generous." This is reflected in Ganieda's epitaph for her husband in *VM*, 730, which refers to him as *Rodarchus Largus*, "Rodarch the Generous." The theme of his wife's infidelity, however, appears in a story constructed on the fish-and-ring motif in Jocelin's *Life of Kentigern*, but Jocelin's work is later than Geoffrey, and may have been influenced by him (Forbes, ch. 36). The wife's name in the *Life of Kentigern* is Langueth, not Ganieda. Ganieda appears to have been Geoffrey's version of Gwenddydd, the name of Merlin's sister in the *Afallennau*, *Hoianau* and the *Cyfoesi*. The theme of the queen's infidelity may have come to Geoffrey through traditions associated with Kentigern. The Welsh traditions of the *Cyfoesi* imparted the idea that Myrddin prophesied concerning the rulers to follow Rhydderch in response to his sister's urging. The same poem also contains information about Myrddin's life and suffering in the forest, the magical protection of an apple tree, to which the *Afallennau* is addressed, the companionship of a pig, and of course, many of Myrddin's predictions.

Late Antique Sources. The pseudoscience that dominates Taliesin's discourse in the second half of the poem derives from a variety of late antique compilations much revered during the Middle Ages and probably reflects the kind of erudition in vogue at Oxford during Geoffrey's residence there during the second half of the twelfth century. Most of the information contained in Taliesin's speech can be traced back to authorities such as Pliny, Solinus, Martianus Capella, Pomponius Mela, and Rabanus Maurus, but probably reached Geoffrey through Isidore of Seville's widely read *Etymologies* (seventh century), Bede's *De natura rerum* (eighth century), and the *mirabilia* chapters of Nennius's *Historia Brittonum* (ninth century), or the twelfth-century humanist encyclopedists such as Bernardus Silvestris, Adelard of Bath, Guillaume de Conches, the *De imagine mundi* (attributed to Honorius of Autun), or the *Liber Floridus* of Lambert of Saint Omer (*Vita Merlini,* ed. Clarke, 6–15; Faral, 2:373–84). No doubt Geoffrey was writing for an audience who delighted in the knowledge of this learned material for its own sake. The library at Lincoln cathedral, which Geoffrey must have known, possessed among its books, copies of Solinus, and Isidore, and a *mappamundi* (*Vita Merlini,* ed. Clarke, 8, and n. 5).

As with his other sources, Geoffrey molded "scientific" texts to his own ends. He based his description of the Fortunate Island, for example, on Isidore of Seville's Islands of Fortunate Women (*insulae fortunatarum*), but has Taliesin identify this place with the Island of Apples (*Insula pomorum que Fortunata vocatur*) to which Arthur was carried after the Battle of Camblan (*Vita Merlini,* ed. Clarke, 147, 182–83). The *HRB* calls the place simply the Island of Avalon (*Insula Avallonis*), but Geoffrey exploited the similarity of the place-name Avalon and the Welsh word for apple (Thorpe, 261; *afal*). Apples grew in abundance on Isidore's Island of Fortunate Women, as did crops and vegetables, which grew in place of grass. This provided Geoffrey with another opportunity to link the *HRB* and the *VM* together, while at the same time exploiting the rich associations of Isidore's Island of Fortunate Woman. Again, where Isidore never explains why the island is called *fortunatarum* ("of fortunate women"), Geoffrey placed Morgen and her sisters there. Morgen appears to have been Geoffrey's own creation, although she may have been suggested to him by the Welsh Modron (= Matrona), derived from the Celtic fertility goddess, or from the Morrígan, the Irish battle goddesses, or from Liban/Muirgein, a dimorphic Irish sea goddess, half-salmon and half-woman. He may also have been influenced by Pomponius Mela's description of the island of Sena, which was inhabited by nine virgins endowed with shape-shifting, medicinal, and prophetic powers (*Vita Merlini*, ed. Clarke, 203–8; Faral, 2:301–8).

The ship that took Taliesin and Arthur to the Island of Apples was piloted by Barinthus, a character whom Geoffrey borrowed from the *Voyage of Saint Brendan* (*Navigatio Sancti Brendani*), either directly from the Latin text (ninth century) or from a vernacular translation, such as the Norman-French version by Benedeit (*Vita Merlini*, ed. Clarke, 165–66).[16] Geoffrey's Barinthus, however, is knowledgeable about the seas and the stars, whereas the Barinthus of the *Voyage of Saint Brendan* arrives quite mysteriously at the Promised Land, an island, after being enveloped at sea by a thick fog. Geoffrey molded both Barinthus and Taliesin to his own purposes in the *VM*, using them to stress the poem's underlying theme concerning the redemptive power of knowledge.

Much of Taliesin's information on cosmology, geography, and the weather came from Bede's *De natura rerum*, but here, too, significant differences are found. The depiction of the five zones of the world are the same as in Bede, but the idea that gems are formed from the passing of Dione's beams through Pisces onto the frigid sea, Taliesin attributes to the Arabs, an acknowledgment perhaps of the growing influence of Arab science on Western European learning during Geoffrey's day (*VM*, 800–4). Adelard of Bath, a contemporary of Geoffrey, translated the astronomical tables of Mohammed ben Musa al-Khwarizmi and the Elements of Euclid from an Arabic source, while his treatise, entitled *Questiones naturales*, sets forth what its author had learned about the natural world from the Arabs.[17] The presence of three distinct orders of spirits inhabiting three celestial regions, including the *cacodemones*, is found in Guillaume de Conches rather than in Bede and is clearly an attempt to link this section of Taliesin's discourse with Maugantius's information in the *HRB* on the *incubi demones*, which he claims to have found in Apuleius's *De deo Socratis* (see chapter 3; *VM*, 771–87; Thorpe, 168; Faral, 2:380).

The nature lore of the *VM* is most fully expounded by Taliesin in the second half of the poem. Taliesin's disquisitions serve a consolatory purpose and have a distinctively Boethian flavor. Like Philisophy's colloquy with Boethius in *The Consolation of Philosophy*, they are intended to assure Merlin, in spite of outward appearances to the contrary, of the justice of

God's stewardship of the universe. They assure him that God is the *conditor orbis*, the founder of the world, whose stabilizing presence mediates opposing forces, maintains dynamic tensions, resolves contradictions and regulates all things (*VM*, 737). Taliesin's discourse stresses the curative qualities of fish, the fertility and abundance of the sea, and the tripartite order of celestial spirits who regenerate the world by renewing the seed of things (*VM*, 786–87). The nature lore of the *VM* is thus brought into the Boethian framework of the poem in its insistence on the order and harmony which God bestowed on all parts of the world.

Geoffrey's refashioning of Boethian vocabulary of order and stability may owe something to the philosophers of the "school of Chartres." Like the Chartrians, Taliesin celebrates the liberating power of knowledge of the physical world. Stars, rivers, springs, and animals all mirror the stability of nature and its curative and restorative properties. Prophetic knowledge, too, was waiting to be unlocked by the learned man or woman who withdraws from the distractions of court with its greed and its amorous and political intrigue.

In celebrating intimacy, friendship, companionship, personal and family loyalty, the interior life, and the renunciation of worldly pleasures, the *VM* thus marks a rather dramatic departure from the concerns of the *HRB*. We learn little of the interior life of individuals in Geoffrey's *HRB*, and while the history is justly esteemed for its colorful representations of action, its sense of character is rather flat. The *VM*, by contrast, is essentially the story of the suffering of one man driven mad by grief. His grief is personal, being precipitated by the death of the three brothers of Peredur.

The company formed in the wilderness at the end of the poem is a learned one. Taliesin has brought back from Brittany a vast storehouse of learning about nature. Ganieda's withdrawal into the wilderness is followed by her acquisition of prophetic powers. All four companions live under the guidance of Merlin who is disciplining his flesh as a means to earn heavenly reward. On the whole, the picture drawn in the *VM* is one of austerity and renunciation undertaken in order to achieve leisure for study, learned conversation, observation of natural phenomena, contemplation, and the close ties of family and friends. This might well be seen as Geoffrey's judgment on the violence of the period of civil war in which he lived, a projection of twelfth-century political conflicts on the distant past of early Britain. The elegiac tone of the narrative certainly suits the mood of the nation during the civil strife of Stephen's reign with its violence, insecurities, uncertain loyalties, and outright betrayals. In Geoffrey's own day the civil war had given rise to deep theological insecurity.

The Anglo-Saxon Chronicle (Whitelock, 200) claims that during the chaos and misrule of Britain under Stephen many people proclaimed openly that Christ and his saints were asleep. Taliesin's comment that no one has seen more fierce civil wars (*fera proelia inter concives*) than Merlin, must have had special resonance for Geoffrey's audience (*VM*, 976–78).

Merlin rejects the allurements of court life and persistently contrasts the self-sufficiency of the forest to the excesses of the court (*VM*, 141–245). His first prophecy, particularly embittered in its denunciatory tone, is a jeremiad against the inveterate habits of violence that have characterized British history (*VM*, 580–688). The future offers no comfort. Merlin foresees that the Normans will fall to the same pattern in their turn.

The presence of numerous hermitages in the England of Geoffrey's day bears testimony to the appeal of the life of quiet withdrawal. Ganieda's decision to abandon court for a life of solitude is rather closely paralleled in the career of Christina of Markyate (1096/98–1155/66), a contemporary of Geoffrey of Monmouth. Christina fled from the betrothal her family arranged for her and obtained the protection of a hermit named Eadwin. Later, with the help of Roger, a hermit at Markyate, she appealed her betrothal and had it officially annulled by Thurston, archbishop of York. Like Ganieda, Christina was a clairvoyant and was often carried away in ecstatic trances (*rapiebatur in exstasim*) where she received revelations from the Holy Spirit.[18] Her dedication to the ascetic ideal earned her great fame. She was sought out by secular and ecclesiastical dignitaries from all over England and abroad. If Geoffrey had Christina of Markyate in mind when writing the *VM*, he may have learned of her through his Lincoln connections, for Christina made her monastic profession before Alexander, bishop of Lincoln, who also consecrated Markyate priory in 1145.

Classical Sources. The *VM* is written in Latin hexameters, the metrical form used by Virgil, Statius, and Ovid, and naturally assumes an audience thoroughly familiar with Latin poetry. Geoffrey had briefly turned his hand to poetry once before in the *HRB* by representing Brutus's ritual invocation to Diana and the goddess's response, both in distichs (Thorpe, 65; Wright, 1984, 9). Not surprisingly for a man who earned the title of *magister* at Oxford, Geoffrey adheres closely to the conventions of classical prosody in the *VM*, lapsing only occasionally into false quantities. In the prologue to the *VM*, Geoffrey calls on the Muses to accompany him in his song and compares his poetic talents unfavorably to Orpheus and a group of Augustan poets whose names he recalled from Ovid's *Ex Ponto*, 4, 16. Elsewhere he turns to Ovid's *Heroides* for the names of three women in antiquity whose suffering he likens to that of Gwendolena and Ganieda, and he later alludes to Minerva and to the myth of Daedalus (*VM*, 191–95, 736, 923). Apart from such occasional allusions, and the poem's language and meter, however, the *VM* does not rely heavily on classical literature. Part of the pleasure of reading or listening to the *VM* still derives from the novelty of its exotic subject matter being expressed in classical metrical form.

The *Vita Merlini* and Geoffrey's Other Works

Geoffrey attempted to show that Merlin of the *HRB* was the same person as Merlin of the *VM*. To begin with, he set the events of his poem during the last days of Constantine, Arthur's immediate successor, and during the reign of the usurper Conan, the second to rule after Arthur, according to his own chronology in the *HRB* (Thorpe, 262–63). This was a wise choice on Geoffrey's part. Having Merlin live through the reigns of Vortigern, Aurelius, Uther, and Arthur, would convincingly make him an old man upon Constantine's accession. Moreover, for a tale of madness occasioned by grief over the death of three brothers in battle, the Constantine-Conan period was the perfect backdrop. The *HRB* states that Conan "took delight in civil wars," and usurped the throne after Constantine's death by imprisoning his own (unnamed) uncle, who should have reigned after Constantine, and by murdering his two cousins. In the *VM* Conan is said to be Constantine's *cognatus* ("blood relative"), and Geoffrey has him rebelling directly against Constantine himself, perhaps wishing to stress the personal nature of his betrayal.

The two prophecies Merlin utters in the *VM* also conveniently link him to Merlin Ambrosius of the *HRB*. In some instances, Geoffrey has Merlin repeat predictions he had made in the *HRB*. Thus, his first prophecy, beginning with the lament *O rabiem Britonnum,* is mostly a réchauffage of *PM* prophecies and post-Arthurian history as found in book 11 of the *HRB* (*VM*, 580–688). Merlin explains to Ganieda that he rehearsed these predictions years earlier in greater detail for Vortigern while they sat on the banks of the drained pool and he interpreted the "mystic warfare" (*mystica bella*) of the two dragons. This refers, of course, to the encounter of Vortigern and Merlin at Dinas Emrys in the *HRB* and to the *PM* (Thorpe, 169). His second prophecy restates the Conan-Cadwallader scenario from the *HRB* (*VM*, 941–1135).

Merlin Calidonius's deep interest in the secrets of nature, one of the chief topics in the *VM,* is also paralleled in the *HRB.* At the outset of Merlin's career in the *HRB,* when yet a boy-prophet, he reveals that fighting dragons, unknown even to Vortigern's wise men, lurk beneath the pool at Dinas Emrys (Thorpe, 169). Merlin Ambrosius in the *HRB* is not only a prophet, but also an enchanter in possession of knowledge of medicines that have extraordinary powers to change one person's appearance into that of another (Thorpe, 206–8). Also, as the architect of Stonehenge, he knew of the ancient medicinal properties of the megaliths. The giants who first brought these stones to Ireland, Merlin explains to Aurelius, cured themselves of their wounds by bathing in herbal water poured over the stones (Thorpe, 196). Much of the nature lore of the *VM* is similarly concerned with the curative power of rivers, lakes, and streams. Merlin himself restores his old friend and companion Maeldin to sanity in the *VM* by commanding that he be administered water from a newly sprung stream (*VM,* 1433–41).[19] Merlin Calidonius's association with springs recalls the scene in the *HRB* when Aurelius's messengers find Merlin in the region of the Gewissei at the Galabes Spring that, we are informed, he was wont to frequent (Thorpe, 195–96). Merlin of the *VM* is no longer simply a prophet and enchanter, but has become king of Demetia, the region of South Wales that included Carmarthen, where Vortigern's agents first found him as a boy in the *HRB.* And, of course, the suggestion in the *HRB* that Arthur will be cured of his wounds is more fully developed in the *VM* when Morgen assures Taliesin that the king can indeed be restored to health if he stays for a long period under her care (Thorpe, 261; *VM,* 932–40). It should be noted, too, that nowhere in Geoffrey's works does he ever bring Arthur and Merlin together.

Moreover, even many of the most opaque prophecies in the *PM,* whatever their political significance may be, demonstrate Merlin Ambrosius rich stock of nature lore. Like the pseudoscience of Taliesin's discourse, Merlin's prophecies frequently mention the extraordinary powers of springs, rivers, and baths. To cite but one example in the *PM,* Merlin foresees three springs rising up at Winchester: anyone drinking from the first will enjoy long life free from illness, the second brings on death from insatiable hunger, while the third causes the one drinking from it to die suddenly and makes burying his body impossible (Thorpe, 177).

The high esteem Geoffrey accords to the Breton people in his history is reflected in the *VM* in Taliesin's sojourn in Brittany under the tutelage of Gildas. Gildas's association with Brittany was not Geoffrey's invention; it dates back to the Breton *Life of Gildas* (ninth or eleventh century), which claims (chapter 19) that Gildas's book was written at the request of British monks who visited him in his retreat at the Ile de Rhuys, north-west of Quiberon Bay in Brittany (*Vita Merlini,* ed. Clarke, 185). Both the Breton Life and the one by Geoffrey's contemporary, Caradoc of Llancarfan, contain stories of Gildas's miraculous healing ability, his rais-ing of a fountain, turning water into wine, his ability to command streams to follow him, and his extreme asceticism (Henken, 135–40).[20] Gildas was known throughout the Middle Ages by the epithet *Sapiens,* "the Wise," and the *HRB* claims that Gildas translated the Molmutine Laws from British into Latin (Thorpe, 94). Some readers have seen in Taliesin's tutelage under Gildas in the *VM,* a veiled allusion by Geoffrey to the preeminence of certain Breton scholars during the twelfth century, particularly Bernard of Chartres and his learned brother Thierry, both of whom were apparently Breton (Faral, 2:381). Otto of Frising said of these two men that they showed that Brittany produced an abundance of brilliant students particularly devoted to the liberal arts.[21] In any case, in the *VM,* a work that exalts the quiet life of learning and prayer, the omnivorous knowledge of Taliesin derives from the school of Brittany. The poem's praise of the life of learning has its analog in the *HRB,* where Geoffrey claims that in Arthur's day in the City of the Legions, there was a "college of two hundred learned men, who were skilled in astronomy and the other arts, and who watched with great attention the courses of the stars and so by their careful computations prophesied for King Arthur any prodigies due at that time" (Thorpe, 226–27). Arthur himself in the *HRB* displays occasional curiosity and learning about the geographical *mirabilia* of Britain. He delivers a learned discourse to Hoel on the fish in the corners of the square pool near Loch Lomond, and remarks on the curious behavior of the pool known as Lin Ligua near the Severn in Wales (Thorpe, 219).[22]

Taliesin's scientific excursus in the second part of the poem is also related to certain passages in the *HRB*. His discourse on the *cacodemones,* the sublunar spirits thought to lie with women and get them pregnant, for example, recalls Maugantius explaining to Vortigern in the *HRB* (Thorpe, 168) that an *incubus demon* may have been Merlin's father. Maugantius claims to have derived his information from Apuleius's *De Deo Socratis,* while Taliesin names no source for his knowledge of the *cacodemones.* Faral, however, pointed out that the term *cacodemones* is used of these intermediate spirits by Guillaume de Conches, a member of the school of Chartres (Faral, 2:379–80).

The Arthurian Matter

The *VM* complements the *HRB* also in providing much circumstantial detail on Arthur's fate following the Battle of Camblan, a topic on which the *HRB,* as we saw in chapter 4, was coy and evasive. After Camblan, according to the *HRB,* Arthur was carried away mortally wounded to the Isle of Avalon, "so that the wounds might be attended to" (Thorpe, 261). The *PM* was even less specific on this subject, stating simply that "his [Arthur's] end will be in doubt" (Thorpe, 172; *exitus eius dubius erit*).

The *VM,* however, provides a more detailed picture (*VM,* (930–40). Here Taliesin tells Merlin that he and Barinthus, a man who knew the seas and the stars, accompanied the wounded Arthur to the Island of Apples, or the Fortunate Island. We learn not only that the king's wounds would be attended to there, but that Morgen had promised to cure Arthur if he stayed a considerable time with her and submitted to her medicine (*medicamine*).

Most important perhaps is Merlin's response to Taliesin, when the latter suggests that Arthur should be called back if he has sufficiently recovered, in order to expel the Saxons and restore the ancient peace to the island of Britain (*VM,* 958–75). Significantly, Merlin rejects this solution and predicts an alternative liberation scenario for the British folk: Conan will arrive in his chariot from Brittany and ally himself with Cadwallader: "They will create an alliance, a firm league of the Scots, the Welsh, the Cornish, and the men of Brittany. Then they will restore to the natives the crown that had been lost. The enemy will be driven out and the time of Brutus will be back once more. The natives will administer their own cities by the time-hallowed laws. They will once again undertake the subjection of distant kings and make a vigorous effort to bring these kingdoms under their sway" (*Vita Merlini,* ed. Clarke, 105).

This, of course, is a reiteration of the idea of the restoration of British sovereignty precisely as Merlin had foreseen it in the *PM* and clearly represents Geoffrey's rejection of Arthur as the revenant hero or as the "once and future king." On the contrary, Merlin's prophecy here in the *VM* reasserts the central role long reserved for Conan and Cadwallader in Welsh vaticinal literature as shown in chapter 2. Given the sensitive political position in which Geoffrey found himself, this was a cautious step for him to take. On the one hand, he refused to put Merlin's authority behind Arthur as a redeemer king, but he did stand behind the general promise of British restoration at some vague future date under the stewardship of the two Welsh leaders. The very idea of British

Restoration could hardly be viewed with indifference by the supporters
of either Stephen or Matilda during the 1150s, but the names Conan
and Cadwallader surely represented far less of a threat to them than did
Arthur, whose fame was in large measure the result of Geoffrey's *HRB*.

The *VM* also elaborates on Arthur's destination following the Battle
of Camblan, which we learn to be the Island of Apples, or the Fortunate
Island (*VM*, 908–40). Geoffrey exploited the Island of Apples as part of
his utopian strategy in the *VM*. Morgen, the most beautiful of the nine
sisters who rule the island with kindly law (*geniali lege*), is, like Merlin,
knowledgeable in the art of shape-shifting and medicine, and ranks first
among her learned sisters. The Fortunate Island in the *VM* represents a
variation on the topos of a lost paradise or Golden Age, and owes much
to Ovid's depiction of the *aurea aetas* in the *Metamorphoses,* and to the
image of the happy otherworld in Celtic mythology. On the Fortunate
Island, the inhabitants enjoy longevity, living to be 100 years old, the
soil produces abundant fruits without labor of the plough, the wounds
received in this world are cured, the king is restored to health, and so on.
Significantly, too, the Island of Apples represents an inversion of patriar-
chal political authority. It is a land ruled harmoniously by a female kin-
group and enjoys the happiness that eludes mortals in this world: peace,
fertility, health, leisure, knowledge, and family solidarity. Merlin's woodland retreat in the *VM* is set up as an analog to Morgen's magical kingdom by establishing its own ascetic ideals: renunciation of the vanities of
court life, prayer, companionship, learning, and spiritual and moral
reformation.

Merlin is followed into the woodland by his sister Ganieda, who abandons her life at court, and dedicates herself to leading a chaste life (*vitam
. . . pudicam*) in the company of her brother and his colleagues; by
Taliesin, who renounces all vanities, and by Maeldin, recently restored to
sanity, who chooses to adopt Merlin's example of living simply.

Geoffrey appears to have wanted to distinguish Ganieda's prophecies
from those of her brother. The first of Merlin's prophecies is brought on
just after he breaks a long fast and wanders through his house gazing on
the stars (*VM* 570–79). In a later reflection on his prophetic gift, Merlin
refers to himself as being "taken out of his true self" (*VM*, 1161–68;
Raptus eram michimet). In this state of suffering and distress, he is
deprived of rest by the "harsh law" (*districta lege*) of his condition, but as
a result of it he comes to know the history of ancient peoples, future
events, and the secrets of nature (*rerum secreta*). He thanks God for sending the healing spring whose waters cure him of his madness, and release

him from the burden of secret knowledge. Madness and isolation, in other words, are the psychic conditions out of which Merlin's prophecies are born. Geoffrey speaks of Ganieda, too, as being swept up (*rapiebat ad alta*) in her own prophetic trance, but this condition is made to appear transitory, being brought on, we are informed, only occasionally (*quandoque*). Moreover, Ganieda's prophecies, unlike Merlin's, are visions, perhaps even self-induced ones, caused by her gazing at the sun's rays glittering in the windows of her brother's house. And there is no evidence that these visions involve mental suffering of any kind. Unlike her brother, Ganieda focuses her prophetic attention exclusively on twelfth-century events familiar to Geoffrey's contemporaries. She foresees armed conflicts in Oxford, Lincoln, and Winchester, and a battle that will take place in the reign of Coel between the men of Deira and Gwent "under the hill of Urien" (cf. Thorpe, 131–32). She bewails a famine that will begin in Wales and soon overspread the entire island, and she exhorts the "Normans" to leave Britain along with their armies, which have consumed the fertile bounty of nature. Her prophecy ends with an appeal to Christ to end war and bring peace to the land.

Ganieda's prophecies have been interpreted variously, but their common theme is the disorder unleashed by the conflict between the partisans of King Stephen and his rival, the Empress Matilda (*Vita Merlini*, ed. Clarke, 21, 153–54). Mention of helmeted troops occupying Oxford while holy men and bishops are restrained in bonds may allude to the capture of Bishops Roger of Salisbury and Alexander of Lincoln by Stephen during the Council of Oxford in 1139. In her prophecy concerning Lincoln (Kaerloytcoyt?), Ganieda envisions one of two men escaping from the besieged town and returning with a fierce people (*cum gente fera*) and their chief to capture the commander of the assaulting army. She bemoans the crime by which the "stars" should thus have power to capture the "sun." These utterances were interpreted by Ward as signifying Stephen's siege of Lincoln in February 1141, when the king blockaded William of Roumare and Randolph of Chester in Lincoln. Randolph, one of the "stars" presumably, escaped and returned to liberate the town and capture the king, the "sun" of the prophecy, with the help of the Welsh, the "fierce people," and their leader Robert of Gloucester. Ganieda next sees two moons over Winchester, two lions raging with great ferocity, and the vagaries of a great battle. This prophecy ends with the Boar of Brittany taking away the moon under the protection of an ancient oak. The prophetic scenario depicted here has been interpreted as a thinly veiled account of the siege of Winchester in September 1141, when the forces of the king and the empress, the "two moons" of the prophecy, clashed. The empress is said to have been saved from being captured by Geoffroi Botrel, a Breton nobleman (hence the appellation *Boar of Brittany*), or perhaps by Brian the son of the illustrious Breton leader Alain Fergant. The allusion to the battle "under the hill of Urien" is difficult to interpret, but may possibly refer to the Battle of Consyllt (Coleshill) in 1150 in which Owain Gwynedd defeated Ranulf, earl of Chester, and Madoc ap Maredudd. Ganieda's indictment of the "Normans" probably is intended to apply to the auxiliary troops brought by both factions to England from Normandy, rather than to the long-settled Anglo-Norman residents, the principal contestants in the civil war. If these interpretations are correct, Ganieda's denunciation of civil strife would have resonances in Geoffrey's own life because he was among the official witnesses to the Treaty of Westminster in 1153, which brought an end to the civil war.

Following Ganieda's prophecy, Merlin concludes that the spirit has chosen to close his mouth and book and to confer the office of prophet on Ganieda. The *VM* thus ends with the suggestion that the silence of this small community is not absolute, but will be broken occasionally by Ganieda, who will use her new office to denounce the follies of the world and to invoke God's help in restoring peace and justice.

The three prophecies of the poem thus strike the same elegiac mood. They lament the inveterate violence to which the land has been and will be subjected before its anticipated redemption. Having Merlin reject Arthur as revenant savior may also be part of Geoffrey's strategy of rejecting naive hopes that the deep-rooted political antagonisms of his day could be resolved so easily. Merlin and Ganieda both envision, on the contrary, a long period of suffering for the island's inhabitants. Moreover, read against the background of the civil war, their prophecies take on a special relevance. They fit well with the gloomy mood of the poem and in its praise of a life of quiet withdrawal from the corrupting influences of the court, with its intrigue, betrayals, and self-interest.

The *VM* thus brings to a close the long career of Merlin and marks a new introspection in Geoffrey's political outlook. Passing the office of prophet on to Ganieda, may have been Geoffrey's way of indicating that he would write no new prophecies for Merlin, and also perhaps to discourage any others from being foisted on him.

In the *VM* Geoffrey turned his artistic attention away from the grand exploits that had been the subject of the *HRB* in order to focus on a smaller, more personal canvas. In place of the great events of history, the

VM emphasizes the importance of learning, companionship, reconciliation, magic, women, and withdrawal from the active life of court. And in place of the long chronological sweep of history, the poem chronicles the suffering and redemption of one man in the twilight of his years. Geoffrey's literary career began with the *PM* and reached its apex with the *HRB*, where Merlin and his prophecies once again played a crucial part. Fittingly, Geoffrey's last work, *VM*, ends by silencing the prophet with whose legend and utterances Geoffrey's own name has become so closely identified.

Notes and References

Chapter One

1. Geoffrey of Monmouth, *The History of the Kings of Britain,* trans. with intro. Lewis Thorpe (Harmondsworth: Penguin Books, 1966), 52, 171 (in the dedication to the *Prophecies of Merlin*), 257; *The Life of Merlin, Geoffrey of Monmouth, Vita Merlini,* ed. with intro. Basil Clarke (Cardiff: University of Wales Press, 1973), 134 (line 1526); hereafter cited as *HRB, PM,* and *VM,* respectively. (All references in text to Thorpe which appear without a date refer to this work.)

2. John Edward Lloyd, "Geoffrey of Monmouth," *English Historical Review* 57 (October 1942): 460–61; hereafter cited in text.

3. On Monmouth, see E. K. Chambers, *Arthur of Britain* (London: Sidgwick & Jackson, 1927; reprint, Cambridge: Speculum Historiale, 1964), 20–21; J. S. P. Tatlock, *The Legendary History of Britain, Geoffrey of Monmouth's Historia Regum Brittanniae and Its Early Vernacular Versions* (Berkeley: University of California Press, 1950; reprint, New York, 1974), 440–41; Edmond Faral, *La légend arthurienne: Études et documents* (Paris: Librairie Ancienne Honoré Champion, 1929), 2, 18; these studies hereafter cited in text.

4. Paul Marchegay, *Chartes anciennes du Prieuré de Monmouth en Angleterre* (Les Roches-Baritaud, 1879), 22.

5. The charters have been published by H. E. Salter, "Geoffrey of Monmouth and Oxford," *English Historical Review* 34 (1919): 382–85; hereafter cited in text.

6. Hans Claude Hamilton, ed., *Historia rerum Anglicana Willelmi Parvi . . . de Newburgh* (London: Sumptibus Societatis, 1856), 1, 4: *"Gaufridus hic dictus est, agnomen habens Arturi; pro eo quod fabulas de Arturo, ex priscis Britonum figmentis sumptas et ex proprio auctas, per superductum Latini sermonis colorem honesto historiae nomine palliavit."* Hereafter cited in text.

7. John Edward Lloyd, *A History of Wales from the Earliest Times to the Edwardian Conquest* (London: Longmans, Green, 1939), 524.

8. For the name *Arthur ap Redr* in a Dyfed genealogy, see P. C. Bartrum, ed., with notes and indexes, *Early Welsh Genealogical Tracts,* (Cardiff: University of Wales Press, 1966), 4, 10, 45, 106.

9. M. Dominica Legge, "Master Geoffrey Arthur," in *An Arthurian Tapestry, Essays in Memory of Lewis Thorpe,* ed. Kenneth Varty (Glasgow: University of Glasgow Press, 1981), 23–24.

10. *The Anglo-Saxon Chronicle, A Revised Translation,* ed. Dorothy Whitelock with David Douglas and Susie Tucker (New Brunswick, N.J.: Rutgers University Press, 1961), 198–99.

11. *"Ergo meis ceptis faveas vatemque tueri/auspicio meliore velis quam fecerit alter/cui modo succedis merito promotus honori"* ("Approve, then, my project, and be ready to be more indulgent to this poet than was that other whom you have just succeeded, attaining an honour well-deserved").

12. On Robert, see Clarke, 1973, 212.

13. On Robert, bishop of Exeter, see D. W. Blake, "The Bishops of Exeter 1138–1160," *Transactions of the Devonshire Association for the Advancement of Science* 114 (1982): 71–78, esp. 72; for John of Cornwall, see Michael J. Curley, "A New Edition of John of Cornwall's *Prophetia Merlini*," *Speculum* 57 (1982): 217–49.

14. See the discussion of this in chapter 2.

15. Christopher Brooke, "The Archbishops of St. David's, Llandaff and Caerleon-on-Usk," in *Studies in the Early British Church,* ed. Nora K. Chadwick et al. (Cambridge: Cambridge University Press, 1958), 228–33. Brooke concludes: "If it [the *Book of Llandaff*] was not written by Caradoc, then I should feel tempted to resuscitate the old and much abused theory that it was the work of Geoffrey of Monmouth himself" (Brooke, 232). For more recent abuse of the idea of Geoffrey's part in composing the *Book of Llandaff,* see E. D. Jones, "The Book of Llandaff," *National Library of Wales Journal* 4 (1946): 154; hereafter cited in text.

16. S. M. Harris, "Liturgical Commemorations of Welsh Saints (II), St. Asaph," *Journal of the Historical Society of the Church of Wales* 6 (1956): 5–24.

17. Gerald of Wales twice refers disparagingly to the small town and church of Saint Asaph. Gerald of Wales, *The Journey through Wales and The Descriptions of Wales,* trans. Lewis Thorpe (Harmondsworth: Penguin Books, 1978), *Travels,* 2, 10; *Description,* 1, 4; hereafter cited in text.

18. A. W. Haddan and W. Stubbs, eds., *Councils and Ecclesiastical Documents Relating to Great Britain and Ireland* (Oxford: Clarendon Press, 1869), 1, 360. Geoffrey's appointment was also noted by Robert of Torigni in his *Chronica* under the year 1152 (R. Howlett, ed., *Chronicles of the Reigns of Stephen, Henry II and Richard I,* 4 vols. [London: n.p., 1884–89], 4, 168). On Robert's possession of a copy of the *HRB,* which he showed to Henry of Huntingdon, see chapter 2.

19. H. W. C. Davis, ed., *Regesta Regum Anglo-Normannorum, 1066–1154,* vol. 3, in *Regesta regis Stephani ac Mathildis Impertaricis,* eds. H. A. Cronne and R. H. C. Davis, (Oxford: Clarendon Press, 1968), 97–99, no. 272.

20. W. Owen, ed., *The Myvyrian Archaiology of Wales,* (Denbigh, 2d ed.), 711. Relevant passages can be found in Tatlock, 1974, 446–47; Lloyd, 1942, 462–64, and Faral, 2:3–6.

21. Geoffrey, however, was witness to charters in the vicinity of Oxford during the early 1150s (Salter, 384).

22. J. Gwenogvryn Evans, *The Text of the Book of Llan Dav, Reproduced from the Gwysaney Manuscript* (Oxford, 1893; reprint, Aberystwyth: National Library of Wales, 1979), xviii–xxvii; hereafter cited in text.

23.   Elissa R. Henken, *Traditions of the Welsh Saints* (Cambridge: D. S. Brewer, 1987), 61–63.

24.   Wendy Davies, *An Early Welsh Microcosm, Studies in the Llandaff Charters* (London: Royal Historical Society, 1978), 2–22.

25.   *Brut y Tywysogyon or The Chronicle of the Princes, Red Book of Hergest Version,* critical text and trans. with intro. and notes Thomas Jones (Cardiff: University of Wales Press, 1955), 132–33: *"Yn y ulwydyn honno y bu uarw Jeffrei, escob Llan Daf, a Rosser, jarll Henffor{d}"* ("In that year died Geoffrey, bishop of Llandaff, and Roger, earl of Hereford"); hereafter cited in text. Lloyd traced the *Brut y Tywysogyon's* claim that Geoffrey was bishop of Llandaff to a scribal error for Llan Elwy (Lloyd, 1942, 466). Nicholas ap Gwrgant was bishop of Llandaff from 1148 until 1163. The variant *ar offern* ("at mass") for *a Rosser* ("and Roger") in certain manuscripts of the *Brut y Tywysogyon* gave rise to the idea (found in the *Strata Florida Brut,* for example) that Geoffrey died while saying mass (Chambers, 21).

Chapter Two

1.   The title of the work *Historia regum Britannie* is that of the editors since Commelin, who was the first to use it in his edition of 1587. The same is true for the divisions of the *HRB* into 12 books. Neither of these traditions, however, is without organic justification in the narrative. Geoffrey calls his work *Historia regum Britannie* in his preface, although elsewhere he calls it *de gestis regum Britannicorum* (Wright, 1984, 73), while in the *VM* (line 1529) he refers to it as *Gesta Britonnum.*

2.   Henry's letter to Warin has been recently edited and analyzed by Neil Wright ("The Place of Henry of Huntingdon's *Epistola ad Warinum* in the text-history of Geoffrey of Monmouth's *Historia Regum Britannie:* a preliminary investigation," in *France and the British Isles in the Middle Ages and Renaissance,* ed. Gillian Jondorf and D. N. Dumville [Woodbridge, Suffolk: Boydell Press, 1991], 71–113, esp. 93). See also Robert de Torigni, *Chronique,* ed. L. Delisle, 97 f. in Howlett, 4, 64. Text in Chambers, 251–52.

3.   On a possible fourth, see Wright, 1984, xii, n. 17.

4.   This was not an unknown practice in Geoffrey's day. Matilda, first wife of Henry I, was the dedicatee of Benedeit's *Voyage of Saint Brendan.* After her death (d. 1118), however, the scribes replaced her name in the dedication with that of the king's new wife, Adelise of Louvain. See M. Dominica Legge, "L'influence littéraire de la cour d'Henri Beauclerc," in *Mélanges offerts à Rita Lejeune* (Gembloux, Belgium: Editions J. Duculot, 1969), I, 683.

5.   Mary-Dominica Legge, "Gautier Espec, Ailred de Rievaulx et la matière de Bretagne," in *Mélanges de langue et de littérature du Moyen Age et de la Renaissance offerts à Jean Frappier* (Geneva: Droz, 1970), 619–23. Legge conjectures that Robert Duke of Gloucester carried to Normandy in 1137 the copy of the *HRB* that Henry of Huntingdon saw at Bec in 1139 (Legge, 1970, 620–21).

6. This very protestation sounds like a borrowing from Terence's *Phormio* 500: "*Ut phaleratis ducas dictis me!*"

7. Valerie I. J. Flint, "*Historia Regum Britanniae* of Geoffrey of Monmouth: Parody and Its Purpose. A Suggestion," *Speculum* 54 (1979): 459–60.

8. Geoffrey Ashe, "'A Certain Very Ancient Book': Traces of an Arthurian Source in Geoffrey of Monmouth's History," *Speculum* 56 (1981): 301–23.

9. See T. D. Crawford, "On the Linguistic Competence of Geoffrey of Monmouth," *Medium Aevum* 51 (1982): 152–62.

10. The word derives from *Kombrogi (sg. *Kombrogos), which yields the Welsh *Cymry* (singular, *Cymro*). See Rachel Bromwich, A. O. H. Jarman, Brynley F. Roberts, ed., *The Arthur of the Welsh, The Arthurian Legend in Medieval Welsh Literature* (Cardiff: University of Wales Press, 1991), 253; hereafter cited in text.

11. Flint thinks it probable that Walter was a "mischievous collaborator" in Geoffrey's pretense to be in possession of an ancient British book (Flint, 459–60). Brynley F. Roberts, "Sylwadau ar Sieffre o Fynwy a'r *Historia Regum Britanniae*," *Llên Cymru* 12 (1972–73), 134–35; hereafter cited in text.

12. On Geoffrey's use of the genealogies see Arthur E. Hutson, *British Personal Names in the Historia Regum Britanniae* (Berkeley: University of California Press, 1940); Brynley F. Roberts, "The Treatment of Personal Names in the Early Welsh Versions of *Historia Regum Britanniae*," *The Bulletin of the Board of Celtic Studies* 25 (1973); Brynley F. Roberts, "Geoffrey of Monmouth and Welsh Historical Tradition," *Nottingham Mediaeval Studies* 20 (1976). These studies hereafter cited in text.

13. Stuart Piggott, "The Sources of Geoffrey of Monmouth. I. The 'Pre-Roman' King-List," *Antiquity, A Quarterly Review of Archaeology* 15 (1941): 276–82.

14. If Piggott is right about the condition of the manuscript from which Geoffrey was working in this instance, it might well have appeared to be "a very ancient book."

15. The stylistic changes of this passage have been analyzed by Neil Wright, "Geoffrey of Monmouth and Gildas," *Arthurian Literature II,* ed. Richard Barber (Cambridge: D. S. Brewer, 1982), 5–7. The anonymous author of the Variant Version relies almost verbatim on Bede for this description of Britain. Neil Wright, ed., *The Historia Regum Britanniae of Geoffrey of Monmouth, II: The First Variant Version: A Critical Edition* (Cambridge: D. S. Brewer, 1988), xlii–xliii.

16. This is a theme that Geoffrey shared with Henry of Huntingdon, who remarks that "the pre-eminent wealth and advantages of England have excited the envy and cupidity of neighboring nations. It has, therefore, been very frequently invaded, and often subdued." Thomas Arnold, ed., *Henrici Archidiaconi Huntendunensis Historia Anglorum, The History of the English, by Henry,*

Archdeacon of Huntingdon, from A.D. *55 to* A.D. *1154, in Eight Books* (London: Longman, 1879), 14, hereafter cited in text.

17. See Tatlock, 1974, 53–56, on the name and its possible origin.

18. There may also have been a Breton-Trojan legend. See Caroline Brett, "Breton Latin Literature as Evidence for Literature in the Vernacular, A.D. 800–1300," *Cambridge Medieval Celtic Studies* 18 (Winter 1989): 17; Bernard Merdrignac, "L'Eneide et les traditions anciennes des Bretons," *Études celtiques* 20 (1983): 199–205.

19. See Faral, 1:262–88; Max Manitius, *Geschichte der lateinischen Literatur des Mittelalters* (Munich: C. H. Beck'sche Verlagsbuchhandlung, 1931; reprint, 1964) 1, 225, on the Trojan story in pseudo-Fredegar.

20. See the allusion to hunting laws in the *PM,* ch. 3.

21. The name *Assaracus* comes from Nennius and the *Aeneid,* 1:284, where he is mentioned as an ancestor of the Trojan people. *British History and the Welsh Annals* [compiled by] Nennius, ed. and trans. John Morris (London: Phillimore, 1980), 19, hereafter cited in text.

22. The name *Alba Longa* may have been a further analogy between the two cities. Britain, according to Bede (*History of the English Church and People,* I, 1, trans. Leo Sherley-Price, rev. by R. E. Latham [Harmondsworth: Penguin Books, 1968], 37) was known originally as *Albion.*

23. Geoffrey's Gomagog is probably a composite of sources such as Ezechiel 38:2–16; 39:4–11; Revelations 20:7–8, the prophecy of pseudo-Mathodius and others. See Faral, 2:86–92 and Tatlock, 1974, 53–56.

24. On the Cyclopes and their lack of civic life, law, and cultivation, see G. S. Kirk, *Myth, Its Meaning and Function in Ancient and Other Cultures* (Berkeley and Los Angeles: University of California Press, 1970), 167–71; for their connection with the idea of possessing land, see Pierre Vidal-Naquet, *The Black Hunter, Forms of Thought and Forms of Society in the Greek World,* trans. Andrew Szegedy-Maszak, with forward by Bernard Knox (Baltimore and London: Johns Hopkins University Press, 1986), 20–22.

25. *Odyssey,* 9:109 ff.; *Aeneid,* 3:612 ff., for the story of the Trojan encounter with the Cyclopes. See also *Aeneid,* 4:58, for the epithet *legifera* (lawgiver) applied to Ceres, showing Virgil's identification of cultivation with orderly social life, as represented by law. See *Georgics,* 1:147 ff. and 338 ff., and Lucretius, *De rerum natura,* 5: 14–15. For the opposition between settled urban culture and the "wild and barbarous" pastoral people, such as the Breton, the Welsh, and the Irish, see Robert Bartlett, *Gerald of Wales, 1146–1223* (Oxford: Clarendon Press, 1982), esp. chs. 6–7; also Robert Bartlett and Angus MacKay, ed., *Medieval Frontier Societies* (Oxford: Clarendon Press, 1989), esp. chs. 4, 8.

26. On the humanity of the giants, see Saint Augustine, *City of God,* bk. 15, chs. 22–23; also John Block Friedman, *The Monstrous Races in Medieval Art and Thought* (Cambridge, Mass.: Harvard University Press, 1981). The land is obviously not entirely rid of giants as Arthur's gigantomachy against Retho demonstrates (Thorpe, 240). For biblical sources for Gomagog, see Paul

Feuerherd, *Geoffrey of Monmouth und das alte Testament mit Berücksichtigung der Historia Britonum des Nennius* (Halle: Ehrhardt Karras, 1915), 31–36.

27. A family trait perhaps? Gwendolen was the daughter of Corineus, who in his own day hurled Gomagog into the sea near Totnes, and the sea was henceforth called after the giant's name.

28. N. E. S. A. Hamilton, ed., *Willelmi Malmesbiriensis Monachi De Gestis Pontificum Anglorum* (London: n.p., 1870), 208–9.

29. This may be Geoffrey's gibe at William of Malmesbury, who claimed that Julius Caesar constructed the hot baths in the city of Bath (Hamilton, 1870, 194). See Flint, 453.

30. For the amusing story of the failed attempt at flight by Eilmer, a monk of Malmesbury, see *William of Malmesbury's Chronicle of the Kings of Britain* (trans. J. A. Giles [London: Henry G. Bohn, 1847], 251–52); and L. White, "Eilmer of Malmesbury, An Eleventh Century Aviator," *Technology and Culture* 2 (1961): 97–111.

31. Suggested perhaps by *Aeneid*, 6:14–19, in which Daedalus lands on a mountain top in Chalcis and later builds a temple to Apollo there.

32. See also Antonia Gransden, *Historical Writing in England c. 550–c. 1307* (Ithaca, N.Y.: Cornell University Press, 1974), 207, for the protection of roads in the *Leis Willelme* and *The Laws of Edward the Confessor*; hereafter cited in text.

33. Dafydd Jenkins, trans. and ed., *The Law of Hywel Dda, Law Texts from Medieval Wales* (Llandysul: Gomer Press, 1986), 120, 268; Rachel Bromwich, *Trioedd Ynys Prydein: The Welsh Triads*, 2d ed. (Cardiff: University of Wales Press, 1978), cxxvi, 232–33; Thomas Peter Ellis, *Welsh Tribal Law and Custom in the Middle Ages* (Oxford: Clarendon Press, 1926; reprint, Scientia Verlag Aalen, 1982) 1, 4–5.

34. Cf. Jacob Hammer, "Note sur l'histoire du roi Lear dans Geoffrey de Monmouth," *Latomus* 5 (1946): 299–301 on biblical and classical parallels in the Leir story in *HRB*. Also Jacob Hammer, "Remarks on the Sources and Textual History of Geoffrey of Monmouth's *Historia Regum Britanniae* with an Excursus on the *Chronica Polonorum* of Wincenty Kadlubek (Magister Vincentius)," *Bulletin of the Polish Institute of Arts and Sciences in America*, 2 (1943–44): esp. 513–18 on Lear.

35. See Nennius (trans. J. Morris, 80, ch. 66a). According to Geoffrey (Wright, 1984, 19), Kaer Leir was known in the Saxon language as *Lerechestria*.

36. Piggott regarded the Leir story as a "complete legend inserted *en bloc,* names and all" into the HRB by Geoffrey (Piggott, 1941, 278).

37. Judith A. Green, *The Government of England under Henry I* (Cambridge: Cambridge University Press, 1986), 11–12.

38. See C. Warren Hollister, "The Anglo-Norman Succession Debate of 1126: Prelude to Stephen's Anarchy," *Journal of Medieval History* 1 (1975): 19–39, reprinted in *Monarchy, Magnates and Institutions in the Anglo-Norman World* (London: Hambledon Press, 1986), 145–69.

39. She is said to have inherited the realm "by hereditary right" (Thorpe, 138).

40. Perhaps the orthography of the name in the *HRB* has to do with the Welsh "brenhin" king.

41. The name *Belinus* probably came to Geoffrey from Nennius (trans. J. Morris, 23, ch. 19), where a Belinus is mentioned as ruler of Britain at the time of Caesar's first invasion of the island. Geoffrey may also have known of the Welsh Beli Mawr, ancestor of a number of dominant Welsh dynasties, whose name frequently appears in the Welsh genealogies. See Bromwich's article on Beli (Bromwich, 1978, 280–81). On Harold and Tostig, sons of Earl Godwin as the models for Belinus and Brennius, see Robert Huntington Fletcher, "Two Notes on the *Historia Regum Britanniae* of Geoffrey of Monmouth," *PMLA* 16 (N.S. 9) (1901): 469–74.

42. C. Warren Hollister, "The Anglo-Norman Civil War: 1101," *English Historical Review* 88 (1973): 315–34; reprinted in *Monarchy, Magnates and Institutions,* 77–96, see esp. 92–93.

43. Younger sons with little inheritance in Geoffrey's day sometimes opted for a career in the church, a path obviously not yet available to Brennius.

44. On this subject, see Georges Duby, *The Chivalrous Society,* trans. Cynthia Postan (Berkeley and Los Angeles: University of California Press, 1977), esp. 112–22.

45. Irving Woodworth Raymond, trans., *Seven Books of History Against the Pagans, The Apology of Paulus Orosius* (New York: Columbia University Press, 1926), 104–6.

46. Amedeo Crivellucci, ed., *Landolfi Sagacis, Historia Romana* (Rome: Tipographia del Senato, 1912), 1, 21–23. The author of the Variant Version appears to have been influenced by Landolf more than Geoffrey was.

47. Making Brennius the leader of the Allobroges was probably Geoffrey's own idea. He betrays his sources, however, when he says that the Roman army, on its way back to defend Rome, was thrown into consternation on seeing its way blocked by what they took to be Brennius and his *Senonian* Gauls (Thorpe, 98).

48. "The seats of the archflamens . . . City of the Legions, the site of which last, by the River Usk in Glamorgan, is still showing its ancient walls and buildings" (Thorpe, 125).

49. See Gustavus Becker, ed., *Catalogi Bibliothecarum Antiqui* (Bonn: Max Cohen and Sons, 1885), 202: Bec catalogue of 1142–64: 100, *gesta Cesaris;* 101, *gesta Cesaris et Orosius.*

50. On the date, see Nancy Partner, *Serious Entertainment, The Writing of History in Twelfth-Century England* (Chicago: University of Chicago Press, 1977), 17–18.

51. Pelagius (late fourth, early fifth century) was a Briton.

52. Caesar, *Gallic Wars,* 4:20 and 5:12.

53. Gildas had observed that when the Romans first attacked, the British "like women they stretched out their hands for the fetters." Michael

Winterbottom, ed. and trans., *Gildas, The Ruin of Britain and Other Works* (London: Phillimore, 1978), 18, hereafter cited in text.

54. The germ of Androgeus's betrayal is found in Mandubracius, the young king of the Trinobantes in Caesar's *Commentaries* (5:20), who comes over to Caesar's army in Gaul to avoid the anger of Cassivelaunus, who has put his father to death. There is no hint of Mandubracius's betraying the British in Henry of Huntingdon.

55. Based apparently on the name for an inhabitant of Gwent "Gwen-hwyss," a region of southeast Wales much beloved by Geoffrey. Perhaps also related to the Gewissei. See Hutson, 1973, 49, and Faral, 2:141.

56. Note how Geoffrey carefully avoids mention of any Roman building apart from the two defensive walls (Thorpe, 126 and 144). See Tacitus (*Agricola*, 21) on the education of the British.

57. Geoffrey changes Asclepiodotus's nationality in order to make him a Briton rebelling against Roman cruelty. In Bede (trans. Sherley-Price, 44), Asclepiodotus is the Roman Prefect of the Pretorian Guards who is sent by the Emperor to crush the usurper Allectus in Britain.

58. Archaeological investigations have uncovered several skulls at Walbrook precisely where Geoffrey claims Asclepiodotus beheaded many Romans. See Ralph Merrifield, *The Roman City of London* (London: Ernest & Benn, 1965), 37, 76, n. 16; also Tatlock, 1974, 33–34, for other explanations.

59. For the creation of "Saint" Amphibalus out of an obscure word for Alban's cloak, see John Tatlock, "St. Amphibalus" in *Essays in Criticism*, 2d series (Berkeley: University of California Press, 1934): 249–57; for the later history of this "saint," see Florence McCulloch, "Saints Alban and Amphibalus in the Works of Matthew of Paris: Dublin, Trinity College MS 177," *Speculum* 56 (1981): 761–85.

60. William states that "Henry . . . so restrained the rebellious, by the terror of his name, that peace remained undisturbed in England. In consequence, foreigners willingly resorted thither, as to the only haven of secure tranquillity (Giles, 443)." Was Geoffrey thinking of the passage in Orosius in which Maximianus Herculius seeks refuge with Constantine (Raymond, 364)? If so, he changed the facts. Constantine is in Gaul, not Britain, at the time, and Maximianus is a persecutor of Christians.

61. The spelling of the name shows the influence of Nennius. The historic personage behind Geoffrey's Maximianus was the Spaniard Magnus Maximus, proclaimed emperor by his troops in Britain in 383. On his frequent appearance in Welsh literature and legend, see Bromwich, 1978, 451–54.

62. For the relevant documents on the legend, see Wilhelm Levison, *Das Werden der Ursula-Legende* (Cologne: Albert Ahn, 1928), esp. 90–107. For Geoffrey's treatment of the legend, see Tatlock, 1974, 236–41; Gransden, 207–8; Flint, 464–65.

63. David Fowler argues that Constantine's murder is modeled on the assassination of Eglon, King of Moab, by Eliud of Israel (Judges 3:19–21), and

that Constan's death is derived from 2 Kings 4:5–12, where Ishbosheth is struck down by Rechab and Baana. David Fowler, "Some Biblical Influences on Geoffrey of Monmouth's Historiography," *Traditio* 14 (1958): 380–83. For other parallels, see Tatlock, 1974, 167–68; Feuerherd, 55–59.

64. On the career of Vortigern, see H. M. Chadwick et al., eds., *Studies in Early British History,* (Cambridge: Cambridge University Press, 1954), 9–46, esp. 21–46; C. A. Ralegh Radford, "Vortigern," *Antiquity* 32 (1958): 19–24; N. K. Chadwick, "Bretwalda Gwledig Vortigern," *Bulletin of the Board of Celtic Studies* 19 (1960–62): 225–30; D. P. Kirby, "Vortigern," *Bulletin of the Board of Celtic Studies* 23 (1968): 37–59; Nora K. Chadwick, "Early Culture and Learning in North Wales," in ed. N. Chadwick et al., esp. 110–18. On Vortigern as an upholder of a native anti-Roman party in fifth-century Britain, see A. W. Wade-Evans, "Vortigern," *Notes and Queries* (13 May 1950): 200–203. For the theory of the two Vortigerns, see J. D. Bu'Lock, "Vortigern and the Pillar of Eliseg," *Antiquity* 34 (1960): 49–53.

65. In the prologue to the so-called Nennian redaction (mid-eleventh century), Nennius claims to have "heaped together" (*coaceruaui*) what he could find out about British history from a variety of sources, including the annals of the Irish and the Saxons, and "the tradition of our elders." He does not call his work a history, but simply "some extracts" (*aliqua excerpta*).

66. J. E. Turville-Petre, "Hengest and Horsa," *Saga-Book of the Viking Society* 14 (1953–57): 273–90.

67. Aldhelm, *The Prose Works,* trans. Michael Lapidge and Michael Herren (Cambridge: D. S. Brewer, 1979), 158.

68. On fasting as a legal means of securing redress, see the passage in the Irish tale *Acallamh na Senórach* (Tom Peete Cross and Clark Harris Slover, ed., *Ancient Irish Tales,* rev. bibliography Charles W. Dunn [New York: Barnes & Noble, 1969], 466) in which Ruide, Fiacha, and Eochaid fast against the Tuatha De Danann for lands and great fortune. Also, Myles Dillon and Nora Chadwick, *The Celtic Realms* (London: Weidenfield and Nicholson, 1967; 2d ed., 1972), 94–95.

69. The biblical parallel to Vortigern, Renwein is found in the book of Esther according to Jacob Hammer, "Geoffrey of Monmouth's Use of the Bible," *Bulletin of the John Rylands Library* 30 (1946–47): 302–4.

70. For a survey of the literature on the incubus, see Nicolas Kiessling, *The Incubus in English Literature: Provenance and Progeny* (n.p.: Washington State University Press, 1977), chs. 1–7.

71. Perhaps alluding to the legend of Saint David's birth. David's mother, Saint Nonita, was from Dyfed (Demetia) and was raped by Sanctus, king of Ceredigion.

72. Kwang-Chih Chang, *The Archaeology of Ancient China* (New Haven, Conn.: Yale University Press, 1963), 159, 173.

73. W. S[tokes], ed., *Three Irish Glossaries. Cormac's Glossary, Codex A. O'Davoren's Glossary and A Glossary to the Calendar of Oingus the Culdee* (Oxford: Williams and Norgate), xli-xlii.

74. Whitley Stokes, "Mythological Notes," *Revue celtique* 2 (1873–8–75): 200–1.

75. H. N. Savory, "Excavations at Dinas Emrys, Beddgelert (Carn.) 1954–56," *Archaeologia Cambrensis* 109 (1960): 13–77, esp. 51. Also Lloyd Laing, *The Archaeology of Late Celtic Britain and Ireland, c. 400–1200 A.D.* (London: Methuen, 1975), 106–7.

76. Leslie Alcock, '*By South Cadbury is that Camelot . . .' The Excavation of Cadbury Castle 1966–1970* (London: Thames and Hudson, 1972), 103, plate 31.

77. Caesar (*Gallic Wars,* 6:16) claimed that the Celts believed that their gods demanded a life to preserve a life. On the Irish sacrifice of their firstborn to Cromm Cruaich, see E. J. Gwynn, *The Metrical Dindsenchas* (Royal Academy Todd Lecture Series, vol. 21; Dublin: Hodges, Figgis, 1924), 18–23, esp. 19–21.

78. On the subject of the king's relationship to the fertility of the land see Annette J. Otway-Ruthven, *A History of Medieval Ireland,* intro. Kathleen Hughes (London: Ernest Benn, 1968), 12–13. Also Proinsias Mac Cana, "Aspects of the Theme of King and Goddess in Irish Literature," *Études celtiques* 7 (1955): 76–114, 356–413; 8 (1958): 59–65; Myles Dillon, "The Consecration of Irish Kings," *Celtica* 10 (1973): 1–8; James Carney, *Studies in Irish Literature and History* (Dublin: Institute for Advanced Studies, 1979), 333–39.

79. Amphion's building the walls of Thebes with stones that he moves with the magic of music is a parallel that has been overlooked. See Statius, *Thebaid,* 10:873–77; Ovid, *Metamorphoses,* 6:177–79; Horace, *Odes,* book 3, poem 11, lines 1–2; Horace, *De arte poetica,* 394–96; see also Dante, *Inferno,* 32:10–12.

80. Among the many studies of Stonehenge, the following are particularly useful for a study of Geoffrey's account of the origin of Stonehenge: H. H. Thomas, "The Source of the Stones of Stonehenge," *Antiquaries Journal* 3 (1923): 239–58; Laura H. Loomis, "Geoffrey of Monmouth and Stonehenge," *PMLA* 45 (1930): 400–15; Stewart Piggott, "The Sources of Geoffrey of Monmouth II. The Stonehenge Story," *Antiquity* 15 (1941):305–19; Tatlock, 1974, 40–42, 362–63, 371, 387; Stuart Piggott, "Stonehenge Reviewed," in *Aspects of Archaeology in Britain and Beyond, Essays Presented to O. G. S. Crawford* (London: H. W. Edwards, 1951); L. V. Grinsell, "The Legendary History and Folklore of Stonehenge," *Folklore* 87 (1976): 5–20; Nikolai Tolstoy, *The Quest for Merlin* (Boston: Little, Brown, 1985), ch. 9, 121–34.

81. J. W. James, ed., *Rhigyfarch's Life of St. David,* 4, 30–31: "*Nam terra, conceptui congaudens sinum suum aperuit, ut et puellę erecundiam seruaret et prolis soliditatem prenuntiaret.*"

82. John Williams ab Ithel, ed., *Brut y Tywysogion; or the Chronicles of the Princes* (London, 1860; reprint, Wiesbaden: Kraus Reprint, 1965), 40–41, hereafter cited in text.

83. A. B. Scott and F. X. Martin, eds. and trans., *Expugnatio Hibernica, The Conquest of Ireland by Giraldus Cambrensis* (Dublin: Royal Irish Academy, 1978), 25–27.

84.   W. J. Gruffydd, *Folklore and Myth in the Mabinogion* (Cardiff: University of Wales Press, 1958; reprint, 1961), 23; also W. J. Gruffydd, *Rhiannon* (Cardiff: University of Wales Press, 1953), 10–19 and ch. 2, 20–46.

85.   Alwyn Rees and Brinley Rees, *Celtic Heritage, Ancient Tradition in Ireland and Wales* (London: Thames and Hudson, 1961), 214–15, hereafter cited in text; W. J. Gruffydd, *Math Vab Mathonwy* (Cardiff: University of Wales Press, 1928), 85–87.

86.   Kuno Meyer and Alfred Nutt, eds., *The Voyage of Bran Son of Ferbal*, 2 vols. (London: D. Nutt, 1895–97; reprint, New York: Ams Press, 1972), 58–84.

87.   Oliver Padel suggests that in locating the story of Arthur's conception at Tintagel, Geoffrey was following preexisting legends about the place as stronghold of Cornish rulers (Bromwich, Jarman, Roberts, 229–34). Whether Arthur was associated with Tintagel before Geoffrey remains unclear.

88.   Rosemary Morris, "Uther and Igerne: A Study in Uncourtly Love," *Arthurian Literature IV*, ed. Richard Barber (Woodbridge, Suffolk: D. S. Brewer, 1985), 70–92.

89.   A. W. Wade-Evans, "The Brychan Documents," *Y Cymmrodor* 19 (1906): 25.

90.   Alexander Penrose Forbes, ed. and trans., *The Lives of S. Ninnian and S. Kentigern Compiled in the Twelfth Century* (Edinburgh: Edmonston and Douglas, 1874), 30–31, 160–61. Also see Kenneth Hurlstone Jackson, "The Sources for the Life of St. Kentigern," in N. Chadwick et al., 335–39.

Chapter Three

1.   Is this one of Geoffrey's arch jokes? How was Alexander to translate from a tongue unknown to him?

2.   Marjorie Chibnall, ed. and trans., *The Ecclesiastical History of Orderic Vitalis* (Oxford: Oxford University Press, 1978), 6, 381–89, esp. 386, n. 4 (on date); hereafter cited in text.

3.   Kathleen Hughes, "British Museum MS. Cotton Vespasian A. XIV ('Vitae Sanctorum Wallensium') its purpose and provenance," in N. Chadwick et al., 183–200.

4.   Sir Ifor Williams, ed., *Armes Prydein, the Prophecy of Britain from the Book of Taliesin*, trans. Rachel Bromwich (Dublin: Dublin Institute for Advanced Studies, 1972).

5.   Migne, *Patrilogia Latina* clvi, col. 983; Chambers, 249. On this passage, see J. S. P. Tatlock, "The English Journey of the Laon Canons," *Speculum* 8 (1933): 454–65. Tatlock concludes, "It seems impossible to doubt that, twenty years or so before Geoffrey of Monmouth wrote his *Historia*, they [the Laon canons] found Cornishmen holding their country to be Arthur's, pointing to his chair and oven, and heartily believing him still alive" (Tatlock, 1933, 465). Tatlock's view is corroborated by William of Newburg's statement that

Geoffrey derived his Arthurian matter "ex priscis Britonum figmentis" (Howlett, 12). For useful surveys of the pre-Galfridian literature on Arthur, see O. J. Padel, "Geoffrey of Monmouth and Cornwall," *Cambridge Medieval Celtic Studies* 8 (1984): 1–28, and A. O. H. Jarman, "The Delineations of Arthur in Early Welsh Verse," in *An Arthurian Tapestry, Essays in Memory of Lewis Thorpe* (Glasgow: University of Glasgow Press, 1981): 1–21. For a contrasting view, see Faral, 225–33. Ditmas conjectures that the person who quarreled with the Frenchman Hagenellus at Bodmin over Arthur's survival was a Breton from one of the local manors rather than a native Cornishman (E. M. R. Ditmas, "Geoffrey of Monmouth and the Breton Families in Cornwall," *The Welsh History Review* 6 [1972–73]: 451–61). The commentator in the Trinity College manuscript, however, states that Cornishmen in his day believed that Arthur still lived on the island of Aval (Jacob Hammer, "An Unedited Commentary on the *Prophetia Merlini* in Dublin, Trinity College MS 496 E. 6. 2 (Geoffrey of Monmouth's *Historia Regum Britanniae*, Book VII))," in *Charisteria Thaddaeo Sinko; Quinquaginta abhinc annos amplissimis . . . ab amicis collegis discipulis oblata* (Warsaw: Philological Society of Poland, 1951), 87): "*Cornubienses ipsum Arturium adhuc credunt vivere in insula Aval; Aval britannice pomum interpretatur latine.*"

     6.   Geoffrey takes this passage from Gildas, 25 (ed. Winterbottom, 28).

     7.   Hammer, "Another Commentary on the *Prophetia Merlini* (Geoffrey of Monmouth's *Historia Regum Britanniaw*. Book VII)," *Bulletin of the Polish Institute of Arts and Sciences in America,* vol. 1, 1942–43, 594; Alanus, *Prophetia Anglicana, Merlini Ambrosii Britanni . . . Unà cum septem libris explanationum in eandem prophetiam . . . Alani de Insulis* (Frankfurt: n.p., 1603), 28. Jacob Hammer, "Bref commentaire de la *Prophetia Merlini* du ms. 3514 de la bibliothèque de la cathédrale d'Exeter (Geoffrey de Monmouth, *Historia Regum Britanniae,* b. VII)," in *Hommages à Joseph Bidez et à Fanz Cumont* (Brussels: Collection Latomus, 2, 1949):113: "*hic notat qualiter sanctus Sampson, Eboracensis episcopus, vel archiepiscopatus rector, cum septum episcopis, vel subditis, Minorem Britanniam adiit, destructa christianitate trans Hunbriam a paganis Saxonibus.*" See also Matthew of Paris, *Matthaei Parisiensis . . . chronica majora* (London: n.p., 1872–83), 2:200.

     8.   Evans, 109: "*Et inde his peractis perrexit sanctus cum suis comitibus adarmoricas gentes & bene continuo susceptus est ab eis. Audiente Samsone dolensis ecclesię archiepiscopo aduentum confratris sui inpatriam occurrit ei cum gaudio. Nam de una regione procreati fuerant & unius linguę uiri & simul cum beato Dubricio archipresule edocti.*" The *Book of Llandaff* appears to have taken the idea of this meeting from the Breton Life of Turiau, which Geoffrey may possibly have known. Henken, 131; G. H. Doble, *Lives of the Welsh Saints,* ed. D. Simon Evans (Cardiff: University of Wales Press, 1971), 186.

     9.   A. W. Wade-Evans, ed. *Vitae Sanctorum Britanniae et Genealogiae* (Cardiff: University of Wales Press, 1944), 262.

     10.   Robert Fawtier claims that Benoit of Gloucester in *Life of Dubricius* (in which Samson becomes archbishop of York) was influenced by Geoffrey, as

was Ralph of Diceto (c. 1183), who states that he saw Samson of Dol's name on a catalogue of archbishops of York. Robert Fawtier, *La Vie de S. Samson: essai de critique hagiographique* (Paris: H. Champion, 1912), 25, 26.

11. Brynley F. Roberts, "Esboniad Cymraeg ar Broffwydoliaeth Myrddin," *Bulletin of the Board of Celtic Studies* 21 (1966): 289.

12. See on this passage, Henken, 34–35.

13. Charles Plummer, ed. (*Vitae Sanctorum Hiberniae* Oxford: Clarendon Press, 1910), 1, 53. Also in Wade-Evans, 1923, 38–39.

14. "Vita Gildae auctore Caradoco Lancarbanensi," in *Chronica Minora Saec. IV, V, VI, VII,* ed. Theodore Mommsen (Berlin: Monumenta Germanica Historica . . . Avctorvm Antiquissimorvm Tomus XIII, Weidmanns, 1898), 107–10. Relevant passages translated in Wade-Evans, 1923, 46–47.

15. "Historia de Vita S. Davidis Archiepiscopi Menevensis," in Giraldus Cambrensis, *Opera,* 8 vols., ed. J. S. Brewer et al. (n.p.: 1861–91), 3, 381–82.

16. D. Simon Evans, ed., *Buchedd Dewi* (Cardiff: University of Wales Press, 1965), 3.

17. These issues are discussed by Dorothy Whitelock in *Some Anglo-Saxon Bishops of London* (Chambers Memorial Lecture delivered 4 May 1974 at University College London; London: H. K. Lewis, 1975), esp. 14 ff., 25–26. For the letter to Pope Honorius II, see James Conway Davies, ed., *Episcopal Acts and Cognate Documents Relating to Welsh Dioceses, 1066–1272* (Cardiff: Historical Society of the Church in Wales, 1946–48), 1, 249–50. Also on this letter, see Brooke, 1958, 201–42; Wendy Davies, "The Consecration of Bishops of Llandaff in the Tenth and Eleventh Centuries," *Bulletin of the Board of Celtic Studies* 26 (1974): 53–73, esp. 58–59; Michael Richter, "Professions of Obedience and the Metropolitan Claim of St. David's," *National Library of Wales Journal* 15 (1967–68): 197–214, esp. 203; R. W. Southern, "The Canterbury Forgeries," *English Historical Review* 73 (1958): 193–226.

18. David Knowles, *The Episcopal Colleagues of Archbishop Thomas Becket* (Cambridge: Cambridge University Press, 1970), 161–62.

19. The prophecy in Gildas states that the Saxons will "hold possession of" (*insideret*) the island for 300 years and lay it waste (*vastaret*) for half of that time. Mindful of the later fate of the Saxon kingdoms, Geoffrey (or his source) subtly extend this to mean that the Saxons would hold possession of the island (*insidebit*) for 300 years, but be in restlessness and subjection (*in inquietudine* and *subiectione*) for 150 years.

20. In Geoffrey it is unclear when the prophecy was originally uttered. When the Saxons left Saxony, as Gildas suggests? Or when they toppled the Man of Bronze? When Cadwallader died in Rome (A.D. 689)? After the 79-year reign of Yvor and Yni, successors to Cadwallader and the last named British rulers in the *HRB*?

21. David C. Douglas, *William the Conqueror, The Norman Impact Upon England* (Berkeley and Los Angeles: University of California Press, 1964), 175–78.

22. William Stubbs, ed., *Memorials of St. Dunstan* (London: Longmans, 1874), 115–17, 127. On Osbern's interpretation, see Gransden, 128, and n. 157.

23. Martin Rule, ed., *Eadmeri Historia Novorum in Anglia* (London: Longmans, 1884), 3–5.

24. On the Breton auxiliaries under Alain Fergant who accompanied William to England in 1066, see Edward A. Freeman, *The History of the Norman Conquest* (Oxford: n.p., 1864), 3:313–14, and Douglas, 230–34, 267–69.

25. For a useful discussion of the attitude of the earliest authorities on Rufus's death, see C. W. Hollister, "The Strange Death of William Rufus," *Speculum* 48 (1973): 637–53.

26. Alanus, 69. Alanus's comment makes it impossible to accept Hollister's view that none of the earliest stories concerning Rufus' death, including Merlin's prediction, "contains any hint of premeditation."

27. See also Alanus (68–69) on these predictions.

28. Jacob Hammer, "A Commentary on the *Prophetia Merlini* (Geoffrey of Monmouth's *Historia Regum Britanniae*, Book VII)," in *Speculum* 10 (1935), 15; "A Commentary on the *Prophetia Merlini* (Geoffrey of Monmouth's *Historia Regum Britanniae*, Book VII) (Continuation) in *Speculum* 15 (1940), 417.

29. The sentiment is shared by a commentator on *HRB* 7 (Hammer, 1935, 16): *"in illis namque diebus fures sunt suspensi, latrones mulctati, corruptores monetae ementulati, quae omnia sunt indicia magnae potentiae et rigidae iustitiae."* Philip Grierson and Christopher Brooke accept Geoffrey's prophecy as evidence for the existence of round halfpennies during Henry I's reign. They may have been struck during the currency reform of 1108 in order to counteract the popular practice of bending and sometimes breaking a coin to determine its quality. Henry's round halfpenny contained an incision ("The surface of the coinage will be cleft"), which revealed the purity of the coinage, thereby making bending unnecessary. Philip Grierson and Christopher Brooke, "Round Halfpennies of Henry I," *British Numismatic Journal* 26 (1951): 286–89).

30. Jacob Hammer, "A Reference to Foppish Coiffures in Geoffrey of Monmouth's *Prophetia Merlini*," *Speculum* 12 (1937):503–8.

31. See also John of Cornwall's version of this conflict in his *Prophetia Merlini*, lines 62–67 (Curley, 1982, 233; on John's commentary, 238).

32. Lewis Thorpe opposed the idea that the PM circulated as an "independent tract." He suggested that Orderic may have copied out portions of the *PM* from a complete copy of the *HRB*, which he may have borrowed from Robert de Torigni at Bec. Lewis Thorpe, "Orderic Vitalis and the *Prophetiae Merlini* of Geoffrey of Monmouth," *Bibliographical Bulletin of the International Arthurian Society* 29 (1977), 191–208.

33. On the dates, see Caroline D. Eckhart, "The Date of the *Prophetia Merlini*," Commentary in MSS Cotton Claudius B.viii. and Bibliothèque Nationale Fonds Latin 6233," N.S. *Notes and Queries* (1976): 146–47.

34. Doris Edel, "Geoffrey's So-called Animal Symbolism and Insular Celtic Tradition," *Studia Celtica* 18/19 (1983–84):96–109; Michael J. Curley,

"Animal Symbolism in the Prophecies of Merlin," in *Beasts and Birds of the Middle Ages, The Bestiary and Its Legacy*, ed. Willene B. Clark and Meradith T. McMunn (Philadelphia: University of Pennsylvania Press, 1989), 151–63.

35.   Geoffrey's later reference in the *VM* (line 967) to Conan's arrival from Armorica (Brittany) and John of Cornwall's statement that he will "sail the seas" (*navigat undas*), indicates that these two writers understood his alliance with Cadwallader as a joining together of Welsh and Breton people on the long-awaited day of reckoning with the Saxons (Curley, 1982, 236, line 138).

Chapter Four

1.   William may be reflecting Welsh tradition as preserved in the *englyn* in the *Black Book of Carmarthen*, which claims that the grave of Arthur is a difficult thing to know about (*anoeth bid bet Arthur*). On this, see Thomas Jones, "The Early Evolution of the Legend of Arthur," *Nottingham Mediaeval Studies* 8 (1964): esp. 17–18.

2.   At least this seems the most likely meaning of Herman's words (Richard H. Barber, *The Figure of Arthur* ([Totowa, N.J.: Rowman and Littlefield, 1973], 124). Henry of Huntingdon notes in his Letter to Warin (1139) that Warin's Breton *parentes* (parents, grandparents, kin?) do not accept Arthur's death, but await his return (Wright, 1991, 105, 112).

3.   For a discussion of Arthur's 12 battles in Nennius and the historic significance of this problematic title ("Duke" or "Leader of Battles"), see Leslie Alcock, *Arthur of Britain, History and Archaeology A.D. 367–634* (Harmondsworth: Penguin Books, 1973), 60–61; Rachel Bromwich, "Concepts of Arthur," *Studia Celtica* 10–12 (1975–76): esp. 167–77.

4.   Bromwich, 1975–76, 172); this would place the battle around the decade 490–500.

5.   For a discussion of Badon see Kenneth Jackson, "The Site of Mount Badon," *Journal of Celtic Studies* 2 (1953–58): 152–55.

6.   On the Arthur of the saints' lives, see Chambers, 80–86. Chambers doubts that Geoffrey made any direct use of these *vitae*.

7.   See also *Aeneid* 12:90–91 on the sword of Daunus, Turnus's father, which was forged by Vulcan.

8.   Nennius (ch. 56) states that Arthur carried the image of the Virgin Mary on his shoulders in the Battle of Castle Guinnion. The *Annales Cambriae*, on the other hand, claim that at the Battle of Badon (anno 516) Arthur carried the cross of Our Lord Jesus Christ for three days and three nights on his shoulders. In keeping with his view of the Battle of Bath as the climactic moment in Arthur's reconquest of Britain, Geoffrey claims that at the Battle of Bath, Arthur carried "across his shoulders" his shield on which the image of the Virgin Mary was painted. Scholars have long suspected that the list of 12 battles derives from a Welsh praise poem, probably originally not associated with Arthur. The awkward image of the king carrying into battle an image or a cross

on his shoulders has been traced to a possible confusion in the putative Welsh source between the Old Welsh *scuit* "shield" and *scuid* "shoulder." If so, Geoffrey's image of Arthur carrying on his shoulders his shield Pridwen, on which was painted an image of the Virgin looks like a clever conflation of the various elements of the story. For discussions, see Barber, 1972, 101–3; T. Jones, 1964, 5–6, 8–9; Bromwich, 1975–76, 170, n. 2; Roger Sherman Loomis, ed., *Arthurian Literature in the Middle Ages: A Collaborative History* (Oxford: Oxford University Press, 1959), 7.

9.   Fulcher of Chartres, *A History of the Expedition to Jerusalem, 1095–1127,* trans. Frances Rita Ryan (Knoxville: University of Tennessee Press, 1969), 66: "For all those going thither there will be remission of sins if they come to the end of this fettered life while either marching by land or crossing by sea, or in fighting the pagans. This I grant to all who go, through the power vested in me by God."

10.   Heinrich Pähler, *Strukturuntersuchungen zur Historia Regum Britanniae Des Geoffrey of Monmouth* (Bonn: Rheinische Friedrich Wilhelms-Universität, 1958), 139–40.

11.   *The Anglo-Saxon Chronicle* has no report on this single combat; it is spoken of only as a challenge in William of Malmesbury. See the description of *holmgang* in H. R. Ellis Davidson, *Gods and Myths of Northern Europe* (Harmondsworth: Penguin Books, 1964), 58–59; and Tacitus, *Germania,* 7.

12.   The *Urbs Legionis* in Nennius is usually thought to refer, not to Caerleon-on-Usk, but to Chester; it is doubtful that Geoffrey took it this way, however.

13.   Green, 22–23; see esp. ch. 2 on the subject of the king's councils.

14.   My translation. Thorpe is too free with this passage: "Britain had reached such a standard of sophistication that it excelled all other kingdoms in its general affluence, the richness of its decorations, and the courteous behavious of its inhabitants" (Thorpe, 229). In particular, the phrase "courteous behaviour" for the Latin *facecia* introduces a resonance that the passage does not have.

15.   Or perhaps, "Their jests (*ioci*) kindled [in the men] the raging flames of love." Thorpe does not capture the clinical directness of Geoffrey's passage: "their womenfolk . . . aroused them to passionate excitement by their flirtatious behaviour" (Thorpe, 230).

16.   For a comparison of Arthur with the Irish hero Fionn mac Umhaill, see A. G. van Hamel, "Aspects of Celtic Mythology," *Proceedings of the British Academy* 20 (1934): 207–48; Gerard Murphy, ed., *Duanaire Finn, The Book of the Lays of Finn* (Dublin: Irish Texts Society, 1953), pt. 3, 213–16.

17.   Stephen Knight, *Arthurian Literature and Society* (London: Macmillan, 1983), 58–59.

18.   Lewis Thorpe, "Le Mont Saint-Michel et Geoffroi de Monmouth," in *Millénaire monastique du Mont Saint-Michel* (Paris: P. Lethielleux, 1967), 2, 381–82.

19.   Thorpe, 1967, 381–82.

20.   *Aeneid,* 8, 563; 9, 496; 11, 397; 12; 14.

21.   Robert W. Hanning, *The Vision of History in Early Britain: From Gildas to Geoffrey of Monmouth* (New York: Columbia University Press, 1966), 170.

22.   Hans E. Keller, "Two Toponymical Problems in Geoffrey of Monmouth and Wace: *Estrusia* and *Siesia,*" *Speculum* 49 (1974): 691.

23.   The same conclusion was reached by William Matthews, "Where Was Siesia-Sessoyne?" *Speculum* 49 (1974): 680–86.

24.   Jones states that the form Camboglanna would normally yield Old Welsh Camglann, rather than the Camlann of the *Annales Cambriae* (T. Jones, 1964, 6).

25.   An interesting verbal parallel to Arthur's being carried from the field of battle occurs in the *HRB* itself when Kay is "mortally wounded" (*letaliter uulneratus*) at Siesia, and is carried back to Chinon following the battle (Thorpe, 252, 257). Unlike Arthur, Kay dies of his wounds, but Geoffrey's application of this same phrase (*letaliter uulneratus*) for Arthur and Kay, may indicate that he had in mind the further parallelism of a French place (or at least place-name) as the destination for the hero after he has been mortally wounded.

26.   Gormund and Isembard are taken by Geoffrey from a chanson de geste (late eleventh century) entitled *Gormont et Isembart.* Alphonse Bayot, ed., *Gormont et Isembart, fragment de chanson de geste du xiie siècle,* 3d ed. (Paris: Champion, 1931). On Geoffrey's use of this text, see Tatlock, 1974, 135–38. Did Geoffrey understand the Saxon Gormont to be a Vandal from North Africa or Spain? Did he perhaps mistake Hibernia (Ireland) for Iberia (Spain)?

27.   Tatlock took this to be a mistake for Chester, but Wright argues that Geoffrey intended Leicester in order to show how far east British rule extended (Tatlock, 1974, 25–26; Wright, 1986, 39–40).

28.   Neil Wright, "Geoffrey of Monmouth and Bede," *Arthurian Literature VI,* ed. Richard Barber (Cambridge: D. S. Brewer, 1986), 51.

29.   See Octavius (Thorpe, 133) who is Duke of the Gewissei during the reign of Constantine; Tatlock (1974, 74–75) for a discussion of the Gewissei. Note Cadwallader's pedigree. His mother is the half-sister of Peanda, hence Cadwallader is partly English.

30.   Some manuscripts add that the return would not be accomplished "until the moment should come which Merlin had prophesied to Arthur," but this is clearly a mistake, because Merlin disappears from the narrative before Arthur is born (Thorpe, 282, n. 1). It is difficult to believe that Geoffrey was responsible for this blunder. Merlin did, of course, prophesy that Britain would one day be retaken by Cadwallader and Conan, but he said this to Vortigern not to Arthur (Thorpe, 175). Wright notes that the phrase "*antequam tempus illud uenisset quod Merlinus Arthuro prophetauerat*" is added at the foot of folio 79r in the Bern manuscript of the *HRB* (Wright, 1984, 146).

31.   Geoffrey hedges on the origin of the term *Welsh* (*Guallenses*). He notes that the word derives either from their leader Gualo, or from their Queen

Galaes, or "from their being so barbarous" (Thorpe, 284). The Old English term *Wealhcynn*, "men of Wales" or "Britons" derives from *wealh* "foreigner," "stranger," or "slave."

32. R. William Leckie, Jr., *The Passage of Dominion: Geoffrey of Monmouth and the Periodization of Insular History in the Twelfth Century* (Toronto: University of Toronto Press, 1981), 5–19, 73–101. See Wright, 1988, lxvi–lxx, on the way the redactor of the Variant Version of the *HRB*, unable to accept such a late date for the transfer of dominion, represents Athelstan as a contemporary of Cadwallader.

33. See Ernst Robert Curtius, *European Literature and the Latin Middle Ages*, trans. Williard R. Trask (New York: Pantheon Books, 1953), 162, 485–86, 515–18.

Chapter Five

1. J. S. P. Tatlock, "Geoffrey of Monmouth's *Vita Merlini*," *Speculum* 18 (1943): 267.

2. J. J. Parry, "The Date of the *Vita Merlini*," *Modern Philology* 22 (1924–25): 413–15.

3. William Henry Black, *Gaufridi Arthurii Archidiaconi, postea vero episcopi Asaphensis, de vita et vaticiniis Merlini Calidonii carmen heroicum* (London: Printed for the Roxburghe Club, 1830).

4. Francisque Michel, *Galfridi de Monemuta: Vita Merlini* (Paris: F. Didot, 1837).

5. These two fragments were edited by H. L. D. Ward, "Lailoken (or Merlin Silvester)," *Romania* 22 (1893): 504–26; Clarke, 1973, Appendix I, 227–34; and more recently Aubrey Galyon and Zacharias P. Thundy in ch. 1 ("Lailoken") of *The Romance of Merlin, An Anthology*, ed. Peter Goodrich (New York: Garland Publishing, 1990), 5–11.

6. On the rich background of the Wild Man motif see N. K. Chadwick, "Geilt," *Scottish Gaelic Studies* 5 (1942): 106–53; R. Bernheimer, *Wild Men in the Middle Ages, A Study in Art, Sentiment and Demonology* (Cambridge, Mass.: Harvard University Press, 1952; reprint, New York: Octagon Books, 1979), esp. 13–15, 142, 166–68; Penelope B. R. Doob, *Nebuchadnezzar's Children, Conventions of Madness in Middle English Literature* (New Haven, Conn.: Yale University Press, 1974), 153–58 (on Geoffrey's *VM*); Charles Allyn Williams, *Oriental Affinities of the Legend of the Hairy Anchorite* (Part I: Pre-Christian, Part II: Christian), University of Illinois Studies in Language and Literature (Urbana: University of Illinois Press, 1925, 1926).

7. See K. H. Jackson, "The Motive of the Three-Fold Death in the Story of Suibhne Geilt," in *Féil-sgríbhinn Eóin Mhic Néill: Essays and Studies Presented to Eoin Mac Neill* (Dublin: n.p., 1940):535–50.

8. The Welsh text is found in *The Poetry in the Red Book of Hergest*, reproduced and edited by J. Gwenogvryn Evans (Llanbedrog, 1911), 1–4;

another version was edited by Ifor Williams ("Y Cyfoesi a'r Afallennau yn Peniarth 3," *Bulletin of the Board of Celtic Studies* 4 [1924–28?]: 114–21); trans. John K. Bollard in chap. 2 ("Myrddin in Early Welsh Tradition") of *The Romance of Merlin,* ed. Goodrich, esp. 31–46.

9. A. O. H. Jarman, "Lailoken a Llallogan," *Bulletin of the Board of Celtic Studies* 9 (1937–39):8–27.

10. On Myrddin see A. O. H. Jarman's essay "The Welsh Myrddin Poems," in Loomis, 20–30. For a survey of the likely chronology of the stages of the legend of Myrddin, see A. O. H. Jarman, "Early Stages in the Development of the Myrddin Legend," in *Studies in Old Welsh Poetry, Astudiaethau Ar Yr Hengerdd,* ed. Rachel Bromwich and R. Brinley Jones (Cardiff: University of Wales Press, 1978), 326–49.

11. For a good survey of issues relating to the Battle of Arfderydd, see Clarke, 1973, 160–62; Bromwich, 1978, 29, 31 W, 44, 84, and esp. 208–10; and Molly Miller, "The Commanders at Arthuret," *Transactions of the Cumberland and Westmoreland Antiquarian and Archaelogical Society* 75 (1975): 96–118.

12. The Welsh text is in A. O. H. Jarman and E. D. Jones, ed., *Llyfer Du Caerfyrddin* (Cardiff: University of Wales Press, 1982), 1–2; for the full scholarly edition of the poem, see A. O. H. Jarman, ed., *Ymddiddan Myrddin A Thaliesin (O Lyfr Du Caerfyrddin)* (Cardiff: University of Wales Press, 1967), esp. 53 for the date. An English translation by Bollard can be found in Goodrich, 18–19.

13. Both the *Afallennau* and the *Oianau* are edited by Jarman (*Llyfr Du Caerfyrddin,* 16–35), and translated by Bollard in Goodrich, 22–30. Bollard's translation of the *Cyfoesi* is found on 31–46.

14. Trans. Thorpe, 1978, 192–93.

15. Léon Maitre and Paul de Berthou, *Cartulaire de l'abbaye de Sainte-Croix de Quimperlé (Finistère)* (Paris: Librairie des Provinces, 1896), 3–7, esp. 4, 6–7. After retreating to the wilderness, Gurthiernus, like Lailoken, was accustomed to sit on a large rock by the water and pray. A hunter finds him there and reports to his father, who promises to build him a monastery, but the surviving version is unclear whether he ever actually does so. Gurthiern is guided in his wanderings by an angel, indicating the religious nature of this life (4–6).

16. Carl Selmer, ed., *Navigatio Sancti Brendani Abbatis from Early Latin Manuscripts* (Notre Dame, Ind.: University of Notre Dame Press, 1959). For an English translation, see John J. O'Meara, trans., *The Voyage of Saint Brendan: Journey to the Promised Land* (Portlaoise: Dolmen Press, 1976; reprint, 1985).

17. On Adelard and the presence of Arab learning in twelfth-century England, see Charles Homer Haskins, *Studies in the History of Mediaeval Science* (Cambridge, Mass.: Harvard University Press, 1924), esp. ch. 2; Lynn Thorndike, *A History of Magic and Experimental Science* (New York: Macmillan, 1929), 2:19–49; Charles Burnett, ed., *Adelard of Bath, An English Scientist and Arabist of the Early Twelfth-Century* (London: Warburg Institute, 1987); R. W. Southern, "The Place of England in the Twelfth-Century Renaissance," *History*

45 (1960): 201–16; Jean Jolivet, "The Arabic Inheritance," and Charles Burnett, "Scientific Speculations," in *A History of Twelfth-Century Western Philosophy,* ed. Peter Dronke (Cambridge: Cambridge University Press, 1988): 113–48 and 151–76 respectively.

    18. C. H. Talbot, ed. and trans., *The Life of Christina of Markyate, A Twelfth-Century Recluse* (Oxford: Clarendon Press, 1959; reprint, 1987), 120. See also the career of Wulfric of Haselbury (d. 1154) as described by John of Ford (d. 1182) in Dom Maurice Bell, ed., *Wulfric of Haselbury* (London: Somerset Record Society 1933), xlvii. Wulfric, like Christina, had a prolific output of "political" prophecies.

    19. On medieval belief in the curative properties of water as a treatment of mental disorder, see Tatlock, 1943, 280–84; Basil Clarke, *Mental Disorder in Earlier Britain: Exploratory Studies* (Cardiff: University of Wales Press, 1975), 25–26, 118, 141–42, esp. 127–33.

    20. For the lives of Gildas, see Chronica Minora, vol. 3, ed. Theodore Mommsen in *Monumenta Germaniae Historia . . . Avctorum Antiquissimorvm,* vol. 13 (Berlin: n.p., 1898), esp. 91–106 (Breton Life), 107–10 (by Caradoc of Llancarfan).

    21. Otto of Freising, *Gesta Freiderici* (ed. B. de Simson): *"ab incolis Brittannia dicitur originem trahens . . . quales fuerunt duo fratres Bernhardus et Theodericus, viri doctissimi";* cited in Manitius, 3:196–202, who discusses their lives and works, and accepts that they were from Brittany. Nikolaus Häring says that Clarenbald of Arras, a student of Thierry, refers to his master on several occasions as "the Breton." Nikolaus M. Häring, *Commentaries on Boethius by Thierry of Chartres and His School* (Toronto: Pontifical Institute of Mediaeval Studies, 1971), 46.

    22. This passage is borrowed with minor changes from Nennius, ed. J. Morris, ch. 69.

Selected Bibliography

EDITIONS

The History of the Kings of Britain

Crick, Julia. *A Summary Catalogue of the Manuscripts of Geoffrey of Monmouth's Historia Regum Britannie.* Cambridge: D. S. Brewer, 1988. A valuable descriptive inventory of more than 200 manuscripts of Geoffrey's works.

Faral, Edmond. *La légende arthurienne: Études et documents,* 3 vols. Paris: Champion, 1929. Still valuable for the introductory material in volume two. Volume three contains an edition of the *HRB* based on an eclectic survey of 10 manuscripts and the *VM* in classicized spelling.

Giles, J. A. *Galfridi Monemutensis Historia Britonum.* London: David Nutt, 1844. Mainly based on 1508 Ivo Cavellatus edition with occasional readings from other manuscripts.

Griscom, Acton and R. E. Jones, eds. *The Historia Regum Britanniae of Geoffrey of Monmouth with Contributions to the Study of Its Place in Early British History Together with a Literal Translation of the Welsh Manuscript No. LXI of Jesus College, Oxford.* London: Longmans, Green, 1929. An edition based primarily on the not-always-reliable Cambridge, University Library, MS Ii.1.14.

San Marte [Schulz, Albert]. *Gottfried's von Monmouth Historia Regum Britanniae mit literar-historischer Einleitung und ausführlichen Anmerkungen, und Brut Tysylio, altwälsche Chronik in deutscher Übersetzung.* Halle: Waisenhaus, 1854. Reissue of Giles's edition. Commentary is still useful.

Wright, Neil, ed. *The Historia Regum Britannie of Geoffrey of Monmouth, I: A Single-Manuscript Edition from Bern, Burgerbibliothek, MS 568.* Cambridge: D. S. Brewer, 1984. The first volume in what will become the first complete scholarly edition of Geoffrey's *HRB.* Valuable introductory material on the manuscript tradition of the *HRB* and other aspects of the history.

The Variant Version of the History of the Kings of Britain

Hammer, Jacob, ed. *Geoffrey of Monmouth: Historia Regum Britanniae. A Variant Version Edited from Manuscripts.* Cambridge, Mass.: Medieval Academy of America, 1951. The first edition of a variant text of the *HRB,* based on a family of four manuscripts.

Wright, Neil, ed. *The Historia Regum Britanniae of Geoffrey of Monmouth, II: The First Variant Version: A Critical Edition.* Cambridge: D. S. Brewer, 1988. Based on a complete collation of the eight manuscripts comprising the First Variant text of the *HRB.* Thorough discussion of all aspects of the Variant texts.

The Life of Merlin

Clarke, Basil, ed. and trans. *Life of Merlin. Geoffrey of Monmouth, Vita Merlini.* Cardiff: University of Wales Press, 1973. Best edition of the poem. Excellent introduction and copious notes.

Faral, Edmond. *La légende arthurienne.* See above.

Parry, John J., ed. and trans. *The Vita Merlini.* University of Illinois Studies in Language and Literature 10.3. Urbana: University of Illinois Press, 1925. The first scholarly edition of the poem, with introduction, notes, and prose translation.

BIBLIOGRAPHIES

Bibliographical Bulletin of the International Arthurian Society/Bulletin bibliographique de la Société internationale arthurienne, vols. 1 (1949)–44 (International Arthurian Society, 1992).

Lacy, Norris J. and Geoffrey Ashe, eds. *The Arthurian Handbook.* New York: Garland Publishing, 1988.

Pickford, C. E., R. W. Last, and C. R. Barker. *The Arthurian Bibliography, Arthurian Studies III,* 2 vols. Woodbridge, Suffolk: 1981–82.

Reiss, Edmund, Louise Horner Reiss, Beverly Taylor, eds. *Arthurian Legend and Literature: An Annotated Bibliography.* New York: Garland Publishing, 1984.

SECONDARY SOURCES

Books and Parts of Books

Alcock, Leslie. *Arthur's Britain.* London: Lane, 1971. This is probably still the best study of the historic and archaeological record for Dark Age Britain, and the "Age of Arthur."

Ashe, Geoffrey. *The Discovery of King Arthur.* London: Guild Publishing, 1985. An expanded and more popular account of Ashe's *Speculum* article associating Arthur with Riothamus.

————. "Merlin in the Earliest Records." In *The Book of Merlin, Insights from the First Merlin Conference, London, June 1986,* ed. R. J. Stewart, 20–46. Poole: Blandford Press, 1987. Speculates that the Welsh Myrddin may ultimately be associated with the pre-Christian god Maponos/Apollo.

Barber, Richard. "The *Vera Historia de Morte Arthuri* and Its Place in Arthurian tradition." In *Arthurian Literature I,* ed. Richard Barber, 62–77. Woodbridge, Suffolk: D. S. Brewer, 1981. Discussion of a thirteenth-century Latin account by a Welsh author concerning the death and burial of Arthur.

Jackson on the Arthur of history and in early Welsh verse; Jarman on the Welsh Myrddin poems; Bromwich on the Triads; Loomis on oral diffusion of the Arthurian legends and on the legend of Arthur's survival.

Partner, Nancy F. *Serious Entertainments, The Writing of History in Twelfth-century England.* Chicago: University of Chicago Press, 1977. A study of Henry of Huntingdon, William of Newburgh, and Richard of Devizes as examples of the concerns and methods of historians writing histories of England during the twelfth century.

_berts, Brynley F. "Geoffrey of Monmouth, *Historia Regum Britanniae* and *Brut y Brenhinedd*." In *The Arthur of the Welsh, The Arthurian Legend in Medieval Welsh Literature,* ed. Rachel Bromwich, A. O. H. Jarman, Brynley F. Roberts, 97–116. Cardiff: University of Wales Press, 1991. Geoffrey's relation to Welsh literary and historic traditions; also good for its discussion of major themes in the *HRB*.

_mer, Walter F. *Die frühen Darstellungen des Arthurstoffes.* Cologne: Westdeutscher Verlag, 1958. A study of the Arthutrian tradition in Geoffrey, Wace, and Layamon. Sees the *HRB* as a reflection of contemporary political struggles.

_k, John S. P. *The Legendary History of Britain. Geoffrey of Monmouth's Historia Regum Britanniae and Its Early Vernacular Versions.* Berkeley: University of California Press, 1950 (reprint, New York: Gordon Press, _974). A magisterial study of Geoffrey. Topical in arrangement and _cyclopedic in scope. The very richness of Tatlock's book in historic _tail, however, sometimes obscures the *HRB* and *VM* as literary works.

_reund, Eduard Gustav Hans. *Vergil und Gottfried von Monmouth.* Halle: _neider, 1913. On Geoffrey's use of Virgil.

_upert. *The Political Prophecy in England.* New York: Columbia _versity Press, 1911. Very dated but still useful as an introduction to _ieval political prophecy.

_ Mary L. H. "A Possible Source of Geoffrey's Roman War?" In *The _rian Tradition: Essays in Convergence,* ed. Mary Flowers Braswell and _Bugge, 43–53. Tuscaloosa: University of Alabama Press, 1988. _ates that Geoffrey's account of Arthur's war in Gaul was influenced _sar's *Commentaries,* perhaps filtered through a Celtic retelling.

_. "Giraldus Cambrensis et le roi Arthur." In *Mélanges de philologie _ératures romaines offerts à Jeanne Wathelet-Willem,* ed. Jacques de _667–78. Liege: Cahiers de l'A. R. U. Lg., 1978. Examines _sceptical attitude toward Geoffrey's portrait of Arthur in the _so discusses Gerald's accounts of the exhumation of the remains _ and Guinevere at Glastonbury in 1191.

_ont Saint-Michel et Geoffroi de Monmouth." In *Millénaire _du Mont Saint-Michel,* 377–82. Paris: P. Lethielleux, 1967. A _eoffrey's possible use of local traditions concerning the island in _Mont-Saint-Michel known as Tumbellana.

Bartrum, P. C., ed. *Early Welsh Genealogical Tracts.* Cardiff: University of Wales Press, 1966. Essential scholarly edition of the Welsh genealogies.

Brinkley, Roberta Florence. *Arthurian Legend in the Seventeenth Century.* Baltimore, Md.: Johns Hopkins University Press, 1932. Includes survey of the impact of Geoffrey's British history on Tudor political concepts.

Bromwich, Rachel. *Trioedd Ynys Prydein: The Welsh Triads,* 2d ed. Cardiff: University of Wales Press, 1978. An essential book on Welsh traditions as preserved in the Triads, but rich in information on a wide rage of subjects related to British history and legend.

Brooke, Christopher. "Geoffrey of Monmouth as a Historian." In *Church and Government in the Middle Ages,* ed. Christopher Brooke, et al., 77–91. Cambridge: Cambridge University Press, 1976. Downplays Geoffrey's attempt to create a genuine history in favor of the view that he was essentially a literary artist.

Bullock-Davies, C. *Professional Interpreters and the Matter of Britain.* Cardiff: University of Wales Press, 1966. An important study of the role of the interpreter in mediating among the various language communities of medieval Britain.

Chambers, E. K. *Arthur of Britain.* London: Sidgwick and Jackson, 1927. Although many of Chamber's views are now somewhat dated this work can still be read with profit. Contains a convenient anthology of Arthurian records at the end of the volume.

Curley, Michael J. "Animal Symbolism in the Prophecies of Merlin." In *Beasts and Birds of the Middle Ages: The Bestiary and Its Legacy,* ed. Willene B. Clark and Meradith T. McMunn, 151–63. Philadelphia: University of Pennsylvania Press, 1989. Traces the use of animal symbolism in the *PM* to a multiplicity of sources, including the Bible, Welsh genealogical material, and a variety of classical and postclassical Latin texts.

Dumville, David N. "An Early Text of Geoffrey of Monmouth's *Historia Regum Britanniae* and the Circulation of Some Latin Histories in Twelfth-Century Normandy." In *Arthurian Literature IV,* ed. Richard Barber, 1–36. Woodbridge, Suffolk: D. S. Brewer; Totowa, N.J.: Barnes & Noble, 1985. Reprinted in *Histories and Pseudo-histories of the Insular Middle Ages.* Aldershot: Variorum, 1990 (ch. 14). A detailed study of the "Bern group" of *HRB* manuscripts, originating in the reign of King Stephen (before 1147).

Eckhardt, Caroline D., ed. *The Prophetia Merlini of Geoffrey of Monmouth, A Fifteenth-Century English Commentary,* Cambridge, Mass.: Medieval Academy of America, 1982. Contains a good introduction to the *PM* and the commentary tradition in addition to an edition of the English commentary.

Feuerherd, Paul. *Geoffrey of Monmouth und das alte Testament mit Berücksichtigung der Historia Britonum des Nennius.* Halle: Ehrhardt Karras, 1915. Basic guide to passages in the *HRB* indebted to the Hebrew scriptures. Feuerherd thought Geoffrey modeled the *HRB* on the history of the Jews.

Fletcher, Robert Huntington. *The Arthurian Material in the Chronicles especially those of Great Britain and France.* Boston: Ginn, 1906. Still valuable for its review of chroniclers who drew on Geoffrey.

Fries, Maureen. "Boethian Themes and Tragic Structure in Geoffrey of Monmouth's *Historia Regum Britanniae.*" In *The Arthurian Tradition: Essays in Convergence,* ed. Mary Flowers Braswell and John Bugge, 29–42. Tuscaloosa: University of Alabama Press, 1988. Argues that Boethius's *Consolation of Philosophy* provided Geoffrey with his basic philosophical outlook on kingship and tragedy.

Goodrich, Peter, ed. *The Romance of Merlin: An Anthology.* New York: Garland Publishing, 1990. Useful for Thundy's translations of the Lailoken fragments, Bollard's translations of the Welsh Myrddin poetry, and a reprint of Parry's translation of the *VM.*

Griffiths, Margaret Enid. *Early Vaticination in Welsh with English Parallels,* ed. T. Gwyn Jones. Cardiff: University of Wales Press, 1937. A survey of Welsh prophetic literature including the Myrddin poetry.

Hammer, Jacob. "An Unedited Commentary on the *Prophetia Merlini* in Dublin, Trinity College MS 496 E.6.2 (Geoffrey de Monmouth, *Historia Regum Britanniae,* Book VII)." In *Charisteria Thaddaeo Sinko; Quinquaginta abhinc annos amplissimis in philosophia honoribus ornato ab amicis collegis discipulis oblata,* 81–89. Warsaw: Sumptibus Societatis Philologae Polonorum, 1951.

———. "Bref commentaire de la *Prophetia Merlini* du ms 3514 de la bibliothèque de la cathédrale d'Exeter (Geoffrey de Monmouth, *Historia Regum Britanniae,* Book VII)." In *Hommages á Joseph Bidez et á Franz Cumont,* 111–19. Bruxelles: Collection Latomus, 1948.

Hanning, Robert W. *The Vision of History in Early Britain from Gildas to Geoffrey of Monmouth.* New York: Columbia University Press, 1966. An essential study of the development of historic writing in Britain. Chapters on Gildas, Bede, Nennius, and Geoffrey of Monmouth.

Hutson, Arthur E. *British Personal Names in the Historia Regum Britanniae.* Berkeley: University of California Press, 1940; reprint, Philadelphia: R. West, 1978. A somewhat dated, though still fundamental, study of Geoffrey's sources through an examination of the personal names in the *HRB.*

Jarman, A. O. H. "Early Stages in the Development of the Myrddin Legend." In *Studies in Old Welsh Poetry, Astudiaethau Ar Yr Hengerdd,* ed. Rachel Bromwich and R. Brinley Jones, 326–49. Cardiff: University of Wales Press, 1978. A reconstruction of five stages in the chronological development of the legend of the Welsh Myrddin.

———. "The Merlin Legend and the Welsh Tradition of Prophecy." In *The Arthur of the Welsh, The Arthurian Legend in Medieval Welsh Literature,* ed. Rachel Bromwich, A. O. H. Jarman, Brynley F. Roberts, 117–45. Cardiff: University of Wales Press, 1991. The best recent survey of the

Welsh (Myrddin), Irish (Suibhne), and Scottish (Kentigern/Lailo⟨ logues to Geoffrey's story of Merlin. *The Arthur of the Welsh* als⟨ valuable articles by Thomas Charles-Edwards on the Arthur⟨ Patrick Sims-Williams on the Welsh Arthurian poems⟨ Caerwyn Williams on Brittany and the Arthurian legends.

Jones, Ernest. *Geoffrey of Monmouth, 1640–1800.* Berkeley and⟨ University of California Press, 1944. A survery of Geoff⟨ and reputation in later centuries.

Keeler, Laura. *Geoffrey of Monmouth and the Late Latin Chronicl⟨* Berkeley: University of California Press, 1946. A stu⟨ influence on some Latin chroniclers.

Kendrick, T. D. *British Antiquity.* London: Methuen, 1950.⟨ of the rise and fall of the "British history" in later En⟨ through the sixteenth century.

Knight, Stephen. *Arthurian Literature and Society.* Londor⟨ Chapter 2 (38–67) views the *HRB* as a "euhemeriz⟨ tion" of Norman brutality in the conquest and ad⟨ from William the Conqueror to Henry I.

Leckie, R. William, Jr. *The Passage of Dominion: Geof⟨ Periodization of Insular History in the Twelfth Cen⟨* of Toronto Press, 1981. A detailed study of h⟨ fined the duration and importance of Celtic ⟨ challenged subsequent historians to incorpo⟨ dard periodization of insular history.

Legge, M. D. "Master Geoffrey Arthur." In *An⟨ Memory of Lewis Thorpe,* ed. Kenneth Varty⟨ of Glasgow Press, 1981. A study of the O⟨ *HRB,* including comments on Walter ⟨ George's, Robert of Gloucester, Walera⟨ and Walter of Espec.

Morris, Rosemary. "Uther and Igerne: ⟨ *Arthurian Literature IV,* ed. Richard B⟨ D. S. Brewer; Totowa, N.J.: Barnes ⟨ of Geoffrey's story of Uther and Ig⟨ Geoffrey of Viterbo, Robert de Bor⟨

Pähler, Heinrich. *Strukturuntersuchungen ⟨ of Monmouth.* Bonn: Rheinischen ⟨ Detailed analysis of the structur⟨

Parry, John Jay, and Robert A. C⟨ *Arthurian Literature in the M⟨* 72–93. Oxford: Oxford Univ⟨ somewhat dated, this essa⟨ Geoffrey's life and works. *A⟨* several other essays by emir⟨

Tolstoy, Nicholai. *The Quest for Merlin.* Boston: Little, Brown, 1985. A wide-ranging and speculative effort to reconstruct the historic Merlin as a druid living during the sixth century in the mountains of South Scotland in an area know as Hart Fell.

Wright, Neil. "Geoffrey of Monmouth and Gildas." In *Arthurian Literature II,* ed. Richard Barber, 1–40. Cambridge, Suffolk: D. S. Brewer; Totowa, N.J.: Rowman & Littlefield, 1982. A detailed study of Geoffrey's debt to Gildas in the *HRB* and the *VM.*

———. "Geoffrey of Monmouth and Gildas Revisited." In *Arthurian Literature IV,* ed. Richard Barber, 155–63. Woodbridge, Suffolk; Totowa, N.J.: Brewer; Barnes & Noble, 1985. Analysis of additional borrowings from Gildas by Geoffrey in the *PM* and *HRB.*

———. "Geoffrey of Monmouth and Bede." In *Arthurian Literature VI,* ed. Richard Barber, 27–59. Woodbridge, Suffolk; Totowa, N.J.: Brewer; Barnes & Noble, 1986. Interprets Geoffrey's borrowings from Bede as a direct challenge to Bede's authority as a historian.

———. "The Place of Henry of Huntingdon's *Epistola ad Warinum* in the text-history of Geoffrey of Monmouth's *Historia Regum Britanniae:* a preliminary investigation." In *France and the British Isles in the Middle Ages and Renaissance,* ed. Gillian Jondorf and D. N. Dumville, 71–113. Woodbridge, Suffolk: Boydell Press, 1991. An edition, translation, and study of Henry of Huntingdon's letter to Warinus (1139), the earliest known witness to Geoffrey's *HRB.*

Ziolkowski, Jan. "The Nature of Prophecy in Geoffrey of Monmouth's *Vita Merlini.*" In *Poetry and Prophecy: The Beginnings of a Literary Tradition,* ed. James L. Nagu, 151–62. Ithaca, N.Y.: Cornell University Press, 1990. Examines the tripartite role of Merlin in the *VM* as a shaman, political prophet, and Christian ascetic.

Zumthor, Paul. *Merlin le Prophète, un thème de la littérature polemique de l'historiographie et des romans.* Lausanne, 1943 (reprint, Geneva: Slatkine Reprints, 1973). A wide-ranging study of the figure of Merlin and the prophecies attributed to him. Not always reliable in detail.

Journal Articles

Ashe, Geoffrey. "'A Certain Very Ancient Book': Traces of an Arthurian Source in Geoffrey of Monmouth's History." *Speculum* 56 (1981): 301–23. Argues that Geoffrey modeled Arthur's Gallic campaign on the career of Riothamus, a fifth-century British military commander.

Bartrum, Peter C. "Was There a British Book of Conquests?" *Bulletin of the Board of Celtic Studies* 23 (1968):1–6. Advances the idea that Geoffrey may have known a simple British king-list recited orally and accompanied by native legendary and mythological lore.

Bromwich, Rachel. "Concepts of Arthur." *Studia Celtica* 10/11 (1975–76): 163–81. Supplement to Thomas Jones's 1964 study of the figure of Arthur in the light of more recent scholarship.

Caldwell, R. A. "Wace's *Roman de Brut* and the *Variant Version* of Geoffrey of Monmouth's *Historia Regum Britanniae.*" *Speculum* 31 (1956): 675–82. Argues that Wace used both the Variant and the Vulgate versions in his *Roman de Brut* (1155) and that the Variant must have been in existence in Geoffrey's own lifetime.

Crawford, T. D. "On the Linguistic Competence of Geoffrey of Monmouth." *Medium Aevum* 51 (1982): 152–62. Particularly good on Geoffrey's knowledge of Welsh and the improbability of his having access to a book "in the British language."

Crick, Julia. "Geoffrey of Monmouth, Prophecy and History." *Journal of Medieval History* 18 (1992): 357–71. A study of the reception of the *Prophecies of Merlin,* primarily during the twelfth century.

Curley, Michael J. "A New Edition of John of Cornwall's *Prophetia Merlini.*" *Speculum* 57 (1982): 217–49. An edition and study of John of Cornwall's *Prophetia Merlini,* showing that John drew on sources other than Geoffrey. The commentary on the *Prophetia Merlini* contains glosses in a Celtic language.

Ditmas, E. M. R. "Geoffrey of Monmouth and the Breton Families in Cornwall." *Welsh History Review* 6 (1973): 451–61. Speculates that Geoffrey may have descended from one of the Breton families settled in Monmouth under Wihenoc. His knowledge of Cornwall may have come through connections with Robert, earl of Gloucester. Breton traditions may have influenced certain episodes in the *HRB.*

———. "A Reappraisal of Geoffrey of Monmouth's Allusions to Cornwall." *Speculum* 48 (1973): 510–24. Concludes that Geoffrey probably did visit Cornwall or was in contact with persons who knew Cornish traditions. His knowledge, however, seems limited to the north coast and the region around the Hayle estuary.

Dumville, David N. "Sub-Roman Britain: History and Legend." *History* 62 (1977): 173–92. Reprinted in *Histories and Pseudo-histories of the Insular Middle Ages.* Aldershot: Variorum, 1990 (ch. 1). A critical examination of the sources on which our history of fifth- and sixth-century Britain is based: Gildas, Welsh romances, "Nennius," the Welsh *Annals,* and genealogies, among others.

Eckhardt, Caroline D. "The date of the *Prophetia Merlini* Commentary in *MSS Cotton Claudius B. VII.* and *Bibliothèque Nationale* Fonds Latin 6233." *Notes and Queries* 23 (1976): 146–47. Dates the earliest complete commentary on the *PM* to 1147 or 1149.

———. "Another Manuscript of the Commentary on *Prophetia Merlini* Attributed to Alain de Lille." *Manuscripta* 29 (1985): 143–47.

———. "Geoffrey of Monmouth's *Prophetia Merlini* and the Construction of Liege University MS 369C." *Manuscripta* 32 (1988): 176–84.

Edel, Doris. "Geoffrey's So-Called Animal Symbolism and Insular Celtic Tradition." *Studia Celtica* 18/19 (1983–84): 96–109. Geoffrey may have derived the idea of using animal symbolism from Insular Celtic tradition, but he was also influenced by biblical and classical sources.

Emanuel, Hywel D. "Geoffrey of Monmouth's *Historia Regum Britanniae:* A Second Variant Version." *Medium Aevum* 35 (1966): 103–11. Identifies a "second Variant Version" of the *HRB* in 15 manuscripts. This version is in many respects closer to the Vulgate text than to the Variant Version, edited by Hammer.

Eysteinsson, J. S. "The Relationship of Merlínússpá and Geoffrey of Monmouth's *Historia.*" *Saga—Book of the Viking Society* 14 (1953–57): 95–112. Argues that Gunnlaugr Leifsson's translation of the *PM* shows an awareness of the *HRB* proper. Gunnlaugr may have worked in Iceland rather than in Norway.

Fleuriot, L. "Old Breton Genealogies and Early British Traditions." *Bulletin of the Board of Celtic Studies* 26 (1974): 1–6. Shows that the legend of Conan Meriadoc's taking possession of Brittany was known in Brittany as early as the early eleventh century and was not the invention of Geoffrey of Monmouth.

———. "Sur quatre textes Bretons en Latin, le 'Liber Vetustissimus' de Geoffroy de Monmouth et le séjour de Taliesin en Bretagne." *Études celtiques* 18 (1981): 197–213. A study of the legendary material in the Breton tradition that preceded Geoffrey and that may have been part of the book Walter the archdeacon brought to Geoffrey from Brittany.

Flint, Valerie I. J. "The *Historia Regum Britanniae* of Geoffrey of Monmouth: Parody and Its Purpose: A Suggestion." *Speculum* 54 (1979): 447–68. Interprets the *HRB* in part as counterpropaganda to the pretensions of twelfth-century monastic literature and society.

Fowler, D. C. "Some biblical influences on Geoffrey of Monmouth's historiography." *Traditio* 14 (1958):378–85. Shows how Geoffrey borrows narratives from the Bible in the HRB, but often turns Biblical heroes into villains, and villains into heroes.

Gallais, Pierre. "La *Variant Version* de l'*Historia Regum Britanniae* et le *Brut* de Wace." *Romania* 87 (1966):1–32. Argues against Caldwell's view that Wace used the Variant Version. Gallais concludes that the Variant Version drew on Wace's *Roman de Brut* and the Vulgate.

Gerould, G. H. "King Arthur and Politics." *Speculum* 2 (1927): 33–52. Geoffrey formed Arthur for the Anglo-Norman aristocracy as a rival to Charlemagne.

Gillingham, John. "The Context and Purposes of Geoffrey of Monmouth's *History of the Kings of Britain.*" *Anglo-Norman Studies XIII, Proceedings of the Battle Conference 1990,* ed Marjorie Chibnall, 99–118. The *HRB* was intended to refute the growing Anglo-French perception of the Welsh as barbarians at a time when Wales was beginning to play an important role in the politics of Britain.

van Hamel, A. G. "The Old Norse Version of the *Historia Regum Britanniae* and the Text of Geoffrey of Monmouth." *Études celtiques* 1 (1936): 197–247.

A study of the translation of the *HRB* by Haukr Erlendsson (d. 1334) and Gunnlaugr Leifsson's *Merlínússpá*, a poetic version of the *Prophecies of Merlin*.

Hammer, Jacob. "A Commentary on the *Prophetia Merlini* (Geoffrey of Monmouth's *Historia Regum Britanniae*, Book VII)." *Speculum* 10 (1935): 3–30.

————."A Commentary on the *Prophetia Merlini* (Geoffrey of Monmouth's *Historia Regum Britanniae*, Book VII) (Continuation)." *Speculum* 15 (1940): 409–431.

————."Another Commentary on the *Prophetia Merlini* (Geoffrey of Monmouth's *Historia Regum Britanniae*, Book VII)." *Bulletin of the Polish Institute of Arts and Sciences in America* 1 (1942–43): 589–601.

————. "Geoffrey of Monmouth's Use of the Bible in the *Historia Regum Britanniae*." *Bulletin of the John Rylands Library* 30 (1946/7): 293–311. Shows how Geoffrey's language throughout the *HRB* was influenced by the Latin version of the Bible.

————. "Note sur l'histoire du roi Lear dans Geoffrey de Monmouth." *Latomus* 5 (1946): 299–301. Finds echoes of the *HRB* story of Lear in Terrence's *Phormio*, the Bible and Vergil's *Aeneid*.

————. "Remarks on the sources and textual history of Geoffrey of Monmouth's *Historia Regum Britanniae*." *Bulletin of the Polish Institute of Arts and Sciences in America* 2 (1943/4): 501–64. Discussion of the dedications, printed editions and sources of the *HRB*. Suggests that the story of Lear in the *HRB* was influenced by the tale of Barlaam and Ioasaph.

Hutson, A. "Geoffrey of Monmouth. Two notes: I, Brychan and Geoffrey of Monmouth's Ebraucus; II, Welsh heroes at Arthur's court." *Transactions of the Honourable Society of Cymmrodorion* (1937): 361–73.

Jackson, Kenneth. "The Site of Mount Badon." *Journal of Celtic Studies* 2 (1953–58): 152–55. Review of sites often identified with Arthur's decisive battle. Jackson suggests the Iron Age hill fort in Dorset, now known as Badbury Rings.

Jones, Ernest. "Geoffrey of Monmouth's Account of the Establishment of the Episcopacy in England." *Journal of English and German Philology* 40 (1941): 360–63. On Geoffrey's use of the *Isidorus Mercator* for the existence of *flamines* and *archflamines* in Roman Britain.

Jones, Thomas. "The Early Evolution of the Legend of Arthur." *Nottingham Mediaeval Studies* 8 (1964): 3–21. Basic study, especially strong on the Welsh background.

Keller, Hans E. "Two Toponymical Problems in Geoffrey of Monmouth and Wace: Estrusia and Siesia." *Speculum* 49 (1974): 687–98. Estrusia as a name for the region around Bayeux reached Geoffrey through Saxon sources. Siesia is a name concocted by Geoffrey to combine the place of Caesar's victory over the Gauls (Alesia) with the nearby Val Suzon, a pilgrimage site in Burgundy.

———. "Wace et Geoffrey de Monmouth: problème de la chronologie des sources." *Romania* 98 (1977): 379–89. Argues that Wace used the Variant Version of the *HRB* and that Geoffrey used the Variant, possibly composed by Walter the archdeacon, as the source of his Vulgate-HRB.

———. "Les conquêtes du roi Artur en Thulé." *Cahiers de civilisation medievale (Xe–XIIe siècles)* 23 (1980):29–35. A discussion of what Geoffrey knew about the "islands of the ocean," which Arthur brought under his sway by conquest.

Le Duc, Gwrnaël. "L'historia britannica avant Geoffrey de Monmouth." *Annales de Bretagne et des pays de l'ouest* 79 (1972): 819–35. Argues that Geoffrey's *HRB* is probably indebted in part to a poem concerned with the early history of Brittany which currently survives only in fragmentary condition of 173 Latin hexameters in a fifteenth-century manuscript.

Lloyd, J. E. "Geoffrey of Monmouth." *English Historical Review* 57 (1942): 460–68. An authoritative review of Geoffrey's biography and literary career; especially good on the connections with Wales.

Loomis, Laura H. "Geoffrey of Monmouth and Stonehenge." *PMLA* 45 (1930): 400–15. Geoffrey's story of the building of Stonehenge was not his invention but was derived from antecedent tradition contained in a folktale.

Loomis, Roger Sherman. "Geoffrey of Monmouth and Arthurian Origins." *Speculum* 3 (1928): 16–33. Argues against Gerould's thesis that Geoffrey's Arthur was conceived mainly as a rival to Charlemagne.

MacQueen, Winifred, and John MacQueen. "*Vita Merlini* Silvestris." *Scottish Studies* 29 (1989): 77–93.

Meehan, Bernard. "Geoffrey of Monmouth, *Prophecies of Merlin:* New Manuscript Evidence." *Bulletin of the Board of Celtic Studies* 28 (1978–80): 37–46. Concludes from a study of the *PM* in Liège University Library MS. 369C that the *Prophecies of Merlin* were originally composed in the 1120s.

Miller, Molly. "Geoffrey's Early Royal Synchronisms." *Bulletin of the Board of Celtic Studies* 28 (1978–80): 373–89. Speculates that behind Geoffrey's claim to have used an ancient book in the British language may have been a short royal pedigree with "British" annotations, which Walter may have brought to England from Brittany.

Minois, Georges. "Bretagne insulaire et Bretagne armoricaine dans l'oeuvre de Geoffroy de Monmouth." *Mémoires de la Société historique et archéologique de Bretagne* 58 (1981):35–60. A study of Geoffrey's references to Britanny. Shows how Geoffrey's history continued to be accepted as veracious by historians of Britanny after it was viewed as legendary in England.

Padel, O. "Geoffrey of Monmouth and Cornwall." *Cambridge Medieval Celtic Studies* 8 (1984): 1–28. The most thorough study of Geoffrey's knowledge of Cornish traditions, history, and geography.

Parry, J. J. "Celtic Tradition and the *Vita Merlini*." *Philological Quarterly* 4 (1925): 193–207. Somewhat dated, but still useful review of the Celtic analogues to Geoffrey's *VM*.

Piggot, Stuart. "The Sources of Geoffrey of Monmouth. I. The 'Pre-Roman' King-List. II. The Stonehenge Story." *Antiquity, A Quarterly Review of Archaeology* 15 (1941): 276–82 and 305–19. Shows Geoffrey's concoction of Britain's pre-Roman kings to be based in part on Welsh genealogical tracts; examines the Stonehenge story in the *HRB* as a variant of the story of Bran the Blessed in the *Mabinogi*. Conjectures that the story may preserve the sacred lore of Bronze Age Wessex concerning the erection of the Stonehenge megaliths.

Reiss, Edmund. "The Welsh Versions of Geoffrey of Monmouth's *Historia*." *Welsh History Review* 4 (1968): 97–127. Attempts to classify the Welsh versions of Geoffrey's *HRB*.

Roberts, Brynley F. "The Treatment of Personal Names in the Early Welsh Versions of *Historia Regum Britanniae*." *Bulletin of the Board of Celtic Studies* 25 (1973): 274–90. Concludes that Geoffrey did not draw extensively on Welsh traditions for the names of personages in the HRB. Shows how influential Geoffrey was on native documents.

――――. "Geoffrey of Monmouth and Welsh Historical Tradition." *Nottingham Mediaeval Studies* 20 (1976): 29–40. Shows Geoffrey's reliance on British/Welsh historic traditions, particularly for the theme of loss and renewal of a people's liberties.

Salter, H. E. "Geoffrey of Monmouth and Oxford." *English Historical Review* 34 (1919): 382–85. Essential study of the biographical data on Geoffrey as revealed in the charters to which he was a signatory.

Schwartz, S. M. "The founding and self-betrayal of Britain: an Augustinian approach to Geoffrey of Monmouth's *Historia Regum Britanniae*." *Medievalia et Humanistica* 10 (1981): 33–53. Examines biblical parallels in the HRB to argue that Geoffrey's historic outlook was shaped by an Augustinian figural concept of history.

Southern, R. W. "Aspects of the European Tradition of Historical Writing: 1, The Classical Tradition from Einhard to Geoffrey of Monmouth." *Transactions of the Royal Historical Society*, Series 5, 20 (1970): 173–96. Contrasts Geoffrey's use of the Trojan legend with that of Widukind and Dudo. Geoffrey's history is distinguished by its vivid details, tragic structure and hope for the future.

――――. "The Place of England in the Twelfth-Century Renaissance." *History* 45 (1960): 201–16. A survey of historiographical and "scientific" learning in twelfth-century England.

Sterckx, Claude. "'Princeps militiae' dans l'Historia Regum Britanniae de Geoffrey de Monmouth." *Annales de Bretagne et des pays de l'ouest* 76 (1969): 725–30. Argues that Geoffrey was influenced by the Welsh office of *penteulu* when making Belinus the *princeps militiae* to Cassivelaunus.

Tatlock, John S. P. "Certain Contemporaneous Matters in Geoffrey of Monmouth." *Speculum* 6 (1931):206–24. A study of the resonances of certain

Bartrum, P. C., ed. *Early Welsh Genealogical Tracts.* Cardiff: University of Wales Press, 1966. Essential scholarly edition of the Welsh genealogies.

Brinkley, Roberta Florence. *Arthurian Legend in the Seventeenth Century.* Baltimore, Md.: Johns Hopkins University Press, 1932. Includes survey of the impact of Geoffrey's British history on Tudor political concepts.

Bromwich, Rachel. *Trioedd Ynys Prydein: The Welsh Triads,* 2d ed. Cardiff: University of Wales Press, 1978. An essential book on Welsh traditions as preserved in the Triads, but rich in information on a wide rage of subjects related to British history and legend.

Brooke, Christopher. "Geoffrey of Monmouth as a Historian." In *Church and Government in the Middle Ages,* ed. Christopher Brooke, et al., 77–91. Cambridge: Cambridge University Press, 1976. Downplays Geoffrey's attempt to create a genuine history in favor of the view that he was essentially a literary artist.

Bullock-Davies, C. *Professional Interpreters and the Matter of Britain.* Cardiff: University of Wales Press, 1966. An important study of the role of the interpreter in mediating among the various language communities of medieval Britain.

Chambers, E. K. *Arthur of Britain.* London: Sidgwick and Jackson, 1927. Although many of Chamber's views are now somewhat dated this work can still be read with profit. Contains a convenient anthology of Arthurian records at the end of the volume.

Curley, Michael J. "Animal Symbolism in the Prophecies of Merlin." In *Beasts and Birds of the Middle Ages: The Bestiary and Its Legacy,* ed. Willene B. Clark and Meradith T. McMunn, 151–63. Philadelphia: University of Pennsylvania Press, 1989. Traces the use of animal symbolism in the *PM* to a multiplicity of sources, including the Bible, Welsh genealogical material, and a variety of classical and postclassical Latin texts.

Dumville, David N. "An Early Text of Geoffrey of Monmouth's *Historia Regum Britanniae* and the Circulation of Some Latin Histories in Twelfth-Century Normandy." In *Arthurian Literature IV,* ed. Richard Barber, 1–36. Woodbridge, Suffolk: D. S. Brewer; Totowa, N.J.: Barnes & Noble, 1985. Reprinted in *Histories and Pseudo-histories of the Insular Middle Ages.* Aldershot: Variorum, 1990 (ch. 14). A detailed study of the "Bern group" of *HRB* manuscripts, originating in the reign of King Stephen (before 1147).

Eckhardt, Caroline D., ed. *The Prophetia Merlini of Geoffrey of Monmouth, A Fifteenth-Century English Commentary,* Cambridge, Mass.: Medieval Academy of America, 1982. Contains a good introduction to the *PM* and the commentary tradition in addition to an edition of the English commentary.

Feuerherd, Paul. *Geoffrey of Monmouth und das alte Testament mit Berücksichtigung der Historia Britonum des Nennius.* Halle: Ehrhardt Karras, 1915. Basic guide to passages in the *HRB* indebted to the Hebrew scriptures. Feuerherd thought Geoffrey modeled the *HRB* on the history of the Jews.

Fletcher, Robert Huntington. *The Arthurian Material in the Chronicles especially those of Great Britain and France.* Boston: Ginn, 1906. Still valuable for its review of chroniclers who drew on Geoffrey.

Fries, Maureen. "Boethian Themes and Tragic Structure in Geoffrey of Monmouth's *Historia Regum Britanniae.*" In *The Arthurian Tradition: Essays in Convergence,* ed. Mary Flowers Braswell and John Bugge, 29–42. Tuscaloosa: University of Alabama Press, 1988. Argues that Boethius's *Consolation of Philosophy* provided Geoffrey with his basic philosophical outlook on kingship and tragedy.

Goodrich, Peter, ed. *The Romance of Merlin: An Anthology.* New York: Garland Publishing, 1990. Useful for Thundy's translations of the Lailoken fragments, Bollard's translations of the Welsh Myrddin poetry, and a reprint of Parry's translation of the *VM.*

Griffiths, Margaret Enid. *Early Vaticination in Welsh with English Parallels,* ed. T. Gwyn Jones. Cardiff: University of Wales Press, 1937. A survey of Welsh prophetic literature including the Myrddin poetry.

Hammer, Jacob. "An Unedited Commentary on the *Prophetia Merlini* in Dublin, Trinity College MS 496 E.6.2 (Geoffrey de Monmouth, *Historia Regum Britanniae,* Book VII)." In *Charisteria Thaddaeo Sinko; Quinquaginta abhinc annos amplissimis in philosophia honoribus ornato ab amicis collegis discipulis oblata,* 81–89. Warsaw: Sumptibus Societatis Philologae Polonorum, 1951.

———. "Bref commentaire de la *Prophetia Merlini* du ms 3514 de la bibliothèque de la cathédrale d'Exeter (Geoffrey de Monmouth, *Historia Regum Britanniae,* Book VII)." In *Hommages á Joseph Bidez et á Franz Cumont,* 111–19. Bruxelles: Collection Latomus, 1948.

Hanning, Robert W. *The Vision of History in Early Britain from Gildas to Geoffrey of Monmouth.* New York: Columbia University Press, 1966. An essential study of the development of historic writing in Britain. Chapters on Gildas, Bede, Nennius, and Geoffrey of Monmouth.

Hutson, Arthur E. *British Personal Names in the Historia Regum Britanniae.* Berkeley: University of California Press, 1940; reprint, Philadelphia: R. West, 1978. A somewhat dated, though still fundamental, study of Geoffrey's sources through an examination of the personal names in the *HRB.*

Jarman, A. O. H. "Early Stages in the Development of the Myrddin Legend." In *Studies in Old Welsh Poetry, Astudiaethau Ar Yr Hengerdd,* ed. Rachel Bromwich and R. Brinley Jones, 326–49. Cardiff: University of Wales Press, 1978. A reconstruction of five stages in the chronological development of the legend of the Welsh Myrddin.

———. "The Merlin Legend and the Welsh Tradition of Prophecy." In *The Arthur of the Welsh, The Arthurian Legend in Medieval Welsh Literature,* ed. Rachel Bromwich, A. O. H. Jarman, Brynley F. Roberts, 117–45. Cardiff: University of Wales Press, 1991. The best recent survey of the

Welsh (Myrddin), Irish (Suibhne), and Scottish (Kentigern/Lailoken) analogues to Geoffrey's story of Merlin. *The Arthur of the Welsh* also contains valuable articles by Thomas Charles-Edwards on the Arthur of history, Patrick Sims-Williams on the Welsh Arthurian poems, and J. E. Caerwyn Williams on Brittany and the Arthurian legends.

Jones, Ernest. *Geoffrey of Monmouth, 1640–1800.* Berkeley and Los Angeles: University of California Press, 1944. A survery of Geoffrey's influence and reputation in later centuries.

Keeler, Laura. *Geoffrey of Monmouth and the Late Latin Chroniclers, 1300–1500.* Berkeley: University of California Press, 1946. A study of Geoffrey's influence on some Latin chroniclers.

Kendrick, T. D. *British Antiquity.* London: Methuen, 1950. A standard review of the rise and fall of the "British history" in later English historiography through the sixteenth century.

Knight, Stephen. *Arthurian Literature and Society.* London: St. Martin's, 1983. Chapter 2 (38–67) views the *HRB* as a "euhemerization" and "mystification" of Norman brutality in the conquest and administration of Britain from William the Conqueror to Henry I.

Leckie, R. William, Jr. *The Passage of Dominion: Geoffrey of Monmouth and the Periodization of Insular History in the Twelfth Century.* Toronto: University of Toronto Press, 1981. A detailed study of how Geoffrey's *HRB* redefined the duration and importance of Celtic sovereignty in Britain, and challenged subsequent historians to incorporate the *HRB* into the standard periodization of insular history.

Legge, M. D. "Master Geoffrey Arthur." In *An Arthurian Tapestry, Essays in Memory of Lewis Thorpe,* ed. Kenneth Varty, 22–27. Glasgow: University of Glasgow Press, 1981. A study of the Oxford background to Geoffrey's *HRB,* including comments on Walter of Oxford, the College of Saint George's, Robert of Gloucester, Waleran of Meulan, Robert of Chesney, and Walter of Espec.

Morris, Rosemary. "Uther and Igerne: A Study in Uncourtly Love." In *Arthurian Literature IV,* ed. Richard Barber, 70–92. Woodbridge, Suffolk: D. S. Brewer; Totowa, N.J.: Barnes & Noble, 1985. Traces the treatment of Geoffrey's story of Uther and Igerne in the works of Wace, Layamon, Geoffrey of Viterbo, Robert de Boron, Malory, Boece and Buchanan.

Pähler, Heinrich. *Strukturuntersuchungen zur Historia Regum Britanniae des Geoffrey of Monmouth.* Bonn: Rheinischen Friedrich-Wilhelms-Universität, 1958. Detailed analysis of the structure of the *HRB.*

Parry, John Jay, and Robert A. Caldwell. "Geoffrey of Monmouth." In *Arthurian Literature in the Middle Ages,* ed. Roger Sherman Loomis, 72–93. Oxford: Oxford University Press, 1959 (reprint, 1979). Though somewhat dated, this essay is still a good general introduction to Geoffrey's life and works. *Arthurian Literature in the Middle Ages* contains several other essays by eminent medievalists on topics related to Geoffrey:

Jackson on the Arthur of history and in early Welsh verse; Jarman on the Welsh Myrddin poems; Bromwich on the Triads; Loomis on oral diffusion of the Arthurian legends and on the legend of Arthur's survival.

Partner, Nancy F. *Serious Entertainments, The Writing of History in Twelfth-century England.* Chicago: University of Chicago Press, 1977. A study of Henry of Huntingdon, William of Newburgh, and Richard of Devizes as examples of the concerns and methods of historians writing histories of England during the twelfth century.

Roberts, Brynley F. "Geoffrey of Monmouth, *Historia Regum Britanniae* and *Brut y Brenhinedd.*" In *The Arthur of the Welsh, The Arthurian Legend in Medieval Welsh Literature,* ed. Rachel Bromwich, A. O. H. Jarman, Brynley F. Roberts, 97–116. Cardiff: University of Wales Press, 1991. Geoffrey's relation to Welsh literary and historic traditions; also good for its discussion of major themes in the *HRB.*

Schirmer, Walter F. *Die frühen Darstellungen des Arthurstoffes.* Cologne: Westdeutscher Verlag, 1958. A study of the Arthutrian tradition in Geoffrey, Wace, and Layamon. Sees the *HRB* as a reflection of contemporary political struggles.

Tatlock, John S. P. *The Legendary History of Britain. Geoffrey of Monmouth's Historia Regum Britanniae and Its Early Vernacular Versions.* Berkeley: University of California Press, 1950 (reprint, New York: Gordon Press, 1974). A magisterial study of Geoffrey. Topical in arrangement and encyclopedic in scope. The very richness of Tatlock's book in historic detail, however, sometimes obscures the *HRB* and *VM* as literary works.

Tausendfreund, Eduard Gustav Hans. *Vergil und Gottfried von Monmouth.* Halle: Schneider, 1913. On Geoffrey's use of Virgil.

Taylor, Rupert. *The Political Prophecy in England.* New York: Columbia University Press, 1911. Very dated but still useful as an introduction to medieval political prophecy.

Thompson, Mary L. H. "A Possible Source of Geoffrey's Roman War?" In *The Arthurian Tradition: Essays in Convergence,* ed. Mary Flowers Braswell and John Bugge, 43–53. Tuscaloosa: University of Alabama Press, 1988. Speculates that Geoffrey's account of Arthur's war in Gaul was influenced by Caesar's *Commentaries,* perhaps filtered through a Celtic retelling.

Thorpe, Lewis. "Giraldus Cambrensis et le roi Arthur." In *Mélanges de philologie et de littératures romaines offerts à Jeanne Wathelet-Willem,* ed. Jacques de Caluwe, 667–78. Liege: Cahiers de l'A. R. U. Lg., 1978. Examines Gerald's sceptical attitude toward Geoffrey's portrait of Arthur in the *HRB.* Also discusses Gerald's accounts of the exhumation of the remains of Arthur and Guinevere at Glastonbury in 1191.

———. "Le Mont Saint-Michel et Geoffroi de Monmouth." In *Millénaire monastique du Mont Saint-Michel,* 377–82. Paris: P. Lethielleux, 1967. A study of Geoffrey's possible use of local traditions concerning the island in the Bay of Mont-Saint-Michel known as Tumbellana.

A study of the translation of the *HRB* by Haukr Erlendsson (d. 1334) and Gunnlaugr Leifsson's *Merlínússpá*, a poetic version of the *Prophecies of Merlin*.

Hammer, Jacob. "A Commentary on the *Prophetia Merlini* (Geoffrey of Monmouth's *Historia Regum Britanniae*, Book VII)." *Speculum* 10 (1935): 3–30.

——. "A Commentary on the *Prophetia Merlini* (Geoffrey of Monmouth's *Historia Regum Britanniae*, Book VII) (Continuation)." *Speculum* 15 (1940): 409–431.

——. "Another Commentary on the *Prophetia Merlini* (Geoffrey of Monmouth's *Historia Regum Britanniae*, Book VII)." *Bulletin of the Polish Institute of Arts and Sciences in America* 1 (1942–43): 589–601.

——. "Geoffrey of Monmouth's Use of the Bible in the *Historia Regum Britanniae*." *Bulletin of the John Rylands Library* 30 (1946/7): 293–311. Shows how Geoffrey's language throughout the *HRB* was influenced by the Latin version of the Bible.

——. "Note sur l'histoire du roi Lear dans Geoffrey de Monmouth." *Latomus* 5 (1946): 299–301. Finds echoes of the *HRB* story of Lear in Terrence's *Phormio*, the Bible and Vergil's *Aeneid*.

——. "Remarks on the sources and textual history of Geoffrey of Monmouth's *Historia Regum Britanniae*." *Bulletin of the Polish Institute of Arts and Sciences in America* 2 (1943/4): 501–64. Discussion of the dedications, printed editions and sources of the *HRB*. Suggests that the story of Lear in the *HRB* was influenced by the tale of Barlaam and Ioasaph.

Hutson, A. "Geoffrey of Monmouth. Two notes: I, Brychan and Geoffrey of Monmouth's Ebraucus; II, Welsh heroes at Arthur's court." *Transactions of the Honourable Society of Cymmrodorion* (1937): 361–73.

Jackson, Kenneth. "The Site of Mount Badon." *Journal of Celtic Studies* 2 (1953–58): 152–55. Review of sites often identified with Arthur's decisive battle. Jackson suggests the Iron Age hill fort in Dorset, now known as Badbury Rings.

Jones, Ernest. "Geoffrey of Monmouth's Account of the Establishment of the Episcopacy in England." *Journal of English and German Philology* 40 (1941): 360–63. On Geoffrey's use of the *Isidorus Mercator* for the existence of *flamines* and *archflamines* in Roman Britain.

Jones, Thomas. "The Early Evolution of the Legend of Arthur." *Nottingham Mediaeval Studies* 8 (1964): 3–21. Basic study, especially strong on the Welsh background.

Keller, Hans E. "Two Toponymical Problems in Geoffrey of Monmouth and Wace: Estrusia and Siesia." *Speculum* 49 (1974): 687–98. Estrusia as a name for the region around Bayeux reached Geoffrey through Saxon sources. Siesia is a name concocted by Geoffrey to combine the place of Caesar's victory over the Gauls (Alesia) with the nearby Val Suzon, a pilgrimage site in Burgundy.

derived the idea of using animal symbolism from Insular Celtic tradition, but he was also influenced by biblical and classical sources.

Emanuel, Hywel D. "Geoffrey of Monmouth's *Historia Regum Britanniae:* A Second Variant Version." *Medium Aevum* 35 (1966): 103–11. Identifies a "second Variant Version" of the *HRB* in 15 manuscripts. This version is in many respects closer to the Vulgate text than to the Variant Version, edited by Hammer.

Eysteinsson, J. S. "The Relationship of Merlínússpá and Geoffrey of Monmouth's *Historia.*" *Saga—Book of the Viking Society* 14 (1953–57): 95–112. Argues that Gunnlaugr Leifsson's translation of the *PM* shows an awareness of the *HRB* proper. Gunnlaugr may have worked in Iceland rather than in Norway.

Fleuriot, L. "Old Breton Genealogies and Early British Traditions." *Bulletin of the Board of Celtic Studies* 26 (1974): 1–6. Shows that the legend of Conan Meriadoc's taking possession of Brittany was known in Brittany as early as the early eleventh century and was not the invention of Geoffrey of Monmouth.

———. "Sur quatre textes Bretons en Latin, le 'Liber Vetustissimus' de Geoffroy de Monmouth et le séjour de Taliesin en Bretagne." *Études celtiques* 18 (1981): 197–213. A study of the legendary material in the Breton tradition that preceded Geoffrey and that may have been part of the book Walter the archdeacon brought to Geoffrey from Brittany.

Flint, Valerie I. J. "The *Historia Regum Britanniae* of Geoffrey of Monmouth: Parody and Its Purpose: A Suggestion." *Speculum* 54 (1979): 447–68. Interprets the *HRB* in part as counterpropaganda to the pretensions of twelfth-century monastic literature and society.

Fowler, D. C. "Some biblical influences on Geoffrey of Monmouth's historiography." *Traditio* 14 (1958):378–85. Shows how Geoffrey borrows narratives from the Bible in the HRB, but often turns Biblical heroes into villains, and villains into heroes.

Gallais, Pierre. "La *Variant Version* de l'*Historia Regum Britanniae* et le *Brut* de Wace." *Romania* 87 (1966):1–32. Argues against Caldwell's view that Wace used the Variant Version. Gallais concludes that the Variant Version drew on Wace's *Roman de Brut* and the Vulgate.

Gerould, G. H. "King Arthur and Politics." *Speculum* 2 (1927): 33–52. Geoffrey formed Arthur for the Anglo-Norman aristocracy as a rival to Charlemagne.

Gillingham, John. "The Context and Purposes of Geoffrey of Monmouth's *History of the Kings of Britain.*" *Anglo-Norman Studies XIII, Proceedings of the Battle Conference* 1990, ed Marjorie Chibnall, 99–118. The *HRB* was intended to refute the growing Anglo-French perception of the Welsh as barbarians at a time when Wales was beginning to play an important role in the politics of Britain.

van Hamel, A. G. "The Old Norse Version of the *Historia Regum Britanniae* and the Text of Geoffrey of Monmouth." *Études celtiques* 1 (1936): 197–247.

names of personages in the HRB against twelfth-century history, particularly the crusades.

————. "The English Journey of the Laon Canons." *Speculum* 8 (1933): 454–65. Accepts the validity of Herman of Laon's account of the Laon canons' visit to Cornwall in 1113. Shows that lore concerning Arthur, including the notion that Arthur was still alive, was flourishing in Cornwall before Geoffrey's HRB.

————. "Caradoc of Llancarfan." *Speculum* 13 (1938): 139–52. A study of the life and works of one of Geoffrey's contemporaries. Critical of the connection sometimes made between Caradoc and the Welsh Bruts.

————. "The Dates of the Arthurian Saints' Legends." *Speculum* 14 (1939): 345–65. A study of the interest that some of Geoffrey's contemporaries took in the Age of the Saints.

————. "Geoffrey of Monmouth's Vita Merlini." *Speculum* 18 (1943): 265–87. A general introduction to the VM, with useful comments on the poem's influence on later literature, the comic spirit of the VM, and remarks on madness in medieval thought and literature.

Thorpe, Lewis. "Orderic Vitalis and The Prophetiae Merlini of Geoffrey of Monmouth." *Bulletin bibliographique de la Société internationale arthurienne* 29 (1977): 191–208. A detailed study of Orderic Vitalis's notations on Geoffrey's PM in bk. 12, ch. 47, of his *Ecclesiastical History*.

Turville-Petre, J. E. "Hengest and Horsa." *Saga-Book of the Viking Society* 14 (1953–57): 273–90. The story of Hengest and Horsa represents a version of a common folk-motif concerning divine twins. The brothers are euhermerized equine divinities newly incorporated into the Saxon settlement legend.

Index

Aaron, British martyr, 31; church at
Caerleon, 85
Aaron, brother of Moses, 40
Aballac, 98
Aber Peryddon, 71
Adelard of Bath, 118, 119
Adso: *Libellus de Antichristo*, 70
Aeneas, 14, 15, 16, 30, 107; forging the
weapons of, 80
Aeneas Silvius, 15, 16, 19
Aeneid, 16, 17, 91–92, 93, 107
Afallennau, 112, 116, 117; apple tree in, 118
Africans, 14, 55
Agicius, 34
Ahab, 40
Ailbe, 57; *Life of Saint David*, 57
aithid (elopements), 43
Alan of Brittany, 54, 81, 106; consults
the prophecies of the Eagle of Shaftes-
bury, the Sybil, and Merlin, 107
Alanus, commentator on *PM*, 56; on the
death of Rufus, 63–64; on Henry I's
hunting laws, 66
Alban/Albania, 20
Alban, Saint, 31
Albanactus, 19
Albany, 86
Albion, 15
Alcmena, 44
Alcock, Leslie, 39
Alcuin, 56
Aldhelm, letter to Geraint, king of
Domnonia, 36
Aldroenus, king of Brittany, 35
Alesia (modern Alise-Seint-Reine), 95
Alexander, bishop of Lincoln, 3, 4, 7, 9,
28, 42, 50, 51, 60; death, 49; dedica-
tee of the *PM*, 3, 48–49, 58, 68; and
Christina of Markyate, 121; interest in
prophecy, 73; in *VM*, 110
Alexander the Great, 44, 45
Alfred, king of England: translates the
laws of Dunvallo Molmutius into
English, 20–21, 27

Ali Fatima, king of Spain, 89
Allectus, 31
Allobroges, 24, 26, 79, 95
Alton, 25
Ambrius, Mount, 40, 41; monastery, 42
Ambrones, 106
Amesbury, 42
Amphibalus, British martyr, 31; church
of, 101
Amphitryon, 44
Andreas Cappellanus, 45
Androgeus, 30, 97, 138
Andromache, 17
Angelsey, 71
Angles, 103, 105, 111
Anglo-Normans, 128
Anglo-Saxon Chronicle, 36, 63, 121; on
Henry I, 65
Anglo-Saxon church, 50, 108
Anguselus, 89
Anjou, 83, 94
Annales Cambriae (Welsh Annals), 28; on
Arthur, 75; on the Battle of
Arfderydd, 115, 116; on the *gueith*
Camlann, 96, 97
Antaeus, 18
Antenor, 14, 15
Apollo, 17
Apuleius: *De Deo Socratis*, 38, 119, 124
Aquitaine, 14; Arthur's conquest of, 83
Arab science, 119
Aravia, Mount (= Mount Snowdon?), 18;
Eagle of, 65; giant of, 91
Archaemenides, 92
Arfderydd, 115; Battle of, 115, 116, 117
Argoed Llwyfain, 111
Arianism, 29
Arles, 35
Armes Prydein, 38, 50; advent of
Cadwallader and Cynan, 71–72; anti-
Saxon alliance, 71; end of Saxon hege-
mony, 62; Geoffrey's knowledge of,
115
Armorica, 32, 33, 55, 56

165